BUSINESS ETHICS IN HEALTHCARE

Medical Ethics Series

David H. Smith and Robert M. Veatch, Editors

Volume 23 in the series

Business Ethics in Healthcare

Beyond Compliance

Leonard J. Weber

INDIANA UNIVERSITY PRESS

Bloomington and Indianapolis

This book is a publication of

Indiana University Press

601 North Morton Street

Bloomington, Indiana 47404-3797 USA

www.indiana.edu/~iupress

Telephone orders 800-842-6796

Fax orders 812-855-7931

Orders by email iuporder@indiana.edu

The paper used in this publication
meets the minimum requirements of American National Standard
for Information Sciences—Permanence of Paper
for Printed Library Materials,
ANSI Z39.48-1984.

Manufactured in the United States of America

Library of Congress Cataloging-in-Publication Data

Weber, Leonard J., date
Business ethics in healthcare : beyond compliance / Leonard J. Weber.
p.   cm.— (Medical ethics series)
Includes bibliographical references and index.
ISBN 0-253-33840-9 (cl : alk. paper)
1. Medical ethics. 2. Business ethics.   I. Title   II. Series.

R725.5 .W43 2001
174′.26—dc21

1 2 3 4 5   06 05 04 03 02 01

To
MARCIA
ROBERT
MICHAEL
BENJAMIN
KATHERINE
ZACHARY

Contents

Acknowledgments   ix

Introduction: Beyond Compliance,
Beyond Integrity, Beyond Clinical Ethics   xi

PART I. BUSINESS ETHICS WITH A DIFFERENCE

One: Healthcare Business Ethics   3

Two: Ethics Is Not Neutral:
A Framework for Making Decisions   13

PART II. THE ORGANIZATION AS CAREGIVER

Three: Ethics, Cost, and the Quality of Care   25

Four: Patient Rights in a Just Organization   35

Five: Clinicians and Conflicts of Interest:
A Focus on Management   44

Six: A Fair Hearing of Appeals of Denied Coverage in
Managed Care Plans   53

Seven: Organizational Ethics:
A Code Is Only the Beginning   62

PART III. THE ORGANIZATION AS EMPLOYER

Eight: Just Wages and Salaries   73

Nine: Ethics and Downsizing   82

Ten: Patient Requests for Healthcare Providers of a Specific
Race or Sex   91

Eleven: Conscientious Objection to Participation in Certain
Treatment Options   100

Twelve: Union Organizing and Employee Strikes   109

Contents

viii

PART IV. THE ORGANIZATION AS CITIZEN

Thirteen: Responsible Advertising   121

Fourteen: Environmental Responsibility and the
Precautionary Principle   130

Fifteen: Community Serving Mergers and Acquisitions   140

Sixteen: Socially Responsible Investing   150

PART V. INSTITUTIONALIZING BUSINESS AND MANAGEMENT ETHICS

Seventeen: Components of a Business Ethics Program   161

Eighteen: The Organizational Ethics Committee   171

Notes   181

Index   189

Acknowledgments

The preparation of this book was supported in part by a grant from the Myrtle E. and William G. Hess Charitable Trust.

I want to express my appreciation as well for the opportunity provided by the University of Detroit Mercy to use a major portion of my time and energy over the years in working with healthcare organizations on practical ethical issues.

Individuals who have contributed in various ways to the completion of this book or who have been particularly effective in influencing my thinking include Thomas Schindler, Paul Reitemeier, Kathleen Bartt, James Tubbs, Robert Guenther, Margaret Weber, Gloria Albrecht, Cheryl Munday, Nancy Prince, and Jessy Seck. Thank you.

I want to thank, as well, the many unnamed members of the different Ethics Committees that I have had the opportunity to be associated with over the last twenty years. The work of these committees has helped to shape my analysis and has highlighted the importance of trying to keep ethics talk practical without losing a commitment to high standards.

I have received gracious permission from the following periodicals to use, in a reworked fashion, previously published articles: *Health Progress, Clinical Laboratory Management Review,* and *HEC Forum.*

Introduction

Beyond Compliance, Beyond Integrity,
Beyond Clinical Ethics

Healthcare business ethics is, in many ways, the meeting of medical ethics and business ethics. There has been much interest in medical ethics in the United States during the last three decades, an interest much more focused on patient care issues and on medical research than on the management of healthcare organizations. The interest in business ethics is also very strong. The attention given to the responsibilities of management has not often been focused, however, on the specific issues of healthcare organizations. The extensive ethical reflection about medicine and business over the years provides significant insight and wisdom for application when we turn our attention to the nature and meaning of healthcare business ethics.

Healthcare business ethics is getting increased attention, but there is no common articulation of the perspectives and principles that the healthcare manager should have and apply. There is no common understanding of the topics to be included in education on healthcare business ethics. It may be useful to begin, then, with a brief description of the approach taken here.

Beyond Compliance

In some healthcare organizations today, business ethics is closely identified with corporate compliance. Hotlines established to encourage employees to report questionable practices are sometimes called "business ethics hotlines." Efforts are sometimes made to implement compliance programs in the context of a broader sense of "organizational ethics," but if the primary focus is on compliance, ethics tends to be defined as compliance.

In compliance programs, the emphasis is on conforming to laws and regulations. The Federal emphasis on preventing healthcare fraud and abuse has provided a strong incentive for healthcare organizations to get their own programs in place to ensure that nothing illegal is occurring.

Compliance is obviously important and is related to ethical business practices, at least as a minimal standard of what should not be done. It may be unfortunate, however, that there is a need to establish corporate compliance programs at the very time that business ethics in the organization is beginning to get more attention. If business ethics is identified with compliance, business ethics has much too narrow a focus.

One danger of such an identification is that a compliance model of ethics might get adopted—as long as the organization is not doing anything illegal, the ethical issues have been addressed. When the primary emphasis in business ethics efforts within the organization is to prevent persons from, knowingly or unknowingly, violating any rules or regulations, there is much missed opportunity.

Business ethics as discussed in this work is not compliance oriented; it is not focused on regulations or on doing what is minimally required. Rather, the emphasis is placed on a variety of issues unrelated to fraud but definitely related to the organization's mission and values and related to management's responsibility to patients, employees, and the community. The emphasis is on trying to understand what it means to manage the healthcare organization according to high ethical standards and ideals, not on complying with regulations.

Beyond Integrity

Theologians have had to acknowledge, frequently over the centuries, that bad things happen to good people. Ethicists have to acknowledge that good people sometimes do bad things. Well-intentioned persons, committed to personal honesty and fairness, can do harm.

Before anyone with management responsibility in an organization can be legitimately described as a person characterized by high ethical standards, there need to be two different traits present. The ethical manager is a person of integrity and a person who takes responsibility for consequences.

A person of integrity can be trusted to be honest, puts doing right by others before personal advantage, puts doing right by others before the organization's advantage, does not exploit power advantage in relationships, and tells the unwelcome truth to persons in positions of power. These are very demanding expectations. Even someone of good character may not live up to these standards at all times, but integrity remains the goal, what we strive to achieve in our relationships in the workplace.

A person who takes responsibility for consequences seeks to understand the impact of business decisions and policies on all affected and makes or recommends decisions designed to minimize the potential negative impact on others. She or he listens to others to understand possible harmful consequences, and accepts responsibility for unintended negative consequences by taking corrective action when harm has been done.

To be a person of integrity requires good moral character. To be a person who takes responsibility for consequences requires, in addition, sensitivity to the meaning an individual decision takes on as a result of institutional and social and community realities. It requires the ability to understand issues from the perspective of those who often have little opportunity to be heard. While an individual's personal integrity often provides the incentive to avoid or reduce harm to others, it takes additional effort and reflection to know what avoiding or reducing harm means in various practices or decisions.

There is an assumption in what follows that individual managers want to do what is best, that they are committed to being ethical. The discussion seeks to identify and clarify what is ethically best in situations where the answer is not always immediately evident. A person of integrity, someone committed to doing what is right, often has to seek information and advice in order to know what it means to do the ethical best in particular circumstances.

Business ethics is about more than personal integrity.

Beyond Clinical Ethics

For most people in American society, healthcare ethics means medical ethics or clinical ethics. The issues that come to mind are those in which there are personal interactions between patients and clinical professionals—treatment decisions (often near the end of life), informed consent, confidentiality concerns, and other issues related to patient rights. Committees that address these issues frequently go by the general name of "Ethics" Committees.

Issues related to patient rights in clinical settings remain very important issues requiring concentrated attention, but they are not the whole of healthcare ethics and are not the primary concern in considering healthcare business ethics.

It is one thing to reconcile the patient's rights, beliefs, and preferences with the responsibilities and interests of clinicians. It is something else to reconcile the individual patient's needs, beliefs, and preferences with the business interests of the organization. In addition, there are a variety of ethical concerns that confront healthcare managers that are not directly related to patient care at all, but have to do with other constituents or stakeholders. Attending to ethics in the healthcare organization requires the development of an informed, sensitive, and practical understanding of the responsibilities to staff and to the community as well as to individual patients.

Healthcare managers need to know something about clinical ethics, simply because these issues are important in the organizations in which they work. But knowledge of clinical ethics is not enough, not nearly enough. Understanding the nature and limits of a patient's right to refuse treatment will not provide much help in determining just wages for nursing assistants. Understanding the requirements for informed consent in therapeutic research does not clarify the nature of responsible advertising.

Practical Ethics

In an article in the *Hastings Center Report* some years ago, Leon Kass commented on the work in ethics in healthcare that he had observed over the last generation: "Though originally intended to improve our deeds, the reigning practice in ethics, if truth be told, has, at best, improved our speech."[1]

I do not agree entirely with Kass about the effects of ethics discussions, but his statement does serve as an important reminder that ethics talk should be designed to affect behavior and practice. Being ethical does require us to pay careful attention to the way that we speak about issues, but the goal in discussing ethics is not skill at articulating theory or arguing positions. The goal is assisting persons to make better practical judgments. This book is designed, therefore, to provide suggestions and recommendations for those interested in the best ethical practices in healthcare business management.

Each chapter in the three central sections of the book is focused on a particular issue or concern. In the discussion of each issue, I have attempted to identify its ethical significance and to propose, whenever possible, guidelines or criteria for good practices. The purpose is not to describe a range of theoretical positions on the issue, but to propose specific ethics-driven perspectives and responses. The basis and framework for the responses given are identified in the first two chapters.

It is not possible, of course, to include in this book a discussion of all relevant and important issues in healthcare business ethics. The issues chosen have been selected to cover a range of different concerns. They have been selected to suggest the kinds of issues that are included in healthcare business ethics when we go beyond a focus on the personal ethics of the manager, beyond a focus on the need to be in compliance with regulations, and beyond a focus on clinical contexts.

Ethics is every manager's business. To resolve complex ethical issues well, however, often requires knowledge, skill, and experience. It does not come automatically with a management position. The last part of the book includes a discussion of ways of promoting, within the organization, increased understanding of the ethical dimensions of healthcare business management. An Organizational Ethics Committee may be a key component of a complete ethics program.

PART I
BUSINESS ETHICS WITH A DIFFERENCE

One

Healthcare Business Ethics

Case 1.1. It was an interesting, though unplanned, discussion at the Board meeting of the managed care plan. The next year's budget was being presented for Board approval and the CFO was explaining some of the assumptions on which the projections were based. One expectation was that the organization would be successful in lowering the "medical loss ratio" by more than one full percent from the current number. (The medical loss ratio is the percentage of premium revenue used for medical expenses for members of the plan.) One Board member asked what the CFO thought the ideal MLR was and what the long-term goal was. Several others voiced their opinions in response and it immediately became evident that a wide range of opinions was represented around the table—everything from "as low as possible" to "as much of the revenue as possible should go to medical care." The Chair suggested that this question be put on the agenda for a future meeting.

One of Emily Friedman's columns in *Healthcare Forum Journal* is entitled "What Business Did You Say We Were In?"[1] In it, she discussed the practice of health insurers excluding certain high-risk individuals from coverage and pointed out some of the implications of adopting a commercial model, as differentiated from a service model, of healthcare. Identifying the appropriate or ideal medical loss ratio seems to require, first, understanding the kind of business healthcare is or should be.

If the healthcare organization is modeled on a business devoted to a high return on investment, the cost of medical benefits will be seen as an expense that should be kept as low as possible. If, on the other hand, the healthcare organization is modeled on a service organization devoted to humanitarian aims, the emphasis will be on using as much of every dollar as possible for the healthcare services that the organization is designed to provide. In fact, in an organization that defines itself as a service organization, management may not even be comfortable with the term medical *loss* ratio, preferring a term like medical *care* ratio or medical *cost* ratio. Providing health benefits is not a "loss" when it is the reason for which the organization exists.

As individuals, we distinguish between investments and contributions. When making investments, we are interested in the potential gains or profits. When making contributions, many of us want to know the organization's record in terms of what percentage of the money received actually is used to provide the services that we want to support; the higher the percentage the better. We tend to think of commercial enterprises as quite different from service organizations. Thinking of healthcare primarily according to the commercial model leads to different expectations from thinking of healthcare primarily according to the service model. Healthcare is no different from any other business in the sense that it cannot be managed successfully without attention to the bottom line. A focus on the practical business implications of decisions is essential. Nevertheless, how one thinks about the nature of the healthcare business sets the ethical tone.

Healthcare Organizations as Service Organizations

The ethical perspectives and guidelines expressed in this book are based on the belief that healthcare is fundamentally and essentially a service. Healthcare organizations have been, historically, humanitarian in nature, and they continue to be understood best as community service organizations. The basic purpose of healthcare organizations is to meet the healthcare needs of individuals and to promote the health of the community.

Healthcare management has long been recognized as a profession unlike the management of most other types of business organizations. The codes of ethics of the American College of Healthcare Executives and the American College of Healthcare Administrators clearly recognize that healthcare managers are professionals whose primary responsibility is to patients and to the community, not to owners or investors. As stated in the Preamble to the ACHE Code of Ethics,

> The fundamental objectives of the healthcare management profession are to enhance the overall quality of life, dignity, and well-being of every individual needing healthcare services; and to create a more equitable, accessible, effective, and efficient healthcare system.[2]

Healthcare management is a service profession.

Healthcare is best understood as a social or public good that should be managed to meet the healthcare needs of the community. Government invests in and subsidizes healthcare extensively (for example, medical education and research); the state licenses health clinicians; the public treasury supports healthcare for (some of) those who are unable to afford healthcare for themselves. How healthcare is distributed and provided is, to a significant extent, a question of the appropriate allocation of a public good. The commodity analogy of a simple purchase exchange between private parties is not an adequate understanding of what is involved in healthcare.[3]

The Tavistock Group (an international multidisciplinary group that met at Tavistock Square in London) drafted a statement of ethical principles to guide decision making in healthcare delivery. They recognize the importance, for practical ethics, of starting with a clear understanding of the nature of healthcare and healthcare services:

> The aim of health care delivery is to maintain and improve health, to alleviate disability, and to provide access to appropriate health services to all persons regardless of their ability to pay.
>   Caring for sick people is a social obligation that extends beyond the commercial realm. Although ownership of health care delivery institutions or other organizations that deliver medical care may be appropriate, care itself cannot be owned and must be viewed as a service that is rendered and remunerated under the stewardship of those in the health care system rather than merely sold to individuals or communities.[4]

Healthcare is a business but it is not just like every other business.

For most people, the term "healthcare ethics" still suggests clinical issues, not management issues. In order to develop a more inclusive understanding of healthcare ethics, many have been suggesting that there should be a strong and visible focus on "business ethics" in healthcare institutions and in the education of future healthcare executives. This is a very good suggestion, but the type of business ethics highlighted needs to be relevant to healthcare.

Mainline academic business ethics, reflected in most books and courses, assumes the context of large corporations in a competitive for-profit environment and includes very little, if any, discussion of service-oriented organizations. The growing interest in business ethics is also found in many corporations. Here the emphasis is often on codes of ethics for employees, efforts to clarify the expectations regarding individual behavior on the job. There is, as well, a push to ensure "compliance" by developing a culture of integrity and by implementing methods of avoiding fraud and other violations of regulations and policies.

While there is much of value in both the academic and the corporate approaches to business ethics, neither is fully satisfactory in meeting the needs of leaders in healthcare organizations. Healthcare management ethics is business ethics, but business ethics with a difference.

Ethics and For-Profit Healthcare

The emphasis on healthcare as a service may raise questions for some readers about the role of for-profit healthcare organizations. This is an important question. Initially, at least, the understanding of the basic nature of healthcare outlined above is more compatible with the traditional understanding of not-for-profit organizations than it is with for-profit organizations.

The difference between for-profit and not-for-profit healthcare is sometimes played down. Individuals who move from one type of healthcare organization to the other often report that they find no real difference between the two. It is to be expected, in fact, that most day-to-day activity is not different for most staff. There are, though, significant differences in the purposes and goals of the organizations, differences which should lead, at times, to different responses to important issues.

Proprietary healthcare organizations may raise ethical challenges beyond those that are found in the more traditional non-profits. In another of her columns, Emily Friedman expresses the most fundamental concern about investor-owned healthcare organizations:

> To look at a town's healthcare providers as simply a good or bad investment is too cold an approach. To view the success of a healthcare organization only in terms of the value of its stock is too simplistic. To make life-and-death decisions about what to close and what to keep, whom to contract with, and whom to enroll on the basis of how much money is to be made is too far from the heart of healthcare. . . . There is a difference between a community and a market.[5]

It is important to note terms used in this statement, such as "simply" and "only" and "how much money." To be a for-profit healthcare organization means that management is accountable to investors to provide a reasonable return on their investments. To be for-profit does not mean, however, that one must be so fixated on profit that management cannot take other considerations into account when making business decisions. To be profit oriented does not mean that one is "simply" concerned about profit, that success is measured "only" in terms of how much money is made. There is a long tradition of for-profit businesses, because of their commitment to being socially responsible, willingly making decisions expected to result in lower profits in order to avoid harm to the community.

It is widely accepted, as a standard of business ethics, that corporations have a responsibility to "balance the benefits to be gained against the cost of achieving those benefits." Recognizing its social responsibility "may require a company to forgo some profits if its social impacts are seriously harmful" to those affected.[6]

The ethical approach presented here is community-based ethics. It requires of for-profits that they be managed with a strong sense of social responsibility, such that they are fully and realistically committed to serving the community at the same time that they are committed to being profitable. Management in for-profit healthcare organizations should be expected to adhere to the standards of the profession of healthcare management, even if that is difficult at times to reconcile with the interests of share-holders. The same community-serving emphasis is, of course, no less a challenge and no less a demand for not-for-profit healthcare.

Justice-Based Ethics

The practical implications of community-based ethics are most clearly recognized by those who have developed an understanding of the nature and meaning of justice.

> Case 1.2. The following situation came to light in a hospital's review of uncompensated care.
>
> A Medicare patient was being treated as an outpatient for a relatively rare incurable immunodeficiency disorder. The physician was treating with repeated IV infusions of immunoglobulin. Medicare did not cover this treatment for this condition; it is considered experimental. The situation was discussed with the physician. He was aware that there is no documented evidence that this treatment is effective, but said that there are no other documented effective treatments either and that the patient has had symptomatic improvement with the treatment so far and both the physician and the patient would like to continue. The treatment costs about $3,000 per month and has already been done for close to a year. None of this cost is reimbursed.

This is a case that would seem to require some careful reflection regarding what is ethically right, but in most hospitals it would probably not be called to the attention of the Ethics Committee.

Many of the Ethics Committees that are in existence in healthcare institutions are, in reality, Clinical Ethics Committees. They serve as important resources in addressing ethical issues related to individual patient care, most notably treatment decision making near the end of life. Typically, cases are brought to the committee only when there is some disagreement (between clinician and patient/family or among caregivers) regarding appropriate treatment or care at a particular point in time. The first reason why this case would probably not be brought to the Ethics Committee is that there is no disagreement involving doctor and patient, no obvious conflict to be resolved.

When the Ethics Committee is consulted on a clinical case, attention is paid, typically, to reviewing the medical condition, the patient's wishes, different medical options, and expected medical outcomes. Much of the focus is on what the patient wants or is said to want. It is uncommon for anyone even to raise the issue of cost and appropriate use of resources in helping to determine what is ethically appropriate in individual cases. The second reason this case would probably not be brought to the Ethics Committee is that Ethics Committees are not thought of as bodies skilled in analyzing cost-related issues.

Those contacted in a situation like this do need to be able to analyze this carefully as an ethical issue. This kind of situation requires the ability to make a decision about what constitutes good quality and fair care in this individual case and to establish the appropriate procedures or processes that can best ensure appropriate decisions in other similar cases. Healthcare business ethics requires a well-developed and practical sense of the organization's responsibility to patients, to staff and employees, and to the community. It is important to have ethics resources available to assist in clarifying what is at stake and how one might best prioritize claims, but the typical Ethics Committee may not yet be well prepared to provide this assistance.

In medical ethics education, it is quite common to discuss four basic ethical principles: 1) respect for autonomy; 2) beneficence; 3) nonmaleficence; and 4) justice. These principles, articulated most fully by Beauchamp and Childress,[7] have been interpreted and applied during the last two to three decades to resolve issues in clinical ethics, where key concerns have been confidentiality, informed consent, and the right to refuse treatment. Given the individual patient care context of clinical ethics, and given the emphasis on freedom and the individual in American culture, it is not surprising that the autonomy principle has received the most attention.

Despite the emphasis on autonomy, there has been a recognition, even in clinical ethics, that individual patients need to be recognized as part of a community and that individual choices are not always the most important factor when making decisions about patient care. Nancy Jecker has expressed the community focus in these terms:

> A tragedy of the commons occurs if members seek to take more common goods than they are entitled to or refuse to make appropriate sacrifices and contributions. A commons flourishes only if each party is willing to acknowledge that resources are shared commodities and respect others' stake in preserving them. Thus, even if competent patients formulate clear preferences, these preferences are not the final word on what constitutes an ethically sound decision.[8]

An understanding of the relationship of individuals to the community is especially important for healthcare business leaders. Those who have stewardship responsibility for healthcare services in a community must be able to use available resources in a way that most effectively achieves appropriate healthcare goals while respecting the rights of employees and other stakeholders. They must be able to design and implement fair processes and procedures for evaluating the claims made by different stakeholders and for establishing the right priorities for making decisions about the organization's resources.

Healthcare business ethics requires an emphasis on the meaning of justice.

Justice has to do with fairness, with recognizing the difference between legitimate and illegitimate claims, with recognizing priorities among different values, with determining who should get what when all cannot get everything they seek. Justice has to do with understanding the potential community impact of decisions made in organizations. Respect for the autonomy of the individual needs to be understood as part of a commitment to justice.

Determining what should be done in the case cited above requires judgments about how best to prioritize different values. It requires a justice analysis. I return to this case later in this chapter. Chapter 2 provides additional perspectives on what it means to understand healthcare business ethics as justice-based ethics.

The Healthcare Organization: Caregiver, Employer, and Citizen

It would be a mistake, in a discussion of healthcare business ethics, to emphasize the unique nature of healthcare organizations to such an extent that issues that are common to managers in different types of organizations are omitted. Some of the most ethically challenging and emotionally difficult ethical dilemmas faced by healthcare managers are not related directly to patient care; they have to do with human resources issues and with challenges regarding what it means for an organization to be a contributing member of the community. The issues selected for discussion in later chapters are placed in three groups, based on the recognition that the healthcare organization has "three distinctive but interrelated roles: it is caregiver; an employer; and a citizen."[9]

Healthcare is the particular kind of business it is because its services are designed to affect the health of persons served. Fundamental to healthcare business ethics, therefore, is a commitment to high-quality services and a commitment to respecting patient rights. This patient care emphasis is, however, somewhat different for managers than it is for clinicians. Managers need to recognize individual patients as part of a community of patients served. Managers have stewardship responsibility for the limited resources available for healthcare services. They need to be able to design and implement fair procedures for evaluating claims made by different stakeholders and for establishing the priorities for decisions about resources.

Management in many different settings struggles with being fair in employing and managing staff in the organization. There are ethical issues related to determining fair wages or salaries, to making decisions about downsizing, to evaluating performance, to setting and attempting to meet diversity or affirmative action goals, to addressing grievances, to responding to unionizing efforts, to applying sexual harassment policies and procedures, to protecting employee privacy. The list could go on. Managing employee-related issues in a just manner is a central element in being an ethical manager and in being an ethical organization.

Employee-related ethical issues are not unique to healthcare, but there are advantages to considering them in the same ethical framework that is used to address business issues more directly focused on patient care. The ethical organization is one in which the needs and interests of all relevant stakeholders are balanced on the basis of a consistent and explicit understanding of priorities.

To describe the healthcare organization as citizen is simply to recognize that it has a responsibility to promote the public good, particularly a responsibility to seek to improve the health status of the community. Acknowledging good citizenship as an important component of ethical healthcare management leads to a recognition of the importance of assessing the impact on the public of institutional or organizational policies and practices. It is not enough to be concerned about the impact of these policies and decisions on individuals directly served by the organization and on individuals within the organization. It is not enough to be a good caregiver and a good employer. One needs also to be socially responsible.[10]

The ACHE Code clearly recognizes that healthcare managers have responsibilities to community and to society. Everyday work pressures and the natural emphasis on the well-being of the organization and on the well-being of patients make it difficult, however, for most managers to understand what this means, let alone place a high priority on these responsibilities.

Organizational Ethics

In making the point in the Introduction that business ethics requires more than being individuals of personal integrity, I noted that "good people" can do "bad" things. Being motivated to do the right thing is not sufficient; one also needs to develop skill and sensitivity regarding the potential harmful effects on others of policies and decisions.

The point to be made here is that "not so good people" often do "good" things, simply by following established patterns and practices in good organizations, even when they are not personally motivated to do right by others. Organizational ethics is as much about attending to "the way things are done around here" as it is about educating individuals regarding their responsibilities. In many situations, the need is for establishing and clarifying the right processes and procedures in order to maintain work of a high ethical quality.

The second scenario in the chapter, the case of unproven and unreimbursed medication, might be a good example of the need to focus on processes and procedures. The physician in the case was making what he thought was a decision in the patient's best interest, one that unfortunately resulted in the institution being stuck with the unreimbursed cost of medicine and being involved in the possible misuse of community-serving resources.

Two of the major concerns regarding this case are the quality issue of using treatments that have not been established as being effective and the question of appropriate use of institutional resources. Since it is reasonable to expect that this is not the only case of this sort likely to occur within the institution, it is good to address the issue as a policy issue. What should be done when a physician wants to treat with medications that are judged experimental for the diagnosis?

Quality standards and responsible stewardship of resources might lead management to institute policy and procedures that would do the following:

1. require that the pharmacy not dispense IV medications that fall outside the standard treatments for the diagnosis, unless there has been explicit approval for an exception in a particular case;
2. establish a clear process for physicians to request these exceptions and a mechanism for quick review of these requests by qualified persons.

There may be good reason, at times, to use drugs for unapproved purposes, but it is questionable organizational practice to allow individual physicians to make this kind of decision entirely on their own, especially if the institution is likely, as a result, to have unrecoverable expenses.

Until there has been a thorough consideration of such proposed policy and procedures by different segments of the institutional community (administration, medical staff, and pharmacy, at least), it cannot be clear that the above suggestions are feasible or the most appropriate. It is fully appropriate, though, for management to suggest a systematic approach and not want to rely on the good will and right education of individuals to lead to the right results. Very often, addressing issues of organizational ethics requires a concern for processes.

The Need for Ethics

In social settings, when someone discovers what their work is, professional ethicists often hear a number of one-liners. In response to "My work is business ethics," the response might be, "Isn't business ethics an oxymoron?" Another common and more sober response, regardless of one's specialization with ethics, is, "Well, attention to ethics is certainly needed."

It is not always clear what individuals mean when they say that we need more attention to ethics. The assumption in this work is that most people want to be ethical and that what is needed is not an effort to persuade someone about the importance of living an ethical life. There are circumstances, though, in which those who want to be ethical themselves and to work in organizations that are ethical are not clear on how to do that, not clear on what is right or best.

There may be a need for more opportunity to learn the insights ethical traditions can bring to bear on issues that individuals face in their work.

There may be a need for explicit and sustained attention to ways of thinking about what is right regarding specific complex situations. There may be a need for more examples of ethics guidelines for addressing specific issues. There may be a need for more attention to what it means to be an ethical organization.

These are the needs, applied to healthcare business, that this book is designed to help meet.

Two

Ethics Is Not Neutral
A Framework for Making Decisions

There are two kinds of ethics concerns that need to be addressed in any organization. And management, accordingly, has two kinds of ethics-related responsibility.

One concern relates to adherence to ethical standards. Management has a responsibility to ensure that established ethical standards are known and observed, that apparent violations of these standards are investigated fairly and promptly, that confirmed violations are corrected in an appropriate manner, and that steps are taken to prevent future violations. There are many situations in which what is right and what is wrong is clear, and managers have a responsibility to act in conformity with this understanding themselves and to ensure that others do as well.

Clear ethical standards need to be established and communicated not only in regard to such traditional expectations as honest documentation, confidentiality of information, and proper use of workplace time and equipment, but also in regard to more recently evolved prohibitions of discrimination and harassment. Adherence to such standards needs to be both modeled and enforced. Even though ethical standards are based on widespread agreement about what constitutes unethical behavior, it would be a mistake to assume that everyone in the organization knows, without reinforcement, what the expectations are or why they are important.

The other ethics-related concern applies to those situations in which it is not immediately clear what is right, even to ethically sensitive persons. Many situations exist which are of clear ethical significance but are not governed by established standards for determining right from wrong. It is not unusual for ethically conscientious persons to disagree about what should be done. These are the hard cases that good managers and employees wrestle with. Making decisions in cases often requires choices that are not between good and evil but between two or more competing values or goods.

This second ethics concern requires that management be sensitive to and educated about the ways that ethical values are inherent in various business decisions. It requires that management promote ongoing reflection of the organization's ethical priorities and commitments. It requires that managers' own decisions reflect high ethical priorities. Management has the responsibility, as well, to promote ethically informed and guided decisions by others in the organization.

Both types of ethics concerns are important. The emphasis in this book is, however, on the second, the situations in which ethical reasoning is required and there is no easy answer to the question of what is right. These are situations not covered in typical codes of conduct.

The ethics framework that is proposed in this chapter is one designed to assist decision makers in identifying and clarifying priorities among the various goods, values, and interests in conflict and in recognizing what is important when reaching decisions about difficult ethical issues.

Thinking about Ethics

When a decision has to be made that cannot respect all legitimate interests that are in conflict in a particular situation, the best decision is one that is based on a recognition of what is of greater ethical importance. If one cannot respect all legitimate interests, a wise choice is one that respects the most important one(s). And what is most important or of highest priority for healthcare management is often directly related to the understanding one has of the nature, purpose, and role of the healthcare organization, as discussed in Chapter 1.

> Case 2.1. A case manager for home care has requested assistance regarding a situation that has just occurred; similar situations have arisen several times before.
>
> She has had an extended conversation with a patient for whom she is arranging home care. All went well until the patient said that he does not want anyone who is black coming into his home. The patient is an elderly European American who says that he does not feel comfortable around black people and that he especially does not like the idea of a black person walking around in his house. "I'm a strong believer in staying with your own kind. Besides," he continued, "I have a right to decide who comes into the privacy of my own home."
>
> The case manager needs to decide whether to make arrangements that specify a white worker or to tell the patient that the home care providers will not comply with this request. She asks for assistance in

deciding what is the right thing to do. She is also seeking suggestions on what to establish as policy in regard to future cases like this.

Whenever I have discussed this sort of case with healthcare professionals, they have raised a variety of concerns and perspectives. Some see the case primarily in terms of racial discrimination. Some express the concern that an African-American employee might suffer harassment or abuse if sent into the home of this patient. Some focus on the healthcare needs of the patient and think that it might be best to avoid distressing the patient. Some raise questions about the revenue implications of refusing to give patients what they seek, whether the agency might lose clients to other agencies. Some emphasize the importance of thinking of a home as a place of privacy where people can admit whom they want. Some raise the "slippery slope" question about other requests patients might make if the organization accedes to this one.

What should, in fact, be done in cases like this is discussed in some detail in Chapter 10. Here it is sufficient to point out that making a good decision in this case requires the recognition of priorities among the various values involved. If the decision cannot both satisfy the patient's interest in not having a caregiver of a particular race and respect the practice of making work assignments without regard to race, which is of greater importance? Or does one of the other considerations override both? Whether one does so explicitly or not, everyone who makes a decision about what to do in a case like this is, in fact, expressing a position regarding what is most important or valuable. The case indicates the need to identify priorities in healthcare business ethics.

Case 2.2. In an alternative model of care for frail elderly, several PACE centers have been established around the country. (PACE = Program of All-Inclusive Care for the Elderly.) For a set monthly fee (paid privately or by Medicare-Medicaid under a managed care arrangement with waivers), the program provides total care for those ill or frail enough to be candidates for nursing homes but not so ill that they require twenty-four-hour care. Services are designed to maintain the patients' ability to live independently in their own homes and neighborhoods. Participants are brought to the center a couple days a week for medical care, nutrition monitoring, bathing assistance, etc. Home care visits are also provided, including some housekeeping assistance where necessary.

The PACE center is responsible for the total cost of the participant's healthcare wherever received. Participants agree to get all of their care through the program and to use other providers only when approved or in true emergencies.

One participant has made repeated, unnecessary, and unapproved use of a hospital emergency room, despite the twenty-four-hour availability of the program's physicians and nurses, at a significant cost to the organization. In one of their regular meetings, program management ask one another whether there is ever justification to "involuntarily dis-enroll" participants like this. The patient's behavior, if it continues, may endanger the viability of the program and, therefore, put the other 100 participants at risk. At what point would it be right to remove a partici-pant from the program because of inappropriate use of the organiza-tion's resources?

Management decides to ask this question of the program's Ethics Committee at its next meeting. (This particular PACE center has an Ethics Committee that advises on ethical issues in management as well as on ethical issues related to patient care.)

This case demonstrates a need to sort through different considerations and to work out the implications of the organization's basic mission. One point is very clear: If a participant were costing the organization money because of necessary and appropriate hospital care, no one should even consider the ques-tion of involuntary dis-enrollment. This is the precise risk that the organiza-tion assumed when it agreed to be "at risk" for the care of these patients. It clearly has a responsibility to cover the cost of the necessary care.

The question, then, is whether there is a decisive difference in the respon-sibility of the organization to the participant when the participant receives unneeded and unapproved care outside the program. If there is a difference, when the participant fails to live up to the conditions of a voluntary agree-ment, does this apply to all participants or only those who are competent to make rational decisions? That is to say, if a participant makes costly decisions that may be attributable in part to (incipient) dementia, is this cost also to be considered part of what the program agreed to be at risk of when enrolling elderly patients? To be skilled at addressing hard ethical dilemmas, one needs to be skilled at thinking through the implications of basic beliefs, commit-ments, and priorities.

What is demonstrated by these two cases is that addressing healthcare business ethics issues adequately requires an approach that involves both clarifying priorities and analyzing or reasoning about specific situations. The next few pages consider each in turn.

_____

Priority Principles of Business Ethics

The following approach to identifying priorities seems especially appropriate in the management of organizations with a service orientation.

There are four major interests, values, or goods that often conflict when decisions need to be made in organizational settings.[1]

1. Basic individual rights
   What everyone, regardless of power, position, or merit, should have re-

spected or provided simply because of being human (human rights) and what is due to persons because of agreements or promises.

2. Individual self-interest
   The good things in life, as individuals define them, which they seek for themselves and for those close to them. What people want.

3. The interests of the organization or the institution
   The good of the organization, normally as defined and interpreted by its leaders.

4. The public good/the community good
   The well-being of the larger community in which the organization exists and which it serves.

Many of the issues in business or workplace ethics involve the need to understand these values carefully and to establish priorities among them. Questions of possible employee "conflicts of interest," for example, require clarification of the relationship between individual self-interest (#2) and the interests of the organization (#3). A proper understanding of the demands placed on healthcare organizations by "patient rights" requires an understanding of the relationship between individual rights (#1) and organizational interests (#3). Similarly, some issues relating to employee rights require an understanding of individual rights (#1) in relationship to organizational interests (#3). The nature of the organization's social and environmental responsibility involves understanding the impact of its activities and the relationship of its interests (#3) to the good of the larger community (#4).

What constitutes the more precise meaning of each of these four values will always need to be clarified in regard to specific situations. It is possible, though, to identify the general relationship about the values, to articulate general priority principles of healthcare business ethics.

1. The organization's interests (#3) generally take priority over individual self-interest (#2).

When there is a conflict between the self-interest of one or more individuals and the interest or the good of the organization, the good of the organization should usually take priority over individual self-interest, no matter who the individuals are or where they are in the organization. While individual wants and preferences are to be considered a good worthy of respect when possible, respecting these wants is not as high an ethical priority as is doing what is best for the organization for which one has some responsibility.

2. Individual rights (#1) take priority over the organization's interests (#3).

When the effort to achieve certain goods for an organization puts basic rights at risk, respect for the rights of individuals takes priority over trying to achieve organizational goals. Respecting basic rights is a fundamental characteristic of ethical behavior for individuals, for professionals, and for organizations. To violate basic rights in the pursuit of organizational goals is to have misplaced priorities.

Rights or needs are, in ethics, very different from wants or preferences. What someone wants is what is understood here as self-interest. A basic right, a true right, is what someone truly needs in order to live a life of human dignity. To say that one has a right to something is to say that one can make a binding claim upon others. There is a strong human rights tradition that is helpful for understanding the differences between rights and wants. Rights relate to freedoms (for example, not to be treated without consent) and to being treated with essential respect (for example, to be paid a just wage). Different human rights are appealed to in this book in an effort to clarify ethical responsibilities.

3. Community good (#4) takes priority over the organization's interests (#3).

When the effort to achieve certain goods for an organization threatens the good of the larger community, the commitment to the public good takes priority over trying to achieve organizational goals. This is the essential citizenship responsibility of an organization. At least in the minimal sense of not doing significant harm to the larger community, any organization's responsibility to the public good is of very high priority. The service orientation of the healthcare organization places a particular emphasis on the centrality of community good.

4. Community good (#4) takes priority over individual self-interest (#2).

Based on what has already been said, this principle is obvious. When there is a conflict between individual self-interest and the good of the larger community, the commitment to the public good takes priority over respecting the individual's pursuit of the good life.

5. Individual rights (#1) take priority over individual self-interest (#2).

If the individual pursuit of the good life puts basic rights of others (or even of themselves) at risk, respect for the rights of individuals takes priority over respecting individual interests. Basic rights and basic needs are essentials. Respecting these rights and meeting these needs is of much greater fundamental importance than promoting something that is not as essential.

It is important to be able to distinguish between individual rights based on essential needs and individual wants based on personal goals or interests, even though it is not always easy to do. An important part of the task of managing an ethical organization is the ability to distinguish between essentials and non-essentials.

It is difficult to put the relationship between basic individual rights (#1) and the good of the community (#4) in a priority statement. In a sense, these are two different sides of the same good: respect for everyone's basic rights is the meaning of the community good. These two goods are of generally equal value. We need to insist on both and try to do the best to respect both at all times. One should not be subordinated to the other.

On the other hand, one cannot say that these two never conflict. If they do, it is not immediately evident how that conflict should be resolved. Careful deliberation on the circumstances and likely consequences is required.

The priority principles identified here can offer guidance when values conflict. They provide both a rationale and a framework for deciding in one direction rather than another.

Resolving Ethical Dilemmas

The goal of education on practical ethics is to assist individuals and groups to make the right decisions, the best decisions when all things are considered. There have been a variety of models proposed regarding the process of making decisions when faced with difficult ethics cases. These models are attempts to assist or guide individuals as they think through a difficult issue and what should be done about it.

In many of these models, however, there is a missing element. The missing element is guidance in deciding which responsibility is most important. The above discussion of priorities can provide that element.

Here is a typical example of a step-by-step model for resolving ethical dilemmas.[2]

1. Gather the facts.
2. Determine the ethical issues.
3. What norms/principles/values have a bearing on the case?
4. List the alternatives.
5. Compare the alternatives with the norms/principles/values.
6. Weigh the consequences.
7. Make a decision.

The model provides a process or method that should help to keep the decision maker focused on the ethical dimensions of the decision that needs to be made. This is often very helpful. The model does not help one to know, however, what to do when relevant "norms/principles/values" point in different directions. We can return to the patient request that healthcare providers of a particular race not be assigned to his care. There are several different potentially relevant norms in this case: 1) one should not discriminate on the basis of race when making work assignments; 2) one should do what is in the patient's best interests; 3) one should not unnecessarily place employees in situations where they may be at risk; 4) one should not unnecessarily endanger the financial stability of the organization. The issue becomes how to interpret the norms and decide which among them is most important. Here the model does not offer much assistance.

Following a good process of decision making does not, by itself, mean that a good ethical decision will be made. If one's most profound workplace commitments are to one's own career advancement, concern about looking good in the eyes of the boss will probably dominate over other considerations even after one has gone through the process of gathering all the facts and answering all the questions. Good ethics is not a neutral process. It requires the right fundamental commitments, which are then put into practice in particular circumstances in a careful and conscientious manner.

A good reasoning process about ethical issues does not lead to an ethically sound conclusion unless one's starting point is ethically sound and unless one has the strength of character to act on the ethical beliefs. Being ethical is about having and implementing a good vision of the world. Addressing specific ethical issues is not just about solving problems; it is about solving problems in a way that is true to the right values and priorities.

Despite the limits to a process approach, models of ethical reasoning are still valuable as aids to individuals as they think about the implications of a particular issue. My own model of ethical reasoning for issues in healthcare business ethics consists of a short list of "Four Reminders":

Reminder #1. Try to situate the particular question or concern in the context of major ethical issues in society.

While it is often possible to define a problem in terms of competing interests in a narrow context, the best ethical insight is often achieved by seeing the issue in the context of related considerations in society. The full implications of the case of the patient who requested that black caregivers not be assigned to his care can best be understood if there is a deep understanding of the nature and impact of racial discrimination in our society. The implications of the case of the unreimbursed experimental treatment (Chapter 1) is probably best understood in terms of criteria for the just allocation of limited healthcare resources. To make good healthcare business ethics decisions often means seeing individual dilemmas in relation to justice concerns in society.

Reminder #2. Don't change the subject.

Those who have been involved in discussions of difficult and complex ethical issues have probably noted how difficult it is to keep the reflection focused on the issue in a sustained and concentrated way. Focusing on all the relevant considerations and only the relevant considerations is not easy. The temptation is very strong to grasp onto one consideration and let that one point bring the discussion or reflection to a stop. The temptation is very strong to get sidetracked by concerns or impressions relating to the persons involved in the case, when this is not relevant to the decision that needs to be made. To make good healthcare business ethics decisions often means disciplining oneself to keep the discussion focused.

Reminder #3. Don't hesitate to consult others.

We all have limited perspectives when we approach situations needing action. We are simply unable to be well informed about all dimensions of all issues, and, perhaps even more important, our perspective is naturally influenced by our own role in society and in the organization. What we see depends on where we stand: this is a simple fact of life. We see through the lenses of our own experiences and of those we associate with most frequently. Managers and employees, for example, often define the very same issue in very different terms. Medical mistakes made in a hospital may be perceived quite differently by the community served and by physicians on staff.

There are two types of assistance from others that may be particularly important in order to make good ethical decisions. The first is assistance that helps enlarge one's perspective, that allows one to hear the points of view of those affected by the decision who are not ordinarily heard. It is especially important to listen to those who are not well represented in the circles in which one regularly moves. The second is assistance that helps one understand the issue more fully, especially in terms of larger justice issues in society (see Reminder #1). This type of assistance may be one of the major contributions that can be made by an ethics consultant.

Reminder #4. Keep the focus practical without losing ethical ideals.

It is easy for many people, when thinking and talking about ethics, to be vague or to engage in generalities. When a decision needs to be made in a particular situation, the purpose of reflection is to determine the best decision here and now. Any concern about employee rights, for example, needs to be practically focused on what specific rights, if any, would be put at risk by a specific decision or policy. The need is not just to think about ethics, but to think about ethics in a way that spells out implications in the nitty-gritty.

To be practical does not mean, of course, that one must leave ethical ideals behind. It means, rather, that one must be concerned about the best ways of translating the ideals into action in a particular situation. It is not "compromising" one's ideal to recognize that what is required in a particular case is the best among several undesirable choices. To do the best, all things considered, is both practical and idealistic.

Conclusion

Perhaps the best way to describe a useful and principled framework for making ethical decisions in healthcare business is to demonstrate it through a discussion of a variety of specific issues. This is the agenda of following chapters.

Because ethics in not neutral, these first two chapters outline a particular understanding of the basic nature of healthcare organizations and a model of establishing priorities that focuses on the relative strength of different values, not on process. These are the ethical commitments that underlie the discussion of issues and cases throughout the book. The highest priorities are to respect basic individual rights and to promote and protect community good. Much of the discussion in the following chapters is an effort to clarify the meaning of basic rights and of community good. It is an effort, as well, to draw out the implications of a commitment to these priorities.

PART II

THE ORGANIZATION AS CAREGIVER

Three

Ethics, Cost, and the Quality of Care

In an essay entitled "Redrawing the Ethics Map,"[1] Richard Lamm argues that medical ethics, "as it is usually understood," is completely inadequate when it comes to the funding of medical care. Medical ethics needs to be revised because of its reluctance to take cost into account and because it tends to focus on only one patient at a time. Neither tendency is satisfactory, he argues, when it comes to constructing a public budget, where the need is to establish priorities and to engage in tradeoffs.

Though Lamm is focusing on public policy and the use of public funds, his basic point also applies to the management of healthcare organizations. Ethics and dollars are connected. What is the right action to take has to do with how financial resources are used just as it has to do with how patients are served.

Many clinicians appear to be uncomfortable including financial considerations when determining what is appropriate care. Most healthcare managers clearly recognize, on the other hand, that it is irresponsible not to take cost considerations into account. Their tendency is not to think that cost does not matter, but to think that cost has to do with the "business decisions," not with "ethics decisions."

Viewing cost and ethics as separate considerations has unfortunate consequences, however. Most importantly, it keeps us from doing the hard work of determining *when and how* counting the cost contributes to the understanding of what is most ethically appropriate. There is a need to become more skilled at including dollars in discussions of ethics and more skilled at including ethics in the discussions of dollars.[2]

Cost control is an ethical value, not just a practical requirement, but it is not the only ethical value at stake in most decisions. The skilled ethical manager knows how to balance considerations of cost with considerations of quality, risk, patient needs, patient preferences, clinician integrity, etc. The question is whether these other considerations should take priority over cost savings. The question is what is the proper balance between cost and other considerations in patient care.

> Case 3.1. The Radiology Department informs the senior management team in the hospital that the department is interested in reviewing the policy regarding the use of contrast media for imaging procedures. The Radiology Department had several years ago gone to the use of high-osmolar contrast media (HOCM) instead of the much more expensive low-osmolar contrast media (LOCM) in cases where there are no known risks. More adverse reactions occur with HOCM, but, it was agreed, the significant difference in cost justified the use of LOCM only in those cases where there are higher risks (such as a history of adverse reactions to contrast media, a history of asthma or allergy, known cardiac dysfunction, severe debilitation).
>
> Now some radiologists are requesting reconsideration, because the difference in cost between the two contrast media is not as great as it used to be.

Given the reality of limited available healthcare resources, providers are required to exercise careful stewardship of resources. Limited resources available to serve the needs of patients means that decisions are always being made about who gets what: it is simply not possible to provide the theoretical "best" for everyone, regardless of cost.

Dollars available for healthcare are limited. We—individuals, businesses, government—are unable or unwilling to invest the resources necessary to provide expensive healthcare for everyone. Meeting community healthcare needs requires, therefore, a conserving approach to the use of resources. Using more resources than necessary to provide good care in one setting means that too few resources remain to provide good care in another setting.

The rationale for wanting to keep the cost of contrast media down is a very important consideration. How that "saved" money will be used is a key concern. In general, however, a basic requirement of the ethical stewardship of limited resources is to use a less costly treatment unless there is "substantial evidence that a more costly intervention is likely to yield a superior outcome."[3] When there is a choice between two treatments and both are good but the considerably more expensive one is somewhat better in some regards, the question should be whether there is sufficient additional benefit to use the additional resources. The ethical use of limited resources places the burden of proof on spending more in these situations, not on using less than "the best."

This fundamental point may merit repeating. The reality of limited resources requires that healthcare providers shift from thinking that they should always try to use the best to thinking that they should try to use the least expensive that works well. Patients are not done a disservice when they are provided with good, competent medical care, even when they are not provided a more expensive intervention that might be marginally better. This recognition of the importance of cost in determining what is appropriate use of medical resources is essential if there is to be just and fair allocation of these resources. Meeting community healthcare needs requires keeping an eye on cost.

At the time that the present policy went into effect, institutional leaders had good reason for making the decision. HOCM is good, high-quality medical care. It may not be as safe as LOCM, but it is within the acceptable range of safety for those with no known indications of abnormal risk. When there are truly limited resources, good care at a much lower cost is better than the best care at a much higher cost. Saving money on contrast media can be a sound ethical judgment as well as a sound business judgment.

Criteria for selecting the more costly (and potentially better) interventions should be clearly identified risks or benefits. Cost-effectiveness studies have indicated that there is a good basis for using LOCM only selectively, that "the universal use of LOCM leads to use of resources that could be more effectively employed elsewhere."[4]

The question now being asked in the case above is whether the present policy remains justified when the cost difference is reduced. As a general rule, they have the burden of proof who propose a more costly intervention; they need to provide "substantial evidence that a more costly intervention is likely to yield a superior outcome." There seems to be a natural corollary to this general rule: The greater the cost differential between treatment options, the greater the required evidence or the greater the improved outcome from the more expensive intervention.

Now that the differential is shrinking in the use of contrast media, is the burden of proof met by showing that the use of LOCM does reduce the number of adverse reactions? Perhaps. It depends on what would be identified in an updated review of both the risks and the cost of the two options. Since LOCM is superior and would be used routinely if it were not more expensive, the lower the difference in cost, the greater the justification for using it on a normal basis. If the radiologists requesting the review are correct and the cost picture has changed considerably since the policy was approved, the question needs to be reconsidered.

As this case discussion suggests, good stewardship of resources requires taking cost effectiveness into account in ethical decision making. The next case, on the other hand, serves as a reminder that there are other considerations involved in the relationship of ethics, cost, and quality of care.

Case 3.2. The Balanced Budget Act of 1997 has resulted in a reduction in the amount of reimbursement for home healthcare for Medicare patients. Many home care nurses think that patients are getting inadequate care. With reduced resources, it is often not possible to provide comprehensive care for patients with complex medical conditions or home situations.

In the midst of this ongoing financial pressure, ABC Home Care needs to make a decision about whether to accept H. M. back as a patient. H. M. had been an ABC patient prior to a recent acute care hospitalization. His previous care resulted in a significant financial loss for the organization, and there is every reason to suspect that his renewed care will result in another loss.

Should ABC refuse to accept H. M. as a patient in order to avoid that risk of loss?

It is difficult to provide detailed commentary specific to this case when additional information is not available. It is possible, though, to identify some general guidelines that might assist in clarifying responsibilities in cases like this.

The reason the cost to the agency was so much more than the reimbursement amount in the care of this patient may be an important consideration. If it was largely the result of non-cooperation on the part of the patient or the result of some incompatibility between the patient and the agency staff, then there is a real question about whether this patient and this agency are a good fit. This is a concern as much about the quality of care as it is about the cost; it is not reasonable to conclude that this organization can provide this patient good care. It is important, however, to recognize that there is enormous potential for self-deception or rationalization. It is easy to say that a decision not to accept a patient is for the patient's good when that patient is both a financial burden and not the easiest patient to care for.

If, on the other hand, the only real reason to consider turning down the request to care for this patient is the desire to avoid additional financial loss, the picture is different. If the patient became a heavy user of resources because of unavoidable complications, there is no reason to think that this agency is not the right setting for this patient to receive high-quality care. Not accepting the patient back in these circumstances is, in effect, dumping this patient because of cost.

There is, however, only so much uncompensated care that an organization can afford to provide. Taking on new high-financial-risk patients may need to be avoided occasionally in order to maintain the organization's viability. This should be done only when necessary, and almost never with patients who already have some relationship with the organization and its staff. It is not fair for the patient, through no fault of his or her own, to be transferred around.

A recognition of one's role in service to the community leads, I think, to the decision to accept some high-financial-risk patients. High on the list of those who should be accepted are those for whom one has already been providing care. Continuity of care is a relevant consideration.

This case also points to another important ethical responsibility. If, as may be the case, the reimbursement rate is simply too low to support an adequate level of care, then there is a clear need to try to change the system or rate of reimbursement. Advocacy for patients requires active efforts to try to improve healthcare financing in order to meet the essential needs of patients.

Case 3.3. Senior management in a community hospital is asked to respond to a situation that has been getting attention both as a utilization and as an ethics issue. A patient has already spent thirty days in the hospital without an immediate end in sight. The patient qualifies for Veterans care, but the attending physician has refused to transfer the patient to the VA hospital because he does not think that the VA will provide the quality of care that the patient is presently receiving. The family does not want the transfer either. The nearest VA hospital is more than a hundred miles away.

The case was referred to the institutional Ethics Committee. At the Ethics Committee discussion, the attending physician indicated that he was not charging the family for his services and suggested that the hospital do the same. He pointed to the institutional mission statement's emphasis on providing care for those in need and challenged the hospital to live up to its rhetoric.

Continuing the healthcare tradition of compassionate service, many healthcare organizations are committed to providing services, when needed, even if patients cannot pay for those services. This stance is a very positive and important one, especially given the reality of so many uninsured in American society. It should not be understood, however, to mean that every request for uncompensated care can or should be satisfied. Uncompensated care dollars are limited and should be used in the most effective manner. The goal is to use these dollars wisely, so that they can have the most positive impact upon the health of the community served.

This patient does have access to care elsewhere, however. Unless the physician is able to provide convincing reasons that the care provided in the VA hospital would not be adequate to this patient's needs (or unless the patient is not stable enough to be transferred), there is no ethical justification not to transfer. One of the major points of this chapter is that high standards of ethics require taking cost considerations into account just as these standards require a clear focus on patient benefit. Since this patient's needs can be met in a different part of the system, it is poor stewardship of resources to continue to care for the patient in the community hospital. Given the information provided in the case description above, the Ethics Committee should recommended that the patient be transferred to VA.

A decision to transfer should, of course, be implemented with sensitivity and compassion. It might be appropriate for the institution to assist the family, depending upon their economic status, in paying for their lodging while the patient is in the VA hospital at a distance from home. This would seem to be compatible with wise stewardship of limited resources in a way that unnecessary long-term inpatient care is not.

Cost and the Quality of Care:
Some Ethical Perspectives

The above cases and commentaries are designed to stimulate reflection upon the need to balance the responsibility to contain cost with the responsibility to provide good-quality care. The following are some principles that can be used as a more systematic expression of a healthcare organization's ethical values and beliefs related to the provision of high-quality care in the face of limited resources. These standards help to sort out the implications of the commitment to community service and to respect for basic rights, key values discussed in Part 1.

1. Good-quality healthcare means cost-effective healthcare.

Since there are limited financial resources available for healthcare, wise stewardship of resources requires that all healthcare be rendered in a manner designed to prevent the unnecessary use of resources. Spending more than necessary in one situation makes it more difficult to meet other healthcare needs.

2. More expensive healthcare does not mean higher-quality healthcare.

Despite the tendency on the part of clinicians and the public to suggest that the emphasis on "the bottom line" is a threat to the quality of healthcare, there is no direct general correlation between providing higher-quality care and providing more costly care. Quality problems include underuse (failure to provide proven effective interventions), overuse (unnecessary interventions or treatment for clearly inappropriate indications), and misuse (interventions causing preventable complications). Some studies on quality suggest that significant cost reductions can be achieved while improving the overall quality of care provided.[5]

3. Certain minimum standards of quality must be met for all patients.

There is a minimum level of basic and essential healthcare service that must be provided to all for whom the organization has responsibility. It may at times be difficult to translate this essential minimum into medical and nursing standards, but this is an important justice standard. When providers do not ensure at least this level of care, a basic patient right is being violated. When insurance does not cover at least this level of care, the coverage is inadequate and unfair and the insurance company has failed to meet its ethical responsibility.

4. Patients are owed the services, if medically appropriate, included in the benefits package of their health plans.

This is simply a matter of contractual fairness. When patients are promised coverage and providers accept the patient under that plan, the covered and needed services are to be provided, even when the provider suffers a financial loss.

5. Patients are not treated unjustly when they do not receive all potentially beneficial care, as long as their basic and essential healthcare needs are met and they are treated fairly in regard to their promised benefits.

In the context of limited available resources, it is appropriate at times to provide less than the theoretical "best" healthcare possible in order to contain cost. There is no ethical obligation to provide the more expensive intervention with marginal additional benefits.

6. As a general rule, the least costly treatment should be provided unless there is "substantial evidence that a more costly intervention is likely to yield a superior outcome."[6]

This statement, taken from principles proposed by a clinician, is perhaps one of the best expressions of the practical meaning of stewardship of resources. The burden of proof is on justifying the more expensive intervention, not the less expensive one, when different acceptable treatment options exist.

7. The greater the cost differential between treatment options, the greater the required evidence of a superior outcome from the more expensive intervention.

In clinical ethics, many have recognized a "sliding scale" regarding competency: The more irreversible and drastic the consequences of a patient's refusal of treatment, the higher the level of understanding required before the patient is accepted as capable of making treatment decisions for her- or himself. A similar sliding scale should be used regarding the cost of different treatment options: The greater the increased cost of the alternative, the more convincing the evidence needs to be that there is a good probability or chance of a significantly better outcome.

8. Good-quality healthcare means delivery of healthcare services in the setting or location that is most appropriate both in regard to the patient's healthcare needs and in regard to cost.

High standards of ethics require taking cost into account, just as these standards require a clear focus on patient benefit. While the publicity given "drive-through" procedures has highlighted the possible abuse of the effort to transfer a patient for cost-saving reasons, caring for patients in less expensive settings remains a stewardship responsibility, as long as it can be done without exposing the patient to unreasonable risk.

9. A commitment to serving patients without regard to the ability to pay or to the source of payment should not be interpreted to mean that cost concerns are inappropriate for such patients.

Many healthcare organizations are explicitly committed to provide services, when needed, even if patients cannot pay for those services. This commitment is not in any way contradictory to the commitment to use limited resources wisely. In fact, uncompensated care dollars are also limited and should be used in the most effective manner, so that they can provide as much good care as possible.

10. Efforts to control costs always need to be evaluated in terms of their impact on patient care.

Where there is evidence that, in fact, cost-saving measures do lead to significantly lower-quality care (in terms of outcomes or respect for patient rights), then the cost-saving measures should not be implemented. Where there are serious quality issues that result from an emphasis on cost saving, there is an ethical responsibility to advocate for a change in practice.

11. It is better to confront problems of fairness and quality directly than to attempt to "beat the system" with "creative" coding or billing.

Most managers, in an age of "corporate compliance," are aware of the risks associated with anything that could reasonably be interpreted as fraud. Another reason why ethical managers avoid manipulating the record to secure payment is that this is often avoiding the need to confront directly issues related to adequate reimbursement for quality care. Deception of payers tends to be less challenging and more accepting of inadequate coverage than open advocacy.

12. The need to provide as good care as possible with reduced resources should not lead to harm or injustices regarding other employees.

Later chapters will address issues related to ethical treatment of employees. The point to be made here is that there is a need to guard against trying to achieve high-quality care and cost containment through staffing patterns and/or compensation rates that are unfair or excessively burdensome to employees.

13. A commitment to high-quality patient care may require advocating for more adequate coverage for individual patients.

Individual healthcare providers as well as healthcare provider organizations need to be advocates for their patients in relationship to payers. When payer decisions mean that truly necessary care will not be covered or that the patient is denied reimbursement available to others with the same coverage, providers have a responsibility to appeal on the patient's behalf (or support the patient's appeal).

14. A commitment to high-quality patient care may require strenuous efforts to get the payment system improved.

In addition to advocating for individual patients, healthcare providers have a responsibility to seek a more just system, a better allocation of limited healthcare resources. This might mean advocating for less coverage for some types of treatment in order to improve coverage for other (more essential) services.

15. Discretionary decisions regarding which patients to accept for care should reflect an acknowledgment of the responsibility of the organization to have one's "fair share" of high-financial-risk patients.

In making these decisions, managers need to determine whether the organization can provide the kind of care that the patient needs and can benefit from. In addition, it is appropriate to take into account the likely financial impact on the organization of the patient's care. It is not an acceptable practice, however, to refuse routinely all patients who appear likely to present a high financial risk. This is fair neither to the patients who need care nor to other provider organizations.

16. There should be mechanisms in place to review routinely the quality and cost-effectiveness of care of patients who are heavy users of resources.

It is important, in good stewardship of limited resources, to identify and review those cases in which the care is, or is likely to become, unusually costly. The purpose of such a review is to ascertain whether good-quality care can be provided at a lower cost.

17. Patients should be informed regularly regarding the relationship between the nature of the care that they are receiving and cost/coverage-related considerations.

The authors of an article in *Archives of Internal Medicine*[7] propose that case managers routinely and frequently meet with patients/families to keep them updated on financial considerations related to their care and their coverage/benefits. Whether or not this particular mechanism is used, it is important that patients and the public become more conscious of the need to take both cost and quality into account at the same time. Explicit rather than unacknowledged consideration of cost factors appears to be necessary in order to improve the ability to provide good healthcare.

Conclusion

Many in healthcare are reluctant to think about cost at the same time that they think about the quality of care. Most in healthcare are inexperienced in articulating the basis for deciding when the cost-saving impact of a decision should be a key factor in that decision and when it should not. Given these realities, the organization needs to encourage and promote a widespread discussion and reflection on ethics, money, and the quality of care. The above principles may be useful in promoting reflection within the organization, just as they may be useful in guiding decisions in individual situations.

Four

Patient Rights in a Just Organization

Respecting the rights of individual patients is a characteristic of an ethical healthcare organization. It is not the only characteristic, however. There is a need to understand clearly the ways in which respect for patient rights relates to a variety of ethical responsibilities.

Medical ethicists have been engaged in ongoing reflections on the nature and limits of patient rights. Concern that patients are sometimes subjected to unwanted treatment, especially near the end of life, has led to an emphasis on the patient's right to refuse treatment. Concern that physicians are being forced to practice bad (futile) medicine has led to an effort to define the limits of the patient's right to demand specific treatment. Recognition of the diversity of cultural values in society has led to efforts to determine the accommodation that healthcare organizations should make to patients with different cultural values. Recognition of the importance of the non-dramatic ethical issues ("everyday ethics") has led to concern about the rights of patients in relationship to institutional practices and concerns. The growth of managed care has led to efforts to clarify the rights of patients as enrollees in healthcare plans. The growing interest in complementary and alternative medicine may well lead to additional refinements of the meaning of patient rights.

I have already explored, in the last chapter, some questions related to the nature of patient rights in regard to cost considerations. This chapter provides a discussion of the extent and limits of the rights of individual patients regarding treatment decisions, regarding accommodations to cultural values, and in relationship to other institutional interests.

As was noted in Chapter 2, thinking carefully about ethical issues requires recognizing the difference between rights and wants or preferences. To say that one has a right to something (using the word "right" in the strict sense) is to say that one can make a binding claim upon others. To honor and protect a true right is a fundamental ethical responsibility; to say that someone's right has been violated is to make a most serious charge. Whether wants or preferences should be honored or accommodated, on the other hand, depends upon contextual considerations; one cannot usually make an ethically binding claim that wants or preferences be honored. Discussion of patient rights requires an effort to clarify, therefore, which interests should be considered rights and which are not at that level of ethical significance.

Patient Rights and Treatment Decisions

Case 4.1. The adult patient announces that his religious convictions as one of Jehovah's Witnesses do not permit him to accept blood products under any circumstances. He is eager to get on with his recovery and does not object to medical treatment of any other sort. He asks for assurance that his beliefs regarding blood will be respected.

Some members of the team caring for the patient later express their frustration about this request. They do not like having their "hands tied" by patients who want to benefit from aggressive medical care but who tell them not to do certain things that are part of that care. It is one thing for a patient to refuse medical intervention, they say; it is something else to tell the doctor what kind of medicine to practice. Medicine should not be looked upon as a menu from which the patient can pick and choose.

The right of informed competent individuals to refuse unwanted treatment is one of the most basic rights of patients in healthcare. Even when a patient consents to other medical treatment as recommended by the physician, his or her refusal of a particular intervention should be honored. Respect for individuals means that they will not be treated, something will not be done to or for them, without their permission. As a basic protection of human dignity, the right to refuse treatment continues to merit the emphasis that it has received in the last three decades in American medical ethics.

The hands of care providers are tied in cases like this only in one sense: they have no choice but to honor the patient's refusal of blood products. Beyond that, however, they need to exercise their professional responsibility as in any other case. If, as a result of the patient's refusal of specific interventions, the proposed treatment no longer meets criteria for safety or effectiveness, it should not be provided. The patient's decision may reduce options, but it does not change the essential relationship between clinician and patient. The patient's right to refuse unwanted treatment does not imply a "right" to get medically inappropriate treatment. The right to refuse what is medically indicated does not mean a "right" to demand (and get) what is not medically indicated. It is one thing to expect others not to treat without consent. It is something else entirely to expect others to practice medicine in ways contrary to professional standards.

It may happen that an alternative treatment that does not involve the use of blood is available but is more expensive.[1] Should that treatment be provided?

Patients do have a legitimate expectation that reasonable efforts will be made to provide them with beneficial treatment at the same time that their refusal of specific treatment is honored. Patients should be able to expect that respect for their deeply held beliefs about healthcare will result in reasonable accommodation when alternative options exist. It should be noted, however, that while the criterion of reasonableness applies in these situations, it does not apply in the same way when the patient refuses unwanted treatment.

Competent patients have a legitimate expectation that others will respect their informed refusal of treatment even when these others judge the refusal unreasonable. The same patient has a legitimate expectation that others will provide an alternative option only when providers judge that option reasonable. Deciding whether to accept recommended treatment is different from deciding what treatment is medically appropriate. Patients do not have a right to have the treatment they want even if such treatment is at odds with the professional responsibility to practice only good medicine and to use resources wisely.

Case 4.2. A young woman sustained a severe closed head injury in a motor vehicle accident. She was treated in intensive care but did not demonstrate any functional neurological improvement, and she remained ventilator dependent with tube feedings. After many weeks and repeated neurological exams, a determination of persistent vegetative state (PVS) was made. Plans were made to transfer the patient to a long-term-care facility.

Throughout the stay in the hospital, the family had insisted that all life-sustaining efforts be maintained or undertaken if necessary to keep the patient alive. They insisted that "as long as there is life, there is hope." They did not want to "give up." Now that the patient was being transferred, the staff at the long-term-care facility wanted clarification regarding future care. The physicians who had been caring for her in ICU thought that any further intensive care would be futile and said that they would not accept her back in the ICU.

Are the rights of this patient being violated if she is refused further ICU treatment that her family (presumably speaking for her) might want? There are really two parts to this question: (1) Does a patient have a right to treatment that is judged futile on the basis of good medical criteria? (2) Is this a case in which an appropriate judgment of futility is being made?

Self-determination in healthcare means that patients have the right to accept or decline proposed treatment and to choose from among proposed treatment options. The right to accept from among medically acceptable options does not imply the right to decide which options are medically appropriate. There are different roles for the clinician and for the patient. Respect for patient autonomy does not mean that the patient is his or her own physician.

This is not to say that the patient should be passive. This is not to say that patients should not inform their physicians about their own insights into their health and that they should not challenge what they consider to be questionable diagnoses and prescriptions. They should be encouraged to do both. Nevertheless, physicians have a responsibility to provide evidence-based treatment. It is not ethical medicine to provide patients with the treatment they want when the treatment is not indicated or there is no reasonable expectation that it will be beneficial.

This point is of relevance to healthcare managers as well as to clinicians. In some business settings it may be appropriate to operate under the assumption that the customer is always right, that the consumer is sovereign. Healthcare is not that kind of business. The patient is the center of attention and, in this sense, is the key "customer." The patient is not always right about medical treatment, however, and should not always get what he or she wants.

It is essential, for good-quality medical care and for the just management of healthcare organizations, to recognize that a patient does not have a legitimate claim to treatment that, on the basis of professional medical judgment, is recognized as futile or non-beneficial. When a patient or family wants "everything" done to extend life, that should be understood to mean everything that is medically appropriate and indicated.[2]

The second question regarding this case, whether further intensive care of this patient is futile, is more difficult to answer. There is no consensus that intensive efforts to sustain the life of a patient with PVS can provide a benefit; there is no consensus that such treatment constitutes a futile activity. As healthcare professionals and the public continue to grapple with the purpose of medicine and the meaning of "medical benefit," greater agreement may gradually result. It is likely, though, to remain very difficult to implement a judgment of medical futility in some specific situations.

Lawrence Schneiderman and his co-authors have emphasized the distinction between an effect and a benefit. An effect is a measurable change on some portion of the patient's anatomy. A benefit is an improvement in a patient's prognosis, comfort, well-being, or general state of health. "The ultimate goal of any treatment should be improvement of the patient's prognosis, comfort, well-being, or general state of health. A treatment that fails to provide such a benefit—even though it produces a measurable effect—should be considered futile."[3]

This is, I think, a very useful approach to understanding futility. It remains true, however, that it is often very difficult to determine which treatment should be considered futile, especially if there is some potential for prolonging a life.

Given the lack of agreement on what constitutes futile medicine in cases like the one described above, patient rights are best protected by procedural fairness. Patients have a right to be informed about decisions to withhold or discontinue treatment efforts against their wishes. They have a right to get a second opinion about the likely benefits of the treatment. They have a right to a clearly defined and timely review by someone (perhaps the Ethics Committee) capable of making a reasonably objective judgment of whether the institutional understanding of futility is being appropriately applied to this case. They have a right to seek a transfer to other providers. They always have the right, of course, to seek legal intervention.

When patients are understood as individuals and as members of a larger community, healthcare organizations need policies in place that permit patient-requested or family-requested treatment to be withheld when it is judged to be medically non-beneficial. To protect from an expanding or an abusive use of the concept of futility, however, these policies should require procedural safeguards. In disputes over whether a particular treatment is futile, patient rights are best protected by ensuring that the decision is not implemented without due consideration and reconsideration, not by simply doing what the patient/family wants.

Respecting Cultural Values

Respect for cultural diversity is becoming more widely recognized as an important personal virtue and an important organizational value. There is, as well, a clearer understanding in healthcare that respect for patient rights includes respect for expressions of cultural differences. The challenge is to respect the cultural values of patients while adhering to professional standards and to ethical business practice. It is often difficult to determine when the cultural values of patients should mean a change in institutional practices and when they should not.

Case 4.3. The rehabilitation patient is reluctant to engage in scheduled whirlpool therapy because she does not think that she would be appropriately dressed for being in the presence of males who are not members of her family. In her culture, she says, women do not appear in swimwear at public beaches or pools. She requests that she be given privacy and female therapists. Therapists take this request to their supervisor and ask what should be done. They state their conviction that it is important to treat all patients equally and that they do not think that patient requests for special treatment should be accommodated.

As a general principle, healthcare organizations should accommodate a patient's request for culturally sensitive special treatment to the extent that this is feasible, provided the special treatment is not likely to be harmful to the patient or others. Patients are not all the same; treating patients fairly does not mean treating them all the same.

There are two provisos in the above general principle: feasibility and the avoidance of harm.

Feasibility in this case has to do with whether facilities, staffing, and scheduling allow for the request to be accommodated in a reasonable way. It is feasible to accommodate the request if it is possible to do so and not pose an unreasonable burden. Respect for patients means that special requested treatment that is of significant cultural importance will be provided unless it is truly not feasible to do so. The request for privacy and female therapists should be honored if it is possible to do so and does not present an unreasonable burden to other patients or to staff.

What constitutes an unreasonable burden? There are no clear guidelines; commonsense judgments are required. Using staff responsibilities as an example, many would agree that simply making adjustments in patient assignments is not placing an unreasonable burden on them, even if they prefer not to have the schedule changed. Making unwanted shift changes, however, especially over a period of time, might well constitute an unreasonable burden.

The second proviso is the avoidance of harm. If the requested special treatment results in significant harm or poses the risk of significant harm, then the request should not be honored. Avoiding unnecessary harm is of higher ethical priority than honoring requests for culturally sensitive special treatment. A clinic that, for example, refuses to refer a patient for "female circumcision" is not violating patient rights even when the request is made on the basis of deeply held cultural beliefs.

It is frequently difficult to know how best to respond to requests for special treatment, and it is tempting to conclude that the best response is to treat all patients "the same." Patients are individuals with different beliefs and values, and their requests for special treatment should be considered on their own merits, not automatically rejected. It is always appropriate, of course, to consider whether alternative therapies could provide benefit without the need to accommodate special values. In the above case, an alternative to whirlpool therapy, if there is one that would provide comparable benefit, might be the best approach.

The question of whether the organization should make reasonable efforts to accommodate patient sensitivities in regard to gender or race or culture of those who provide care is considered in Chapter 10.

Institutional Interests and Patient Rights

Case 4.4. Mr. O., a mentally competent resident in a long-term-care facility, has a habit of walking to a nearby coffee shop a couple days a week. This has been going on for several years. He has become generally more frail, walks very slowly, and, despite new glasses, has problems with peripheral and depth vision. He needs to cross a street at a stoplight on the way to the coffee shop and he has been observed several times having trouble making that crossing. He starts out when the light is red, or it is red before he gets across. No accidents have occurred, but the director of nurses is concerned about the risks that he is taking. She is concerned, as well, with the home's liability if a car should hit him.[4]

There is a real tension at times among the various ethical responsibilities of the organization. In this case, for example, home management has a responsibility to protect the resident from foreseeable harm. They have a responsibility to respect the freedom and independence of the resident. If possible, management would like to do both at the same time. If it is not possible to fulfill both responsibilities, a decision about ethical priorities needs to be made.

There may be options available that would allow a win-win situation in which the nursing facility is able to ensure Mr. O.'s safety and he is able to retain his independence. He may, for example, agree to take his walk to the coffee shop only at specified times when a volunteer will be available to assist him in crossing the street. The goal is to find the least restrictive alternative to protect his safety. As a competent person, Mr. O. needs to be included in the decision-making process.

There are some alternatives that are clearly not ethically acceptable. Preventing him, against his will, from leaving the building or the property is unjustifiable. Manipulating him, through deception, to do what the staff wants is a clear affront to his dignity. Claiming that he has consented to restrictions on his freedom when he agreed to abide by the institution's policies is no justification to control his behavior. One cannot sign away basic rights.

Informed competent adult patients have the right to act in ways that may place them at unnecessary risk of harm. In addition to the right to refuse treatment discussed above, patients have a right to choose not to comply with recommended practices and procedures that are designed to protect them from harm, as long as their behavior does not pose a significant risk of harm to others. Only when such acts of "noncompliance" truly interfere with the ability of the organization to provide beneficial care should such behavior be considered as possible reason for discharge. Patients should not have to lose basic freedoms to accept professional care.

Putting the emphasis on patients' freedom to act in ways that may put them at risk of harm is not to say that other considerations are irrelevant. It is important to keep ethical priorities straight, however, and respecting a competent patient's freedom of movement is a higher-priority responsibility than protecting patients from accidental harm. Patient rights are fundamental and do make binding claims upon management of healthcare organizations.

It is not clear that the risk of harm to others (occupants of vehicles that may hit Mr. O.) is sufficiently great to justify restricting his freedom.

Honoring Patient Rights:
Some Proposed Guidelines

The discussion in this chapter has been designed to add to Chapter 3 in clarifying the nature, extent, and limits of patient rights in healthcare. It may be of value to conclude here with some general guidelines for respecting patient rights in relationship to treatment or care. Except for #5, which is discussed in Chapter 3, these guidelines summarize the points made in previous sections of this chapter.

1. Honor informed competent adult patients' refusal of treatment (except when such refusal puts others at serious risk of significant avoidable harm), even when the refusal appears to be putting them at unnecessary risk of harm and even when their values are not accepted in the dominant culture.

Except in the very unusual circumstances when the refusal of treatment for self may put another at significant risk of serious harm, respect for patient rights means accepting the informed competent patient's decision.

2. Honor informed competent adult patients' decisions to act in ways that might place them at risk of accidental harm.

Exercising normal control over one's own life should also be recognized as a right, not just a preference or want.

3. Refuse to provide or facilitate an intervention that is expected to cause harm to the patient, even when the patient requests the procedure with full knowledge of the likely harmful consequences.

Professional responsibility not to harm takes priority over satisfying the patient's request for specific treatment. There is no right to harmful treatment.

4. Avoid useless treatment, treatment not expected to be beneficial, or treatment not appropriate to health goals, even when requested or demanded by the patient.

Professional responsibility to practice good medicine takes priority over satisfying the patient's request for specific treatment.

5. Provide cost-effective treatment when treatment is paid for from shared resources, even if the patient does not want cost to be taken into account.

See Chapter 3.

6. Accommodate a patient's request for culturally sensitive special treat-

ment to the extent that this is feasible and reasonable, provided that the special treatment is not likely to be harmful to the patient or others.

Patient cultural preferences are important and worthy of respect, but they do not take priority over all other considerations. Patients have a general right to have their cultural and religious values respected, but there is not a clear right to have their specific requests honored in individual cases.

The interpretation of these guidelines and their application to particular situations sometimes requires experience and skill. In some cases, it may be helpful to seek assistance from an Ethics Committee or an ethics consultant.

Five

Clinicians and Conflicts of Interest

A Focus on Management

In their role as caregiver, healthcare organizations employ clinical professionals or enter into other contractual working relationships with them. Management decisions may have an impact on the ability of clinicians to act in the patients' best interests and on the likelihood that they will do so. The purpose of this chapter is to consider some management decisions and policies that might affect the way clinicians do their job. There are important ethical concerns that can help guide decisions that might affect either the incentive or the ability of clinical personnel to act in the patients' best interests.

"Conflict of interest" is a useful concept for facilitating a discussion of some of the ethical issues and responsibilities of concern here. Not everything in the chapter fits neatly into a discussion of conflict of interest, but this is a good place to start.

Conflict of Interest

Conflict-of-interest analysis underlies the policies in many employee codes of ethics on gifts and honoraria, on relationships to suppliers, and on outside employment. Employees are expected to subordinate their self-interest to the interests of the organization. They have a responsibility to avoid situations in which some personal interest is in conflict with their responsibility as employees or, if such a situation cannot be avoided, to protect against actions that are contrary to the organization's interests.

Manuel Velasquez has described conflicts of interest in a business setting in this manner:

> Conflicts of interest in business arise when an employee or an officer of a company is engaged in carrying out a task on behalf of the company and the employee has a private interest in the outcome of the task 1) that is possibly antagonistic to the best interests of the company, and 2) that is substantial enough that it does or reasonably might affect the independent judgment the company expects the employee to exercise on its behalf.[1]

The discussion of conflicts of interest in this chapter takes a somewhat different approach from this customary focus on the private interests of individual employees in potential conflict with their workplace responsibility. The focus here is on management's role as a possible contributor to conflicts of interest.

There are two ways in which this consideration of conflicts of interest differs from the more common one. First, the interest that should be subordinate and not permitted to become dominant is not something private or outside the organization. It is, rather, an interest promoted by the organization itself or resulting from a practice or policy within the organization. Second, the interest that should be dominant is not the organization's interest but professional responsibility to patients. In other words, the question is whether healthcare management is contributing to conflicts of interest through its decisions, policies, and practices.

Healthcare professionals sometimes find themselves in conflict-of-interest situations related to their private or business interests. There has been much attention given over the years to such practices as physician referral of patients to testing facilities in which the physician has an ownership interest.[2] Conflict-of-interest analysis is useful, as well, in considering the responsibility of clinicians who are offered gifts by drug company representatives and when dealing with the question of dual relationships with patients or clients.

The discussion here, however, focuses on those personal interests resulting from or contributed to by organizational practices or policies (such as incentive and reward systems) that may be in conflict with professional responsibility. As indicated, the analysis here is of the organization as a possible contributor to conflicts of interest.

For purposes of this discussion, I offer the following reworking of Velasquez's statement:

> Healthcare organizations contribute to conflicts of interest when the healthcare professional is engaged in service to patients and the professional has a personal interest 1) that results from practices or policies of the healthcare organization, 2) that is possibly antagonistic to the best interests of patients, and 3) that is substantial enough that it does or reasonably might affect the independent judgment patients should expect the professional to exercise on their behalf.

Management's responsibility, then, is to avoid contributing to conflicts of interest for those providing direct care for patients, if possible. When it is not possible, when contributing to some conflict-of-interest situations is necessary in order to achieve some other essential goals, then management's responsibility is to keep the conflicts as insubstantial as possible and to assist in finding methods of preventing behavior that is actually antagonistic to the best interests of patients.

Financial Incentives for Physicians

One of the Patient Rights and Organizational Ethics standards of the Joint Commission on the Accreditation of Health Care Organizations is that

> The Hospital's code of ethical business and professional behavior protects the integrity of clinical decision making, regardless of how the hospital compensates or shares financial risk with its leaders, managers, clinical staff, and licensed independent practitioners.[3]

The example of physician compensation is used here to explore the issue of protecting patients from harmful effects of financial incentives.

It is very difficult, if not impossible, to devise a compensation system for physicians that does not involve them in some conflict-of-interest situation. In "the good old days," the solo practitioner who earned a living through fee-for-service medicine was involved in a constant conflict of interest. The more services the doctor performed, the greater the income—and the doctor was the one who recommended that patients should have additional medical care. When combined with insurance, which reduces the financial incentive for patients to go without medical treatment, fee-for-service leads to a significant overuse of medical services.[4]

The point is not that physicians, in fee-for-service medicine, consciously prescribe more services than needed or warranted. The ethical importance of avoiding conflict-of-interest situations results from the recognition that, even for the most ethical among us, financial self-interest may have a subtle impact on objectivity of judgment, an impact that we do not recognize ourselves. The method of compensation may, in fact, have an impact on what is considered good practice. The issue is not personal ethics as much as compensation arrangements that promote, or work against, good medical practice. The issue has to do more with how the system works than with the personal integrity of individuals.

U.S. physicians have developed practice patterns that result in high utilization of costly medical services. These patterns appear to be so deeply ingrained that, in efforts to keep cost under control, most payers have decided that it is necessary to make use of financial incentives to achieve a more conservative use of medical services. Without such incentives, they believe, there is almost no hope of reducing unnecessary treatment and in achieving cost-effective treatment.

Financial incentives to use medical services more conservatively put the patient at some risk by placing the physician in a different kind of conflict of interest. If a managed care plan withholds a percentage of physicians' payment and releases it at the end of the year only if the physician group did not provide more than the projected number of services, there is a definite incentive not to provide unnecessary services. This is a desirable outcome, but the incentive might carry over to a reduction in necessary services. If providing appropriate care is more than rarely contrary to the physician's financial interest, the incentives are wrong. "Something is perverse in a payment system when it makes well-intentioned physicians look at sick patients they treat as a drain on their income."[5]

If some financial incentive is truly essential to reduce unnecessary treatment and promote the most cost-effective treatment, it is appropriate to use such an incentive. Incentives need to be used carefully, however, so that they do not result in care contrary to the patient's best interests. Using the example of a withhold system, guidelines like the following suggest important protections against putting patients at too great a risk by putting physicians in too great a conflict of interest.

1. Incentives should not be too high.

The amount of any financial incentive designed to promote a particular type of behavior needs to be calculated very carefully. In order to be effective in affecting behavior, it needs to be of some significance, more than just a nominal or token amount. On the other hand, the higher the amount of the incentive, the greater the potential that it will encourage "cutting corners" or other deviation from professional standards. Ezekiel Emanuel suggests a 20 percent limit: "the higher the financial incentive, the larger the conflict; at some point the financial incentive is simply too large . . . when the salary withhold or bonus exceeds 20 percent of a physician's salary, it is too large."[6]

Twenty percent may well be a reasonable limit. The amount of the incentive should not be too high, but the determination of what is too high depends, in part, on what other safeguards are built into the payment system to protect against rewarding inappropriate behavior.

2. Incentives should be based on meeting quality criteria, not just reduction in resource use.

Physicians should use resources when appropriate, according to quality standards, and not use them when inappropriate. This is the message that should be conveyed by financial incentives. To do so, it is not enough to focus on the overall volume of services, to focus on simply reducing expenditures. What incentive programs should do is discourage inappropriate services and encourage the use of the fewest resources needed to achieve beneficial results. Incentives should be related to quality guidelines and to cost-effectiveness criteria and focused on specific practices rather than global use of resources. Both overuse and underuse of services would then be factors. "Such incentives would discourage both skimping and waste, would reward physicians for providing good medical care, and would not undermine fidelity to patients."[7]

Good-quality healthcare means cost-effective healthcare. Payment incentives for physicians are appropriately focused on evidence of cost-effectiveness. At a time when there may still be a need to change patterns of medical practice that involve overuse of services, it is understandable that someone may choose to promote more cost-effective healthcare by providing incentives to reduce overall use of services. The problem with this method is that it is too blunt and it sends the wrong message. It fails to protect patients against the underuse of services, and it communicates to physicians that the only thing the payer is really interested in is the bottom line, regardless of quality. The payer organization's commitment to good-quality healthcare needs to be built into financial incentives. Quality criteria and data collection methods have been developed to the extent that this is now clearly feasible.

3. Financial incentives should be used sparingly as a method of influencing physician practice patterns.

There is something at least a little problematic about using strong financial incentives to promote good practices by physicians or by any other service professionals. What these incentives do is promote good practice (when they do, in fact, promote good practice and not just cost cutting) by focusing on the professional's self-interest. It is characteristic of service professions to place a strong emphasis on service to others and to play down self-interest. It is characteristic of service professions to stress the importance of adhering to high standards of professional responsibility/professional ethics, even at some cost in terms of one's financial self-interest. This is not to imply that such professionals are not motivated by financial interests; of course they are. And it is ideal when financial self-interest and professional responsibility both point in the same direction.

Nevertheless, to focus primarily on financial incentives as the motivator to provide good service is to risk distorting the nature of service professions. A basic starting point of healthcare business ethics, as I have noted, is that healthcare is not just like any other business, primarily because of the service orientation. The financial incentive model of promoting desired behavior may have more appropriate use in the commercial world than in healthcare services. One does not need to be naive about the impact of self-interest and one does not need to have romantic notions about the altruism of medical practice to recognize that using financial self-interest as a key motivator carries with it the risk of subtly changing the model of professionalism.

Many of the points made here about physician incentives in managed care plans are relevant to other situations as well, such as compensation of physicians by hospitals. They also apply, with appropriate translation, to compensation of many non-physician healthcare professionals. The reward system, the incentives and disincentives, should be such that professionals are not distracted from their responsibility to provide high-quality services but are reinforced in that responsibility. If this is not the case, management of healthcare organizations is contributing to conflicts of interest.

Management Decisions and Patient Best Interests

Healthcare managers make frequent decisions that have an impact on the ways in which clinical professionals do their work. It is not always easy to know which decisions put patients at unnecessary risk. The following cases (two of which appeared in slightly different forms in earlier chapters) provide the opportunity to think further about what is ethically appropriate when management makes decisions that might affect the incentive or the ability of clinical personnel to do what is in the patients' best interests.

Case 5.1. Several years ago the hospital, following consultation between management and the Radiology Department, established a policy regarding the use of contrast media for certain imaging procedures that was based on considerations of cost-effectiveness. According to the policy, high-osmolar contrast media (HOCM) is to be used instead of the more expensive low-osmolar contrast media (LOCM) in cases where there are no known risks. Though there is a higher risk of adverse reactions to HOCM, it is considered good-quality care. The significant difference in cost is recognized as justifying the use of LOCM only in those cases where there are particular risks (such as a history of adverse reactions to contrast media, a history of asthma or allergy, known cardiac dysfunction, severe debilitation).

Recognizing that good-quality healthcare means cost-effective healthcare, it is important to point out that policies like this do not place physicians in ethically compromising situations. Such policies, assuming that they are based on good information and judgments appropriate to the cost and the seriousness of the risks, do not put the physician in the position of having to choose between providing high-quality patient care and following the organization's policies. There is no real conflict. Good-quality care is precisely what good policies on cost-effective care promote.

A good principle of healthcare ethics is that one should provide the least costly treatment to care for a particular condition unless there is "substantial evidence that a more costly intervention is likely to yield a superior outcome."[8] There can be, and often should be, debate about what constitutes "substantial evidence" and how to understand "likely," but the principle is still an important one. Given the reality of limited available resources, good medicine in this case does not mean the safest care available regardless of cost.

There are individual physicians, of course, who do not agree that cost should be taken into account in situations like this. They may think that policy decisions, such as in this case, interfere with their efforts to carry out their professional responsibility. Cost-effective care policies are not always well received by clinicians. Nevertheless, as long as such policies are based on recognized quality standards and are developed with the participation of the appropriate clinicians, they are appropriate. They do not prevent clinical professionals from fulfilling their responsibilities to patients.

> Case 5.2. Various factors, including some changes in reimbursement rates, have put the hospital in the red. At a meeting of the management team, a decision was made to cut costs by reducing the payroll. The major cuts are to be in the nursing budget, the largest labor cost in the institution. Nursing management is told to reduce the number of RN positions and, if necessary, increase the number of unlicensed assistants.[9]

Management affects the quality of healthcare provided by clinical professionals through decisions about staffing and working conditions. The responsibility not to act in ways that compromise the quality of care should be a major consideration when staffing and workload decisions are made. The appropriate number of registered nurses on various units, the length of their shifts, the number of patients employed physicians are expected to see, the hours of residents: these and similar questions relate very much to the quality of patient care.

Not every claim that "the quality of care is going to suffer" if something is done means, of course, that this is true. Nevertheless, staffing practices are related to the ability of professionals to provide good care. Similar to decisions about cost-effective medical care, staffing and scheduling decisions should be evidence-based whenever possible. They should take into account studies on the patient care impact of particular staffing patterns. Many times, however, these studies are not available or not conclusive. As one nurse consultant acknowledges, "Studies are not yet complete that support the premise that eliminating professional nurse positions and adding UAP [unlicensed assistive personnel] will negatively affect quality care."[10]

What should be done in the absence of clear data? Caution is necessary when making decisions that may have a negative impact on the quality of patient care. On the question of reducing the nursing staff, it may be somewhat reckless to assume, in the absence of good information, that there is likely to be no significant negative patient care impact from such a move. In addition, there is need to give attention to the process of decision making. Just as medical treatment guidelines should not be introduced without appropriate consultation with and agreement from physicians, so nursing staffing patterns should not be established without a similar consultation with and agreement from nurses.

When nursing staff is spread too thin, nurses are not able to provide professional-quality services to all patients. It is important to recognize that staffing decisions, not just financial incentives, can put clinical staff in a position of compromising their professional standards.

Case 5.3. In an alternative model of care for frail elderly, several PACE centers have been established around the country (PACE = Program of All-Inclusive Care for the Elderly). For a set monthly fee (paid privately or by Medicare-Medicaid under a managed care arrangement with waivers), the program provides total care for those ill or frail enough to be candidates for nursing homes but not so ill that they require twenty-four-hour care. Services are designed to maintain patients' ability to live independently in their own homes and neighborhoods. Participants are brought to the center a couple days a week for medical care, nutrition monitoring, bathing assistance, etc. Home care visits are also provided, including some housekeeping assistance where necessary.

The PACE center is responsible for the total cost of participants' healthcare wherever received. When participants are cared for in hospitals or in long-term-care facilities, their care is much more costly to the program than when they stay in their own homes. The program physicians make most decisions about hospitalization or nursing home placement.

Does this arrangement put a program physician in an ethically compromised position? There is no doubt that caring for these patients in a full-risk arrangement means that there is incentive, for the financial well-being of the organization, to keep patient cost down. There is incentive to keep a patient out of the hospital or the nursing home. The incentive is present even when the cost of patient care is not directly tied to the physician's own income, because a physician working in such a center is likely to have a strong personal investment in the success of the program. She or he cannot help but be aware of the fact that program participants who need institutionalized healthcare are much more of a financial burden on the program than those who do not. There is a risk that the physician's objectivity of judgment may be affected.

In this case the risk to quality patient care may be acceptable, provided that certain precautions are taken. Persons who choose to be participants experience many benefits in the program as a result of the full-risk arrangement and of the Medicare/Medicaid waivers. Their independence is valued and supported, and attention is paid to quality-of-life concerns. They have access to a variety of healthcare professionals without being institutionalized and without additional fees.

As was noted earlier, any method of payment for healthcare services involves some incentives to provide one kind of care or another. The payment system here provides incentive to keep patients out of the hospital and out of the nursing home. The incentive is to keep participants healthy and to provide support for them to stay in their own homes. The incentive appears, by and large, to promote good quality of care, though it may result, at times, in a significant reluctance to put a patient in a hospital or nursing home.

Even when institutional factors affecting clinician behavior are appropriate, it is important to prevent negative impacts on the quality of care. It might be useful, for example, to have clear criteria or indications for placing a patient in a hospital or nursing home and to involve more than one clinician in the evaluation of questionable cases. It is also important that salaries, fees, and benefits for clinicians not be tied too closely to the financial well-being of the organization.

Organizational Ethics

The reader may have noted that nothing has been said in this chapter about one usual response to potential conflicts of interest: disclosure. Boards members of healthcare organizations are asked to disclose their financial interest in companies with which the organization does business. Speakers in continuing medical education programs who have a financial interest in a particular company are expected to disclose that interest if they discuss a product or service provided by that company. Disclosure is a common method of managing potential conflicts of interest. Letting others involved in a situation know that a person has a financial stake allows steps to be taken to prevent this interest from influencing decisions.

While disclosure has value at times as a way of protecting against harm that may result from conflicts, it is not a key response to the very specific focus of this chapter. The goal here is to reduce the extent to which management contributes to conflicts of interest for clinical professionals. The issue here is how the organization should be managed so that it is not the source of unnecessary conflicts that put patients at risk.

The issue here is not so much how the individual behaves as how the organization is managed.

Six

A Fair Hearing of Appeals of Denied Coverage in Managed Care Plans

Managed care has grown rapidly in the United States during the last decade and has, in recent years, been subjected to widespread criticism. Much of the criticism is directed at practices that are perceived as denying patients needed care. One issue related to that concern, tying physician compensation to resource use, is discussed in Chapter 5. This chapter is related to another aspect of the question of limiting care for patients—denial of coverage for desired services. Specifically, the question here is what constitutes a fair hearing and a fair response when members request reconsideration following denial of coverage.[1]

Legislative efforts to protect the rights of managed care members often include the proposal that members have the right to have their appeal for coverage of denied services heard by an outside independent party. There is much to be said for the opportunity for an external appeal once a member has completed the internal appeal process, but this chapter is focused exclusively on the internal process. This is where most cases are resolved, and this is the arena in which management has responsibility to ensure that the appeal hearing is fair.

A commitment to fairness requires an understanding of the criteria to be used in making decisions. A commitment to fairness requires the implementation of the appropriate procedures. This chapter, therefore, includes consideration of procedures followed as well as reflection on the meaning of fairness in hearing various types of appeals.

Before proceeding further, a brief comment on the benefits package may be in order. The determination of covered benefits and the level of benefits does not start with a clean slate, as we might prefer in order to design the most rational system of allocating limited resources. There are certain mandated benefits that regulations require. There are also marketplace constraints that result from a number of factors, including the type of coverage provided by other plans in the geographical area, the impact on the membership mix (and, therefore, on the financial risks) involved in offering services not covered by other plans, and the perspectives and expectations of the benefits managers at corporations where the plan is marketed.

The result is a subscriber contract that may not always be fully consistent and/or clear in terms of the rationale used for determining which services and benefits to include. It might be useful to discuss the ethics of benefit package design further, but that is another agenda. What is important to note here is that the hearing of appeals takes place in the context of contracts that are not always as conceptually clear and consistent as might be desired.

Hearing Appeals: Procedures

It is inevitable that there will be some situations in which plan enrollees think that they are being denied coverage that should be provided. Given the imperfect nature of any benefits contract and the need to reconsider it or its interpretation at times, and given the potential devastating effects of some decisions made regarding healthcare coverage, it is absolutely essential that plan members have the opportunity to appeal benefit decisions. In a good healthcare plan, members are well-informed regarding their right to appeal and the procedures to be followed, procedures which are designed to be user-friendly: clear, simple, and timely.

A good appeal response process requires a commitment of resources. Plan members are owed not only a quick response, but one that is thorough, involving a review of all relevant data. To provide a fair response, one that is both timely and thorough, requires that appropriate mechanisms are put in place to see that this happens.

The initial review of an appeal, to assess whether the contract stipulations appear to have been appropriately applied to this case, is a management responsibility. Fairness to the member requires more than consistent application of contract language; it also means that the appeal will be considered, if the member wishes, in terms of any extenuating circumstances that may require a unique response in this case. Plan members should have the option of appealing the initial decision on their appeal to another level within the organization.

The final internal option is usually the appeals or grievance committee, a body with authority to overrule any earlier denial. The primary advantage of using a committee is that there are different perspectives brought to the review. Another major advantage of a committee is that in a committee setting, individuals need to explain their perceptions and reasoning to others, a process that often leads to a helpful testing of one's thinking.

The committee needs to be sufficiently independent, in fact as well as in role description, so that it feels no obligation whatsoever to confirm management's decisions. There are various models of appeals committees in use in different plans. One good one is a committee made up primarily or entirely of persons who are themselves participants in the plan, but who are not employees of the managed care organization. As persons who themselves get their healthcare through this plan, grievance committee members should be able to recognize the need to be fair to subscribers and to identify with subscribers. On the other hand, it is also important that grievance committee members recognize a commitment to the well-being of all members of the plan, not just those appealing a decision. This means, among other things, that they recognize the reality of limited resources and the importance of consistent applications of the subscriber contract. One interesting model is to use subscribers who are elected by other subscribers to the Board, where this practice exists, as the grievance committee. They represent members, and they have Board responsibility for the plan as a whole.

Providing a good grievance procedure requires careful attention to the details of the process. Those appealing denials of coverage should have the opportunity to make their case in person. While the committee often needs the presence of management and medical directors for clarification of issues related to the case, it is important that the committee carry out its final deliberations and decision making only after management personnel have been excused. This promotes candidness in deliberation and independence in judgment. These sorts of procedural concerns are important in maintaining fairness in the appeal process. They increase the likelihood that attention will be focused on basic rights and on community service more than on organizational self-interest.

Types of Appeals

The appeals for reconsideration when coverage has been denied cover a wide variety of situations. It is possible, however, to identify some of the types of cases that occur and to offer examples of interpreting the demands of fairness in these situations.

1. *Coverage for out-of-plan providers.* One type of appeal that is fairly common is the appeal for coverage for services provided by physicians or other professionals who have not contracted with the managed care organization. One of the ways in which managed care organizations are able to manage both the quality and the cost of care is to provide services through a restricted number of professionals. Yet plan members sometimes have their own reasons for seeking exceptions to the requirement that their healthcare services be provided by professionals in the plan. Some of the appeals make the claim that the outside provider is "the best" for a particular type of treatment. Sometimes the appeal is based on the claim that the desired provider (outside

the plan) has developed a new technique that is not (yet) available within the plan. Sometimes it is a desire to return to someone who has provided good service in the past (when the subscriber had different coverage).

> Case 6.1. A 75-year-old patient has severe degenerative joint disease, and her orthopedist within the HMO has recommended hip replacement. The patient requests approval to have the procedure done by an outside orthopedist (at a nearby university hospital) because of a conviction that he is the best in the area. The HMO has several qualified and experienced orthopedic surgeons (though none with the national reputation of the university surgeon), and the patient is told that this procedure will be covered only if it is done by one of the HMO's surgeons. The patient appeals the decision, asking that the plan cover surgery by the university physician.

The question here is whether subscribers should be covered for services provided outside the plan when similar services are available within the plan. The general guideline is this: It is not appropriate use of shared resources to pay the extra costs associated with going outside the system for treatment that can be provided by competent and experienced persons within the system. Without evidence that the patient is at risk of getting inadequate care within the plan, those reviewing the appeal should uphold the denial. Plan members are not being treated unfairly if they do not get what they judge to be "the best" treatment available anywhere when high-quality treatment and skilled practitioners are available within the plan. In fact, spending extra plan money to pay for the patient's choice in this case might reasonably be judged ethically wrong. It would be at odds with the responsibility to exercise wise stewardship of resources.

2. *Coverage for alternatives to inadequate care.* Sometimes subscribers will seek coverage for treatment received (these are usually after-the-fact cases) because they thought that it was necessary to go outside the system for treatment they had first sought through normal plan channels. These are out-of-plan cases, but with a difference. The only reason for going out of plan is that they have been unable to get what they considered appropriate care within. "Appropriate care" might mean medically appropriate: for example, a patient who thought that she or he had been misdiagnosed and decided, in an emergency, not to return to the same provider. "Appropriate care" might also mean ethically appropriate: for example, a patient who thought that the right of an adult Jehovah's Witness to refuse blood products was not understood or was not likely to be respected by the plan provider.

In cases like these, those hearing the appeal need to make a judgment on whether it was reasonable for the patient to conclude that adequate treatment or care was not being provided and that it was reasonable to seek that treatment or care where he or she did. This is a somewhat different kind of judgment—not whether the type of treatment or care should be recognized as something owed to the member, but whether the member had a reasonable basis for concluding that good care was not likely to be provided within the system.

> Case 6.2. A woman began seeing an out-of-plan OB/GYN when she became pregnant for the third time. She returned, in fact, to the physician (Dr. A) who had followed her during her first pregnancy. After the first baby was born, her husband changed jobs, and they became members of the HMO. She began seeing an HMO OB/GYN (Dr. B). She didn't feel as comfortable with Dr. B. but was willing to stay with him— until she totally lost confidence. A few weeks into her second pregnancy, she began bleeding. She called the doctor and described her situation to the nurse. After consulting with the physician, the nurse returned to the line and told her that bleeding was normal early in the pregnancy, and that she need not seek immediate medical attention. The next morning, she miscarried.
>
> When she again became pregnant eight months later, she went back to Dr. A. (not part of the HMO) and requested that the plan cover this care. She was told that she should choose from among other OB/GYN physicians within the plan if she was dissatisfied with Dr. B. She appealed this decision.

An appeals committee is not likely to find this an "easy" one. While there are physicians other than Dr. B. within the plan who could provide good care for this patient, she has had a bad experience with one HMO doctor and a good experience with the out-of-plan doctor. Her confidence and comfort are important to her well-being and to her satisfaction as a member of the plan. This is the type of case in which reasonable and sensitive persons may well disagree regarding the extent of the organization's responsibility to the plan member. She should not be required to return to Dr. B., but there are other doctors available in the plan. It is reasonable that she does not want to seek another new doctor in her third pregnancy. Still, it remains important to receive care within the plan when that care is available and meets quality standards.

Even when the member has a reasonable basis for going outside the plan, the need for cost control remains important. The greater the amount of extra cost, the greater the need for a compelling reason for going outside the plan.

If the appeals committee decides that coverage should be provided in a case like this, it should also impose some limits (in regard to future coverage for outside-the-plan care for mother and baby). It will likely need to find some way to balance the recognition of the unique circumstances of the individual plan member with the need to get the person back in the system in order to manage the care.

3. *Coverage for explicitly denied procedures.* Sometimes plan members appeal denials of coverage for procedures that are explicitly excluded in the subscriber contract. The claim is that the particular procedure should be covered in their case, that their case should be recognized as an exception, because it meets the larger goal and purpose of healthcare coverage. For example, a woman may seek coverage for breast reduction surgery out of a belief, supported by a physician, that the pain and discomfort associated with breast size make such surgery in this case "medically necessary" rather than "cosmetic" (the reason for the exclusion).

The appeals for covering the cost of explicitly excluded services or procedures might seem to be among the easiest ones that come to appeals committees: If the contract is clear, what else needs to be said? As a matter of fact, these cases are often very difficult. A contract is obviously extremely important, but it is not the final word on fair and appropriate coverage. What justifies covering a service that the contract says is excluded is the recognition that the overall commitment to the plan member requires that this service be provided in an individual case. The appeals committee has the responsibility to make that assessment.

There is another very important ethical issue related to appeals on explicitly excluded procedures or services. There are likely to be other subscribers who did not appeal because of the contract language but who may also have strong cases. There is a fairness issue when those who challenge get treatment not available to those who try to abide by the literal terms of the contract. This is an issue that I return to in the section on consistency below.

Case 6.3. A plan member seeks coverage for surgery related to TMJ (temporomandibular joint) dysfunction. He claims to be in extreme pain as a result of this problem and to be unable to open his mouth to any significant extent. He has lost weight over the last several months. An oral surgeon has recommended surgery. When authorization was sought for the surgery, plan administrators pointed out that surgery for TMJ dysfunction was specifically excluded in the subscriber contract. They told the subscriber that they were not saying that the surgery would not benefit him, but that it was specifically listed as a contractual exclusion and was outside the benefits of the contract.

This case exemplifies some of the real-world messiness in which persons responding to appeals need to do their work. The contractual exclusion for TMJ-related surgery may have little to do with whether patients need this kind of surgery and are likely to benefit from it. It may have little to do with whether it is medically appropriate. It may have more to do with attempts to distinguish between what should be considered dental care and what should be considered general healthcare and with what "the competition" covers.

There is something unacceptable, however, about a situation in which someone with healthcare coverage is in constant pain and is denied the treatment that is judged by appropriate physicians to be the best way of trying to solve the problem. If review of the medical facts and physician recommendations lead to the conclusion that oral surgery is the most appropriate treatment in the circumstances and is very likely to correct the problem, then there is good reason to approve coverage for that treatment, even if there is a specific exclusion in the contract. It is possible that, in an individual case, oral surgery is an essential level of care. Members have a legitimate claim to the minimum level of essential medical care, regardless of contract language.

It is possible, of course, that a careful review of this case would lead to a different conclusion. The point to be made, though, is that, while the contract is very important, it is not the final word on justice or fair treatment of patients. Exceptions to the contract are not be made arbitrarily and inconsistently, but the contract should not prevent people in need from getting the essential level of care that can truly benefit them.

4. *Coverage for experimental "last-chance" therapy.* One type of explicitly excluded treatment merits special discussion. This is experimental treatment in the case of a patient who is dying and for whom there is no proven effective treatment. What should be done when a plan member seeks coverage for an experimental procedure based on the claim that it is the only option left and might be beneficial?

Case 6.4. The patient is a 34-year-old woman with advanced breast cancer. She has requested coverage for treatment that involves high dose chemotherapy with autologous bone marrow transplant, an experimental procedure which her doctor has told her may be her "only chance." The treatment is very expensive and considered unproven, though promising enough for various clinical trials to be undertaken.

The plan initially responded to her request by saying that this treatment is considered experimental and therefore is not regularly covered, but that if the patient qualifies for participation in a scientifically valid trial, the plan would cover the treatment as part of a trial. Unfortunately, the patient's condition is so poor that she did not qualify for any of the scientific studies to which she applied. She has appealed, seeking that this treatment be paid for anyway as her "last chance."

The ethical intensity of the decision that needs to be made in a case like this is caught in a comment by Norman Daniels and James Sabin:

Not covering treatments that ultimately prove to be effective lets curable patients die prematurely, and even if a treatment ultimately proves to be ineffective, not covering it may create the impression that critically ill patients are being abandoned in their moment of need. Covering treatments that ultimately prove to be ineffective or harmful reduces the quantity and quality of the patient's remaining life, wastes substantial resources, and undermines clinical research. These are the moral stakes in the decision.[2]

In the case, as described, plan management has recognized that research regarding last chance therapies that have shown some promise should be supported. They have also taken a reasonable position in their interpretation of the responsibility not to provide coverage for unproven treatment. If someone is judged not to be a good candidate for this experimental treatment by those doing the research, there is very little reason to think that the treatment will benefit the patient.

There appear to be good reasons for the appeals committee to support management's decision in this case. There often comes a time in someone's dying when the treating physician needs to acknowledge that nothing more can be done medically that is reasonably expected to be beneficial. These may be tragic situations, but the patient is not being treated unfairly when that judgment is based on good medical knowledge. It is the same with covered services. The member is not being treated unfairly when a decision is made not to pay for what cannot reasonably be expected to be beneficial. The willingness to cover the treatment if it is part of a scientifically valid research program is a good way of protecting against a too quick or too harsh judgment that something that might hold some chance should not even be tried.

The objective of a good healthcare plan is to maximize the health of the population served, subject to available resources.[3] I would judge the coverage decision in this case to be in line with this objective.

Given the climate of opinion about managed care organizations, decisions not to cover "last chance" treatment in a particular case may lead to some bad publicity for the plan. While it is both understandable and tempting to do what appears necessary to avoid adverse publicity, it is more important to concentrate on the ethical integrity in decision making. The desire to avoid publicity does not provide ethical justification for a deviation from the decision that one would make on the merits of the case.

Hearing Appeals: Consistency

Those hearing appeals for coverage need to be constantly aware of the need for consistency. A basic principle of fairness or justice is that similar cases should be treated in a similar manner. If similar cases are not treated in a similar manner, there is reason for someone to suspect that the decision is based not on the facts of the case but on some personal factors unrelated to the legitimacy of the claims. Without a commitment to consistency in reviewing grievances, an organization cannot expect anyone to respect its procedures and its interest in treating people fairly or with respect.

It is not easy to be consistent. One member's situation may sometimes arouse much more compassion than another's. One member may make a much stronger case than another in writing or in personal presentation. Protecting against inconsistency requires a constant check on whether one is basing the decision on relevant factors. If there is no clear reason for distinguishing between the two cases in terms of health condition or the treatment (or other factors relevant to the organization's responsibility to the plan member), it is hard to justify treating the cases differently.

One particular consistency issue relates to clearly excluded coverage. If an appeal regarding an excluded benefit seems to indicate that an exception should be made in an individual case, the appeals committee has a very difficult decision to make. If it approves coverage in this case, the plan is providing a benefit for this patient that others (who never appealed) do not have. It may be appropriate at times for the appeal committee to approve coverage for something excluded in the contract, as discussed earlier. If the decision is made to pay for a specifically excluded procedure, that decision seems to imply that the specific contract exclusion might be questionable. Follow-up review of the contract exclusion is indicated, as is a willingness to consider other requests for exceptions. Consistency does not mean that nothing can change or that there can be no exceptions, but it does mean that the implications of making an exception in one case need to be considered and applied in similar cases.

Another possible challenge to consistency occurs when a member in a particular case threatens to go to the media or to sue if coverage is denied for a particular procedure. While one may well want to avoid the publicity and/or the lawsuit, this does not provide ethical justification for a decision that one would not make on the merits of the case. Inconsistency in response to these sorts of threats is not only ethically questionable but also difficult to defend to the public.

Hearing Appeals: An Ethics Function

This quick review of the general types of appeals on which rulings have to be made indicates the extent to which this responsibility is an ethics function. Hearing appeals involves making decisions about whether plan participants have legitimate moral claims to be covered for particular services in particular situations. Hearing appeals means making decisions about what is fair and what is not. Though an appeals committee is not usually referred to as such, it is an Ethics Committee in a very real sense of the term. Both those actually hearing appeals and those having responsibility for ensuring that appeals are handled appropriately might do well to think about the process and the criteria explicitly in terms of the meaning of fairness.

Seven

Organizational Ethics
A Code Is Only the Beginning

In 1995 the Joint Commission on the Accreditation of Health Care Organizations began to include accreditation standards related to organizational ethics. These standards now require a code of ethical behavior that addresses, at a minimum, marketing, admission, transfer and discharge, billing, and the relationship of the organization and its staff to other providers, payers, and educational institutions. In addition, JCAHO expects the code to protect the integrity of clinical decision making from undue influence brought about by methods of compensation.

The primary purpose of these standards is to ensure, to the extent possible, that business practices related to patient care are conducted in a manner that is honest and proper. These standards do not cover the whole range of ethical concerns that exist in any healthcare organization. They do not, for example, address most of the ethical issues facing the organization in its roles as employer or as a member of the larger community. JCAHO standards are selective and focused on the organization's role as caregiver. Meting these standards does not mean that the healthcare organization has adequately addressed organizational ethics in the full sense of the term.

There is a second way in which getting a good score on these standards is not a sufficient indication that the organization has attended adequately to organizational ethics. Written codes in and of themselves do not ensure anything. Even when the code is disseminated to all the right people within the organization, it does not usually by itself have a major impact on behavior, as is discussed below. The expectation that behavior will be affected by codes is especially questionable in the cases of codes being developed quickly, without much opportunity for consultation and careful reflection, as is sometimes the case in preparation for a Joint Commission site visit.

JCAHO's decision to include organizational ethics is, nevertheless, an important development in the accreditation standards and presents a good opportunity for management to assess and improve its efforts to promote ethics within the organization. Doing what is necessary to satisfy JCAHO is not sufficient, but it can be a good start. A code of ethics in business practices communicates the importance of doing things the right way at all levels in the organization. It sends the message that administration is interested in results *and* in how they are achieved. A well-constructed code provides real guidance to management and employees for actions in some difficult situations. A good code that is well publicized says that in this organization, it is very important to think and talk about ethics and that this thinking and talking is expected to have a direct impact on behavior.

The Culture of the Organization

In an important article in the *Harvard Business Review*, Lynn Sharp Paine argues that the ethical behavior of individual employees, even when ethics is defined in terms of minimal standards of behavior, is very much the responsibility of management. It is rare, she writes, that it is an individual character flaw that fully explains misconduct. "More typically, unethical business practice involves the tacit, if not explicit, cooperation of others and reflects the values, attitudes, beliefs, and behavioral patterns that define an organization's operating culture."[1] To improve individual ethical behavior in the organization requires a focus on the organization's culture.

The way that individual decisions get made is often the result of the organization's culture: what is usual practice, what is rewarded, what is "the way things work here." The culture, more than any expressed beliefs or written standards, shapes decisions. Managing ethics means modifying the organization's culture, if necessary, so that it supports behavior that matches the ethical standards.

Emphasizing the importance of organizational culture is not to excuse individuals or to imply that they should not be held accountable for their own behavior. It is, rather, to recognize that a strong ethical culture and organizational systems supporting and rewarding appropriate behavior are extremely important, certainly more important than codes alone. In another important article that appeared in the *Harvard Business Review*, Robert Jackall describes how managers in organizations often come to understand that success and failure are defined in social and political terms (what is acceptable and approved by those who have control over one's future in the organization) and not in terms of performance.[2]

The goal, according to Paine, is "organizational integrity," the true integration of expressed values into practical decision making at different levels in the organization. Among the hallmarks of an effective integrity strategy are these:

The espoused values are integrated into the normal channels of management decision making and are reflected in the organization's critical activities: the development of plans, the setting of goals, the search for opportunities, the allocation of resources, the gathering and communication of information, the measurement of performance, and the promotion and advancement of personnel.

The company's systems and structures support and reinforce its values. Information systems, for example, are designed to provide timely and accurate information. Reporting relationships are structured to build in checks and balances to promote objective judgment. Performance appraisal is sensitive to means as well as ends.

Managers throughout the company have the decision-making skills, knowledge, and competencies needed to make ethically sound decisions on a day-to-day basis. Ethical thinking and awareness must be part of every manager's mental equipment. Ethics education is usually part of the process.[3]

When leaders see to it that resource allocation, performance evaluations, and educational opportunities all reflect a commitment to high ethical standards, they are sending a message loud and clear that the translation of the organization's values into everyone's everyday behavior really does matter.

Though the two cases found in this chapter are related to activities in which JCAHO has a particular concern (admissions and discharge), the intent is not to describe what should be included in a code of ethics. Rather, it is to consider issues that may very well not be clearly included in codes of ethics. An ethical organization is one in which individual managers and institutional culture encourage, support, and reward conscientious efforts to apply high ethical standards in responding to issues, whether or not the issue is specifically addressed in a code.

Admission to a Hospitalist System of Care

It is easy, when thinking of "admissions," to think of the admissions function and those who have "admissions" in their job description. It may be more useful, in organizational ethics, to think of what is required to meet patient needs and to respect patient dignity when someone is first admitted. This includes attention to, for example, the availability of interpreters for someone who does not speak English; the criteria for admission to intensive care units; the availability of records and advance directives from earlier admissions; responses to patient questions about the cost of care and possibilities of financial assistance; and the criteria for assigning specific staff to specific patients.

There are many decisions and practices that affect a patient when she or he is first admitted that are of ethical significance. They should not necessarily all be included in the section of the code that addresses "admissions," but they are all attended to in an organization that seeks to ensure that the treatment of patients and the community is consistently fair and respectful of rights. The question of the patient's relationship to the physician upon admission is one such concern.

> Case 7.1. Management of a community hospital, together with the Medical Executive Committee, has been reviewing a proposal to implement a hospitalist approach to inpatient services. In a hospitalist system, primary care physicians do not manage the care of their patients who are hospitalized. They concentrate on outpatient care (presumably doing what they do best) while another physician, the hospitalist, manages the care of inpatients. The proposal has the support of many physicians who see this as an opportunity to improve patient care. Because hospitalists focus exclusively on the care of patients in the hospital, they can provide higher-quality care for hospitalized patients, it is maintained, than primary care physicians who work primarily with outpatients. In addition, the use of hospitalists is expected to offer cost savings in inpatient care.
>
> There are some concerns that have been raised about the hospitalist model, concerns related to the discontinuity of care, to the impact on doctor-patient relationships, to the ability of patients to choose their own doctor, and to informed consent. Patients often choose their primary care doctors and/or develop a long-standing relationship with them. They may then find themselves in a situation, when they need hospital care, of being in the care of a physician whom they did not choose, with whom they do not have an established relationship, and with whom they may have to repeat any advanced planning that they did with their "own" doctor.[4]

The identification of the physician who will have primary responsibility for managing the patient's care is an important component of the way that a patient is treated. The decision to adopt a hospitalist model has a potential impact on the quality of care, the cost of care, and respect for patient rights. In making a decision on this question, the following suggestions might help to contribute to a decision that reflects the organization's commitment to high ethical standards.

1. An objective review of available and relevant information on the impact of this model should take place before a decision is made.

Relevant information means information on the impact of the hospitalist model in other community hospitals. Relevant information also means information that covers the whole range of considerations, including quality, safety, cost, the ability of patients to exercise their rights, and patient satisfaction. Decisions of this sort should be evidence-based, to the extent possible, and should recognize that evidence of the impact on the patient's role in health-care decisions is every bit as important as evidence regarding the impact on other quality factors, on safety, and on cost.

2. A decision to adopt the hospitalist model should involve implementing a version of the model that protects as much as possible against the disadvantages of the approach.

There are advantages and disadvantages to the hospitalist model. When a decision is made to implement it because the advantages are seen as outweighing the disadvantages, it is important to build in mechanisms to reduce the disadvantages as much as possible. In regard to patient rights, for example, the organization might stipulate the following: patients whose primary care physicians do not provide inpatient care management will be informed of this as early as possible in their relationship to their physicians; patients who request a different hospitalist will have that request honored if possible; the hospitalist has access to the patient's office records; the hospitalist will involve the primary care physician in situations in which familiarity with previous history is relevant to decisions that need to be made in the hospital. Patients have a legitimate expectation that every effort will be made to provide continuity of care and to respect their values even if their primary care physician does not manage their inpatient care.

3. The new system, if adopted, should be thoroughly and regularly evaluated as the organization gains experience.

As with any other significant change, it is quite possible that the implementation of the hospitalist system in a particular institution will lead to unanticipated consequences. The process of implementing the system should also include the implementation of an ongoing assessment that, as in the original review, focuses on the full range of relevant considerations.

An institutional culture that expects and promotes sustained, informed, open, and patient-centered reflection on the impact of different arrangements for delivering care is a good indication that ethics is important in the organization.

Discharge as a Fairness Issue

The most important ethical concern related to discharge or transfer is the appropriateness of the decision. Patients should be discharged or transferred when the appropriate level of care can best be delivered elsewhere and when the discharge/transfer is to a setting adequate to meet their continuing needs. The financial interests of the organization or of physicians should not be permitted to lead to discharges or transfers that deny patients access to an essential level of care. Discharge decisions, like other quality-of-care decisions, should be based on the best available information regarding outcomes and cost-effectiveness.

Case 7.2. A Utilization Review specialist in an inpatient rehabilitation unit has brought a length-of-stay concern to her supervisor. The patient is an executive in a major corporation, and the self-insured company is covering the cost of rehabilitation care. The UR specialist tells the supervisor that nurses and therapists on the unit and she herself think that this patient is being given special treatment, that he would have been discharged some time ago if the criteria applied to other patients were applied to him. Despite the fact that the patient has achieved the gains in functioning that normally signal that it is time for discharge, the stay has been extended twice. The patient has indicated that he would like to stay as long as possible, because he believes that this is the best way to hasten his complete recovery, and the UR specialist thinks that this patient is being allowed to exercise inappropriate influence over the discharge decision. It is an issue of fairness, she says, and it is having a negative impact on staff morale.

The supervisor has discussed the situation with the responsible physician, who indicated that he thinks the patient is continuing to improve and that inpatient care is appropriate given this fact and the fact that the home environment presents obstacles (stairs, no family) to optimal improvement. He would like to keep all patients with this sort of injury and similar home settings as long, but financial resources usually do not allow this kind of rehabilitation program. The supervisor also knows that the rehabilitation facilities are not being fully used, so the length of this patient's stay is not preventing someone else from receiving care on the unit. The case manager for the patient's company (the payer) is not expressing any judgments about the patient's length of stay.

For many, this case presents no dilemma. The patient, according to the physician, is benefiting from continued in-patient care; no one is being deprived of needed care; the hospital is not losing money on the case; there is no problem. There is a potential problem, though; there is a real need to address the question of fairness that has been raised.

The physician in this case indicates that other patients could benefit from longer stays as well, but that they do not get them because of their limited coverage. Are they being treated unfairly? Even if they could benefit from a higher level of care, they are not treated unfairly if they receive good-quality care. To repeat the point made in Chapter 3: Patients are not treated unjustly when they do not receive all potentially beneficial care, as long as their basic and essential healthcare needs are met and they are treated fairly in regard to their promised benefits. If the usual discharge criteria for rehabilitation treatment for a particular condition are based on good information on quality and cost-effectiveness, the fact that someone else receives special care does not mean that those who receive the usual have been treated unfairly. They *are* being treated unfairly, of course, if they are being discharged before they meet criteria.

There remain, however, several considerations regarding fairness in this case.

First, there is an ethical limit to the length of stay for this type of patient. When the point is reached at which there is no reasonable basis to expect that the patient will benefit more from continued inpatient care than from outpatient care, then inpatient care is clearly inappropriate, whatever the patient wants. To continue beyond this point is to waste healthcare resources. Company healthcare budgets are shared resources, and others may well be adversely affected at some point by this waste.

Second, there may be a need to get a second opinion regarding the continued appropriateness of inpatient care when the length of stay goes beyond the usual for the condition. When a patient with social standing, wealth, or power requests a longer stay, the circumstances may affect objectivity of judgment, especially when there appears to be no financial disadvantage to the organization to comply with the request. In order to protect against subtle influences on judgment brought about by the circumstances, it would be good practice to have another physician evaluate the appropriateness of further inpatient treatment.

Third, it is important to prevent a decision to allow a longer stay for this patient to carry over to other types of special care by the professional staff. The special treatment accorded this patient regarding length of stay may signal that the patient is a VIP who should, for example, have his nurse calls answered more quickly or be allowed to dictate changes in the physical therapy schedule. The patient's needs in regard to professional care are no more important than those of any other patient, and there is no justification for this special treatment.

This discussion of a discharge case raises an important question related to admissions and, perhaps, to marketing: When should designations like "VIP" be used for patients? What should they mean? The staff is this case is described as being bothered by questions of fairness. This almost always happens when patients receive special treatment. Before there is special treatment given to any patients in the organization, the fairness issues should be addressed carefully and explicitly.

Race, Gender, Income, and the Quality of Medical Care

Among the commitments that healthcare organizations make is one of nondiscrimination: The provision of healthcare and the quality of the healthcare provided within the organization will not be influenced by such factors as the age, race, gender, religion, ethnic origin, and income of the patient.

This is a standard organizational commitment, but it is not always the practice. Studies show that inequality in healthcare services does exist. One major research project, for example, found significant inequality related to race and income: African-Americans and lower-income whites are at risk for treatment associated with less than optimal management of diseases.[5] Other studies have indicated that women do not receive the same quality of health-care as men; women, for example, are not nearly as likely as men to be re-ferred for cardiac catheterization.[6] Given the real possibility in any healthcare organization of a divergence between the principle and the reality of equal care, this concern should be high on the agenda of all involved in organiza-tional ethics.

To acknowledge that inequalities exist that are related to race, sex, and in-come does not explain the reasons for these inequalities. To acknowledge these inequalities is not to say that the differences result from conscious judg-ments to discriminate. To the extent that these inequalities are the result of biases, they are likely to be based on unconscious assumptions that we have about persons of a particular race, gender, or income level. Unintended dis-crimination is, however, discrimination. De facto discrimination, regardless of the cause, is of great ethical significance and needs to be addressed.

There are several methods of seeking to bring about better compliance in medical care with the ethical standard of non-discrimination, methods that recognize the importance of addressing institutional culture when seeking to affect behavior.

The close connection between organizational ethics and non-discrimination is demonstrated, first, by having only those persons in leadership roles in eth-ics in the organization who have and are known to have a demonstrated sen-sitivity to inequalities and a commitment to meeting the challenge they pose. If the persons who have been selected for leadership roles in clinical ethics and in business or organizational ethics are not known to have an interest in issues of inequality and subtle discrimination or, worse, are known not to have such an interest, the message is clear that this is not an important ethical commitment in the organization.

Another method of seeking to raise the level of awareness of the need to be more non-discriminatory in practice is to undertake a systematic educational effort. If management, perhaps through its organizational ethics mechanisms, sponsors and promotes education on ways in which the race, gender, and class of patients might be related to the quality of the care they receive, it will be demonstrating its own sensitivity to this concern and will be providing an opportunity for others to deepen their concern. It will be putting the issue on the agenda in a very public manner.

Most important of all, in seeking to ensure that the principle of non-discrimination gets translated into practice, is to find ways of monitoring practice in order to prevent inequality in healthcare within the institution. The organization might, for example, accept the recommendation made by H. Jack Geiger in the *New England Journal of Medicine:* "the routine and on-going examination of racial disparities in the use of services and in the choices of diagnostic and therapeutic alternatives should be part of the quality-assurance protocols."[7]

In discussions of ethical issues related to the higher education administration, the term "shadow curriculum" is sometimes used (for example, by the Association of University Leaders for a Sustainable Future) to describe the institutional culture, structure, and practices that exercise a powerful educational influence. Students learn ethical values from the shadow curriculum or the informal curriculum as well as from the formal curriculum; they learn by what they observe about what is rewarded at the university, what behaviors are encouraged, reinforced, and permitted by the predominant institutional culture. What the institution recognizes as acceptable practices, especially practices that are the result of decisions on the part of university leaders, express a position on ethics, whether intended or not. The shadow curriculum may be more powerful than the formal curriculum. What we do can be so loud that others cannot hear what we are saying.

Codes of ethics in an organization are the equivalent of the formal ethics curriculum. They represent one important way of trying to promote certain values in the organization. Attention needs to be paid to the shadow ethics curriculum as well. Unless there are clear signals in institutional practices that inequalities related to patient race, gender, or income are totally unacceptable, the words in the code about non-discrimination can be expected to have little impact.

Ethics in the Organization

I have suggested in this chapter that a major commitment to organizational ethics in healthcare requires attention to more issues than those identified in JCAHO's standards and requires going beyond the adoption of codes of ethics. Management can take advantage, though, of the opportunity presented by JCAHO's requirements to clarify the ethical values of the organization and to develop mechanisms to implement these values whatever issues arise.

The last section of this book returns to the question of how best to ensure that ethical issues get adequately addressed in the organization. Before doing that, however, it is important to develop a more complete picture of the range of ethical issues that are significant in the business of healthcare today. The issues discussed in this chapter and in this section have remained basically within the general framework of JCAHO's focus on ethics in business practices that impinge on interactions with patients. There are many other ethical issues facing healthcare management that are not as immediately related to patient care. Some of these are discussed in the next two sections of the book.

PART III

THE ORGANIZATION AS EMPLOYER

Eight

Just Wages and Salaries

It hardly needs to be said that wages and salaries are of great importance when considering ethical issues in any organization. Though there are many reasons for working in addition to the money earned for the job, the level of pay is very important for employees throughout the organization. Responses to the question of whether employees are treated fairly usually begin with a consideration of compensation.

There is a long tradition in ethics, though not a well-known one in every environment, regarding what constitutes a fair or just wage at the low end. In recent years, with the rapid increase in executive compensation, attention has also been paid to ethically appropriate salaries at the high end. A third major consideration relates to the fairness of the compensation of employees relative to others in the organization, sometimes referred to as "equity." This last issue has received particular attention because of the fact that many occupations traditionally dominated by women do not pay as well as occupations traditionally dominated by men.

Just Compensation: Introduction

Case 8.1. The Director of Human Resources has recently begun to make use of "human capital cost" as a measurement for helping to assess how well the organization is doing related to human resources. HCC is the organization's total payroll-related expenses (pay + benefits + cost associated with absences and turnover) divided by the total number of full-time equivalent employees. The resulting number is the cost per FTE.

The Director proudly reported that the HCC for this organization last year was "benchmark" when compared with the average in the health-care industry as whole; it was lower than 90 percent of the organizations for which information was reported.

Thinking about this report from the perspective of a commitment to fair wages and salaries, one might wonder whether it is really "best" to be among the very lowest in the industry. That could mean, after all, that the organization is underpaying (some) employees.

Arriving at a number that can be compared with numbers from other organizations does not give much information about the fairness of compensation in the organization. Human capital cost is like medical loss ratio, discussed in Chapter 1. Being able to calculate a number and compare that number with other organizations does not answer the question of what the goal should be. To describe something as "benchmark" does imply that the goal is to have a low HCC factor compared to others. It is a big and unwarranted step to go from comparing costs with other organizations to concluding that organizations with the lower costs are doing "better" than those with higher costs. Numbers can sometimes be dangerous. Comparing "our numbers" with "their numbers" often involves the competitive effort to make our numbers higher or lower, whatever the case may be, in order to be better than the competition. While there is a way in which the wages or salaries paid to those in similar positions in other organizations can be used to help determine fairness in compensation, the average across all employees is not helpful information for determining what is just compensation in any particular job category. The implication that a low HCC means a good organization works against efforts to set wages and salaries on the basis of explicitly determined fairness criteria.

The goal of the ethical organization is not to pay as little as possible, but to pay well enough to attract good employees, to keep turnover down, to recognize the contributions made by employees, and, above all, to ensure that all employees are paid enough to allow for a decent standard of living.

Salary and wages in businesses in the United States are characterized by a wide and growing pay gap between those at the top and those at the bottom. Whether these salaries and wages, at either end, are to be judged just or fair depends on our understanding of the meaning of justice in compensation. Statistics like HCC that average the pay of all employees say nothing about compensation at different levels in the organization, just as per capita income says nothing about the distribution of income within a country.

Efforts to clarify the nature of justice in society and in organizations have led, over the years, to a developing understanding of how we might best think about just compensation. These concepts and principles do not lead to a simple formula for determining fair salaries and wages in individual cases, but they do help managers recognize the kinds of considerations that need to be included.

The Minimum: A Living Wage

Case 8.2. The hospital CEO in a major metropolitan area has been reviewing the results of a recent employee satisfaction survey and is not at all surprised to note that, especially among hourly employees, the number one complaint is about wages. That was to be expected, but she decides that it needs some follow-up. She contacts the Director of Human Resources and asks him to meet with her to discuss wages. She suggests that they use nursing assistants as an example: How much are they paid, and how do we determine whether these wages are fair?

The HR Director reports that nursing assistants start at $8.05 an hour and that the average wage for the position in the organization is now $8.78. The starting wage is determined by the market, he says; anything less and we would not be competitive enough to fill positions. "We pay basically what other similar institutions in the area pay." He adds that the $8.05 is nearly $3 an hour more than the legal minimum wage of $5.15 and that benefits include health insurance. If we paid any more, he concludes, there would be upward pressure on wages for other positions in the institution and a real stress on the budget.

The industry standard, what employees would likely earn doing similar work in similar organizations in the area, can be of some value at times in helping to determine fair compensation. It is not entirely satisfactory, however, as the basis for determining the minimum that one should pay for the lowest-paid positions in the organization. Here the key question is whether the industry minimum wage standard is sufficient to allow someone to live in dignity and whether it is in conformity with the organization's commitment to treating employees in a way that recognizes their contributions. Justice may require paying workers at the low end of the wage scale more than the industry standard. The market is not the ultimate determiner of justice in compensation.

A just minimum wage has long been understood to be a living wage, one that permits a full-time employee to earn enough to meet the basic living needs of the worker and a small family. In 1933 Franklin D. Roosevelt said, "No business which depends for its existence on paying less than living wages to its workers has any right to continue in this country. By living wages I mean more than a bare subsistence level—I mean the wages of decent living."[1]

In Article 23 (#3) of the United Nations Declaration of Human Rights (1948), the principle is expressed in these words: "Everyone who works has the right to just and favourable remuneration ensuring for himself and his family an existence worthy of human dignity."[2] In 1989, the Commission of the European Community in their "Social Charter" expressed their belief that "Workers should be paid wages sufficient to support a decent standard of living for themselves and their family."[3]

The determination of what is a just minimum wage is determined, then, largely by the cost of living. The U.S. federal *legal* minimum wage is not based on the cost of living. It is set the way legislation gets made; it reflects a variety of criteria and influences and compromises. This can be contrasted with the U.S. federal poverty threshold, which is based explicitly on a cost-a-living analysis. Families are defined as poor if they do not have enough income to pay for the cost of basic needs (such as inexpensive food, shelter, clothing). A just minimum wage is usually calculated in terms of the ability to support a family of four persons. A fair minimum wage is one that allows an employee to cover the basic cost of living for a family and to have a little "extra" to pay debts or to set aside for the future.

At the federal legal minimum wage of $5.15 an hour, a full-time employee paid the minimum wage earns $10,712 a year (40 hours a week, 52 weeks a year). This is significantly below the federal poverty threshold for a family of three or more.[4] In 1998 the U.S. Census Bureau's poverty income threshold was $16,588 for a family of four ($7.98 per hour). The fact that someone can work full-time and not be above the poverty level for a small family means that the legal minimum is not sufficient to meet the standard of a living wage. It is not a just wage.

The Census Bureau has used a simple calculation to draw the poverty line since the 1960s: Multiply an economy food budget by three. This seems quite unrealistic today. The total cost of living for a family is usually more than three times the cost of food alone. A more realistic formula suggests that a family of four needs about $20,000 to meet basic living expenses.[5]

In recent years, there has been an active "living wage" campaign in the United States, a movement that is attempting to raise the legal minimum wage by bringing it more into conformity with the cost of living. The campaign has been focusing on local jurisdictions, where it is often easier for voters to translate their beliefs into law through ballot initiatives.[6] Such efforts have been successful in many cities around the country, including Baltimore, Boston, Los Angeles, Milwaukee, and Detroit.

The Detroit effort can be used as an example. In the fall of 1998, voters overwhelmingly approved a ballot proposal that applies to employers who do business with the City of Detroit worth $50,000 or more a year—through contracts, tax breaks, or other economic aid. They must pay their workers at least at the federal poverty level, and at 125 percent of the federal poverty level if they do not provide health benefits. This was calculated to be, at the time, $7.70 per hour for an employee with health benefits and up to $9.63 for an employee without health benefits.

One of the objections to the living wage standard (and to the living wage campaign) is that it may cause some non-profit organizations to suffer because they cannot afford to pay wages at this level. Non-profit organizations often do have very tight budgets, but they have no more justification for paying unjust wages than anyone else. From the perspective of what is minimally owed to any worker, the standard must apply to non-profits as well as to for-profits. Basic rights need to be respected in all organizations.

The Detroit example points to the importance of healthcare benefits when considering just minimum wages. In considering whether compensation is sufficient to meet the needs of individuals and families in the United States, where healthcare insurance is so closely tied to employment, the analysis of just wages needs to include healthcare insurance. It is unreasonable to expect that poverty level wages will permit families to purchase health insurance, along with everything else that they need. Yet it is clear that access to healthcare is one dimension of a decent standard of living.

The following, in summary form, should guide decisions establishing the very lowest wage that will even be considered in the organization.

1. The lowest wage paid within the organization will be based on the principle that the person working full-time should earn at least enough to be above the federal poverty level (adjusted for regional differences in the cost of living where this is significant). At the very minimum, the organization will pay wages that exceed the federal poverty threshold for a family of four in order to allow the family to meet its basic needs and to have a minimum of discretionary income.
2. Since employment is the normal manner of acquiring health insurance for the working-age population, the minimum compensation package will include health coverage (or the equivalent additional amount of income).
3. In order to earn a living wage, low wage hourly workers need to have the opportunity to work 40 hours a week, if at all possible. If they work less than 40 hours, payment at the per hour poverty threshold level will clearly not provide a living wage.

The wages for nursing assistants, in the case above, are very near the poverty level, even according to the traditional way of calculating that level. The wages are, in other words, very near the minimum that is fair in any organization in the U.S. Taking into account other criteria for determining just wages (such as the level of responsibility required, the contribution to the quality of care provided by the organization, the training or experience required, or the stress involved in the job), a strong case can be made for concluding that they are not being paid a just wage.

One additional point should be made. If the move to ensure that all employees are paid a living wage requires a significant increase in the wages of those at the bottom of the wage scale, managers need to be prepared for the reaction of other employees, perhaps especially those at the next-higher wage level. If the compensation of some employees is raised more quickly (a higher percentage) than others, there is likely to be a sense on the part of other employees that they are not being treated fairly. They may feel the factors that were originally used to differentiate their "worth" to the organization are not receiving adequate attention. It is probably necessary, therefore, to be very explicit about the reasons for raising wages at the low end and, at the same time, to give consideration to the pay differential throughout the organization.

Executive Compensation

In the United States during the last two decades, there has been a rapid growth in the wage gap between the high-paid and the low-paid. When inflation is taken into account, those at the low wage end actually earned less in the mid-1990s than in the mid-1970s, while the compensation packages of those at the high end have grown radically. This income gap, much higher than in most other countries, raises serious ethical issues for American society.[7] The major differences mean an unequal distribution of power and influence in society, which raises serious questions about the possibility of true democracy. Democracy requires that citizens have the ability to participate as equals in the governance of society.

This large income gap is the context within which the effort to provide fair compensation takes place in organizations. The previous section provided some perspectives on the minimum that justice requires. It is important to give serious attention, as well, to ethical criteria for determining appropriate compensation for those who are the highest-paid. Though it is not always the case that the CEO is the highest-paid person in the organization, most of the ethical analysis has been focused on executive compensation.

Case 8.3. The Executive Committee of the Board has been reviewing a bonus program for senior management that was put in place a few years ago. The program has been closely tied to financial performance: senior management is awarded a bonus if financial goals for the year are met, a larger bonus if "stretch goals" are met.

The proposal being considered for the next year would add a variety of other criteria. These include goals related to accreditation, several other quality-of-services indicators, employee absences, and voluntary resignations, in addition to financial goals. Further, the proposal requires that no management bonuses be paid in any year in which it is necessary to eliminate jobs through layoffs or in which all employees are not given at least a cost-of-living increase.

The CEO expresses mixed reactions to this proposal. He welcomes the expanded criteria, he says, because this better represents management's range of responsibilities. He is not supportive of the layoff and wage provisions, however, because, he argues, taking decisive action in order to protect the financial viability of the organization is a sign of good management in difficult situations and should be rewarded.

As was discussed in Chapter 5 in regard to physician incentives, compensation based partially on the achievement of specific goals is one way, often an effective way, of communicating the importance of these goals and improving the likelihood of their achievement. Incentives define priorities and accentuate certain responsibilities. It is important, therefore, that the right priorities be established in any bonus package.

For a healthcare service organization, the most important achievement is the provision of good-quality healthcare services. Making sure that bonus criteria include appropriate measurements of quality is just as important for healthcare executives as it is for physicians. The employee absences and turnover provision is also fitting as a way of stressing the importance of the organization's role as employer. Adding these goals does not deny or undermine the importance of senior management's financial responsibility.

The CEO has made a good point about the difficulty of managing well those situations in which the payroll needs to be cut or frozen. Nevertheless, it is very difficult to justify paying senior management more at the very time when others are being laid off or are not receiving any increases. When payroll cost is the issue, there is an inherent fairness question when executives get bonuses and lower-paid employees get laid off or their pay decreases relative to the cost of living.

One of the ways in which just executive compensation is sometimes discussed is in terms of the ratio of the highest- to the lowest-paid (job classifications) within the organization. When the highest-paid makes 100 times or more the wage of the lowest-paid, there is a judgment being made and a message being sent about the worth of the contribution of some individuals compared to others. When the ratio is 10 to 1 or less, there is a very different judgment and message.

It is difficult to determine equity or fairness when comparing very different types of positions in the organization. Building on traditional understandings of justice and seeking to balance such considerations as need, contribution, equality, effort, and value in the labor market, it seems clear that the burden of proof is on those who defend a higher rather than a lower ratio or gap. While a commitment to fair or ethical compensation does not immediately lead to a clear answer regarding the most appropriate ratio, a high multiple does raise a red flag, ethically speaking.

It is often a very enlightening experience for an organization to identify the present ratio of highest-paid to lowest-paid and to engage in a deliberative conversation about whether the organization should set a particular ratio as a standard for itself. This can be a very useful part of the ongoing reflection on the meaning of just compensation.

In the case above, the bonus to be paid if goals are met was to go to senior management only. At least some of the goals are organizational goals, goals that can be achieved only if many persons do their jobs well. If there is to be a bonus system, consideration should be given to expanding the number of employees who are eligible to receive a bonus if organizational goals are met.

Internal Equity

When individuals claim that their wages are not fair or just, they are sometimes making the claim that their wages are too low compared to what others are being paid for the same or similar work in the organization. The following are a few comments on the issue of internal equity, fairness relative to others in the same organization.

Differences in compensation between different employees are fair when they are based on ethically relevant differences. An employer should be able to explain why one employee is making less or more than another employee, and the reasons need to be able to withstand ethical scrutiny.

Most of us can easily recognize some criteria for differences in compensation that are irrelevant and unethical. To pay a woman less than a man or a single person less than a married person for the same work is a violation of the principle of equal pay for the same work. The same principle is violated when one employee is paid more than another doing the same work because the first was permitted to negotiate a higher salary. Justice requires that differences in compensation be based only on job-related considerations and that the same criteria be applied to all.

Often the basic principle of internal equity is stated in this way: "equal pay for equal work." This phrase can have different interpretations, including equal pay for the same work, equal pay for work of equal value to the organization, and equal pay for work of equal difficulty/responsibility/skill.

It is much more difficult to understand equity when two very different types of jobs are compared (for example, a job requiring physical labor skills and a job requiring office clerical skills) than it is to understand equity between two employees doing the same job. The tendency when comparing different types of jobs is to use the marketplace determination of compensation. The compensation for a particular position in comparable organizations is useful information, but the going rate in the industry is not always a sufficient basis on which to justify differences in compensation. Deeply ingrained biases in society can and do get reinforced in the marketplace. Accepting the marketplace as an arbiter of justice is risky.

The "comparable worth" campaign is an effort to address the fact that jobs which have been traditionally understood as women's jobs tend to have relatively low wages and salaries. In an effort to determine whether these pay levels are based on ethically relevant differences, comparable worth proponents seek to identify and apply relevant criteria for comparing wages in different types of jobs. A point system is used to rate each job category in terms of skill requirements, difficulty, accountability, knowledge requirements, and other factors that most would judge pertinent to compensation decisions. Jobs that are found to have roughly equal total points should pay about the same. Comparable worth programs have found that this kind of analysis confirms that traditional women's jobs are often underpaid and that significant adjustments need to be made in order to achieve equal pay for jobs of comparable worth.[8]

There are no easy answers to what constitutes equity in compensation within an organization. Consultants can contribute to the delineation of job classifications, but management has a responsibility to make sure that the appropriate criteria are used. The fact that there are no easy answers does not mean, however, that addressing issues of equity is not worth the effort. There is very little that shows more respect for employees and a greater commitment to the organization's responsibility as an employer than a serious effort to apply justice criteria to compensation decisions.

The Big Picture

I suggested in Chapter 2 that good healthcare business ethics often means seeing specific issues in a large frame of reference. Situating a particular question or concern in the context of significant justice issues in society is one way of keeping the focus on ethical considerations. It helps us to avoid the temptation of trying to define and solve problems primarily in terms of competing interests in a narrow context. Ethics is about doing the right thing. Being able to understand what the thing is—or might be—often requires an understanding of the big picture.

A major point of this chapter is that those who make decisions about wages and salaries in the healthcare organization should make these decisions with an awareness of the implications of a commitment to just wages in any setting.

Nine

Ethics and Downsizing

Perhaps the greatest obstacle to empowerment today is downsizing. . . . downsizing strikes fear into the hearts of all workers because it reminds them of the fundamental way in which they are totally powerless over their lives when business leaders act as if they are powerless to do anything but downsize. It would seem virtually impossible to empower people in organizations that do not make a strong commitment to keeping their workers employed through good times and bad.[1]

Much of a person's identity and sense of contribution and accomplishment are related to the work that she or he does. . . . Losing a job is a threat to one's sense of identity and self-worth, as well as to financial well being and security.[2]

The ethics of the decisions surrounding the downsizing implementation strategy are the new paradigm. They become the model. They tell all employees what the new rules are. These decisions set the standard for the ethics of future decisions.[3]

The announcement informing employees that layoffs will occur is one of the most difficult memos the CEO can write. The news that layoffs will occur is among the most dispiriting pieces of news that employees can hear. Downsizing is an extremely difficult situation for all involved. The way in which downsizing-related issues are handled has an impact on the workplace that lasts for years. When an organization is faced with a need to cut costs, a knowledge of and commitment to fairness and sensitivity to employees is fundamental to ethical leadership.

Ethical Issues in Downsizing

There are a variety of ethical issues related to downsizing, all of which require careful consideration and preparation. The questions of whether and how to downsize arise in stressful times, usually when the organization is facing a serious financial condition. The temptation may be to get the necessary hard decisions made as quickly as possible to reduce costs immediately and to avoid extending the time during which employees wait, wonder, and talk about what is going to happen. Getting the downsizing decisions over quickly is not nearly as important as attending to all aspects and ramifications well.

There are great costs associated with downsizing. Even when it is handled well, some persons get hurt, and there are likely to be significant negative impacts on the organization's climate. Frequently it is not handled well. Then those who lose their jobs are doubly hurt because of a sense that they have been treated unfairly, and morale among those who remain suffers even more. Distrust of management grows. As noted in the third quote above, how downsizing is done sends a message to employees about what management really thinks about them, despite what mission-related words they mouth.

> Case 9.1. A Task Force has been appointed by the hospital CEO to make recommendations regarding a reduction in the workforce. They are asked to make recommendations in regard to the criteria to be used in deciding which positions should be eliminated, which employees should be let go, and how best to implement the decisions. One member of the Task Force is a senior-level manager who sees the whole question of downsizing as filled with ethical issues. He convinces the other members of the Task Force to ask a business ethicist to meet with them at the very first working meeting to assist in identifying the key fairness issues to which the organization needs to be particularly sensitive.
>
> This Task Force member identifies one issue of particular concern. Should employees who have been selected for layoff be asked to depart immediately (after being informed of the decision), or should there be a week or two of advance notice of the effective date of separation?

The manager who sees downsizing as filled with ethical significance is right on target. In addition to the specific (and important) issue that he has identified, there are a variety of other issues that need careful attention if all employees are to be treated with fairness and respect during the whole downsizing process. A good ethicist would, I think, suggest that there are four major components of downsizing that might benefit from explicit attention to ethical considerations:

1. The decision to downsize
2. Selection criteria
3. The process of letting employees go
4. Rebuilding morale among remaining employees

It does not require a high level of ethics education to understand what should be done in these circumstances. What is required are practical wisdom and courage. What is required is the ability to apply commonly accepted principles of respectful behavior to difficult situations, sometimes in opposition to "experts" and "consultants" who have other recommendations.

The following sections review some of the implications of practical ethical wisdom in regard to each of the four components.

The Decision to Downsize

Since labor costs are usually a major controllable part of the budget, downsizing is often considered as an appropriate response to financial pressures on the organization. Downsizing has enormous employee costs associated with it, including decline in morale and changes in the organization's climate and culture, in addition to the burden of loss of employment for some. Because of these great costs, it is essential not to make the decision to reduce the number of employees too quickly.

It is difficult to maintain trust in management after a downsizing decision is made. Downsizing almost always means both short-term pain and long-term loss of confidence and commitment. There needs, therefore, to be abundant evidence of the need to downsize in order to justify the negative consequences. Reducing the number of employees is justified when it is the best alternative available, keeping in mind the tremendous damage to employee commitment inevitable in most such decisions. A too quick decision to downsize sends the signal that the organization does not have a commitment to its employees.

Management can be satisfied that the decision to downsize is the right one if, after the decision has been made, an honest assessment reveals the following to be true:

1. The reasons for the decision to downsize are understood throughout the organization. This includes an understanding of the problems and pressures facing the organization and of the available alternatives to workforce reduction.
2. Employees at different levels in the organization participated in reviewing alternatives.
3. Employees at different levels in the organization agree that the downsizing decision is necessary or appropriate.[4]

It is only natural for both those who lose their jobs and those who remain to question whether there really was a need to make cuts. It is natural for them to wonder whether the resources of the organization are being allocated appropriately and to suspect that management sees employees simply as costs to be kept as low as possible. Communication with employees needs to be very explicit and candid regarding the threats to the stability of the organization that require action and the possible options for responding to these threats.

In a decision of such importance as this, consideration of the various options in order to select the best should involve more than just top management. We are all influenced by our place in the organization and may not see the whole picture when we listen only to those who occupy similar positions. When persons from different levels of the organization have the opportunity to review various alternatives, there is likely to be an enriched understanding of the implications of each option.

If a decision to downsize does not have some support among employees at different levels in the organization, there is serious reason to doubt that it is the best decision. The question is not how management sells the alternative of downsizing; the question is whether downsizing sells itself as the decision that, given candid information about threats and options, is most reasonable and appropriate. This does not mean, of course, that everyone agrees. Without widespread agreement, however, there remain serious doubts about whether downsizing is the right decision. To proceed without widespread agreement is to add to the already enormous costs of downsizing.

Selection Criteria

A major fairness issue is the selection of the employees who will leave. Individuals who lose their jobs because it is necessary to reduce the workforce in order to meet organizational goals bear the biggest burden of the reorganization. It is essential that there be good (that is, fair) reasons for the decisions made.

Though there is no clear-cut formula for selecting which employees to keep and which to let go in downsizing, there are some important considerations regarding fairness to keep in mind.[5]

1. Clearly identified criteria are needed.

Managers making decisions about specific individuals need to have clearly articulated criteria. There is too great a risk of arbitrariness or inconsistency or favoritism if different divisions or departments are free to make such important decisions on the basis of selection criteria that have not been carefully identified, reviewed, and put into writing.

2. "Across the board" cuts are questionable.

It may sometimes be appealing to think that the fairest way of reducing the workforce is to reduce equally "across the board," the same FTE percentage in each division or department. But equal does not always mean fair, and fair does not always mean equal. A thorough review of needs in terms of services provided by the organization and of appropriateness of the current staffing levels within different divisions will usually indicate that cuts in one area would be more damaging to the mission of the organization than cuts in some other area. Front-line care providers in an already lean healthcare organization, for example, may have a legitimate claim not to be reduced as much as some others.

The same concern about treating all areas of the organization alike also applies to any hiring freezes that are proposed. Not every position is as central to the mission, and not all departments are as appropriately staffed. An "across the board" freeze may not be the best allocation of resources.

3. Downsizing is different from performance review.

It is reasonable, when decisions need to be made about which employees to retain and which to let go, to want to keep the most effective, the most reliable, the best performers. There is a need to be careful, though, in basing downsizing selection decisions on performance evaluations or reviews.

Employee performance concerns should be addressed on their own merits, in a process that provides for step-by-step discipline and due process. To select someone for separation in a time of downsizing because of a manager's perception of poor performance or behavior problems is highly questionable. Performance evaluations can be inaccurate or unfair. When poor performance has not been substantiated and the employee has not had the opportunity to respond to concerns or to correct deficiencies, the employee should not be let go for performance-related reasons, even though a decision to downsize provides the opportunity to do this. Performance-related layoffs require due process.

4. Diversity goals remain important.

As the criteria are identified, it is important that all employee-related organizational commitments be recognized, including diversity goals. It is often easier to be committed to increasing the percentage of minorities and women in management positions in times of expanding the workforce than when reducing the workforce. Well-considered diversity goals are important to the organization. Selection criteria need to be chosen that do not undermine efforts to achieve these goals.

5. Seniority is relevant but not always decisive.

The organization should recognize greater loyalty, a greater commitment, to employees who have served for longer periods of time. It is appropriate to take seniority into consideration in making downsizing decisions. If all else is equal in terms of meeting the organization's needs, there is strong ethical support for retaining the employee with greater seniority. In some cases, however, everything else will not be equal. Respect for seniority need not be seen as decisive in making selections among different employees in these cases. It is different, of course, if collective bargaining or other prior agreements have specified that seniority will be decisive.

6. Criteria should be made public throughout the organization.

There are two very important reasons for informing employees of the selection criteria that are used in making decisions about downsizing.

Communicating the criteria is, first, a sign of justice and respect. Employees who are losing their jobs despite the fact that they are performing satisfactorily have a legitimate claim to know why they were selected. The question "Why me?" deserves an honest answer. Those who remain also need to know what the reasons were for the decisions made; future trust requires this sort of openness.

It is traditional in this country for employers to insist upon their status as at-will employers. This means that, in the absence of a specific law (like an anti-discrimination law) or a contract, employers have the legal right to hire or fire whomever and whenever they please. Regardless of what one thinks about this traditional legal doctrine, it is hard to justify it as the basis for understanding the ethical responsibilities of employers in relationship to their employees. Employees are owed an honest explanation of the reasons for their departure from the workforce.

The second reason for communicating the selection criteria to employees is that the decision to do so functions as a powerful incentive to make sure that the criteria make good sense, are fair, and are consistently implemented. Knowing that employees will learn the selection criteria helps to concentrate attention on the legitimacy of the criteria. Awareness of employee knowledge of the selection criteria increases the likelihood that the criteria will be applied consistently and that they will not be manipulated to protect the job of some favorite.

The Separation Process

Even with a clear need to downsize and with carefully developed and carefully applied employee selection criteria, the employees selected to be laid off will bear a heavy burden. The process should be designed to maximize the extent to which these employees are treated with respect and dignity at this difficult time.

The employees who remain after downsizing have come to be called "survivors." Though survivors do not experience downsizing in the same way as those who depart, they are also affected by the way the separation process is managed. This process communicates a strong message about the way employees are treated in this organization.

In the case above, the one specific issue identified for further ethical reflection is the question of whether employees who have been selected for layoff should be asked to depart immediately after being informed of the decision or whether there should be advance notice of the effective date of separation. This is an important question. The answer given speaks loudly and clearly about management's understanding of employees and of the proper treatment of employees.

It sometimes occurs that affected employees are asked or required to depart the same day that they are informed of being let go. This is a practice that is highly questionable in most workplace settings, including healthcare organizations. The reason for this practice, where it is used, seems to be a fear that laid-off employees who remain in their workplaces for a week or two will "sabotage" the organization or poison morale. Sabotage is rarely a realistic fear, and there may well be more damage done to employee morale by the demand that dismissed employees depart immediately than by their being around for a week or two.

Requiring separated employees to leave immediately is an insult to them as persons with professional and ethical standards. It denies the affected employees the opportunity to finish projects and to prepare for a smooth transition. It denies them the opportunity to say good-bye. It suggests to all employees that, at least in tough times, management does not have confidence in employees and does not trust them to act with integrity. Except in unusual circumstances, respecting employees' dignity and their contributions to the organization is incompatible with demanding that they depart immediately.

1. Employees who are "downsized" should be given advance notice of the effective date and encouraged to continue to work until the effective date.

This is an indication that management recognizes their contributions, respects their professionalism, and wants their assistance for as long as possible. Frank Narvan is correct, I think, in recognizing that the decisions surrounding the downsizing implementation strategy tell all employees what the new rules are.[6] How the departure time is managed symbolizes and models the employer's attitude toward employees.

There are a few other points that can be made briefly about the treatment of employees who are being "separated."

2. Management should inform all laid-off employees of the criteria used in their selection.

This point, made earlier, is worth repeating. It is only fair to individuals to explain why they are being asked to bear a larger burden of organizational restructuring than some others. If management is reluctant to make the true selection criteria known to employees, those criteria probably need to be reconsidered.

3. Management should inform laid-off employees that they may appeal the selection decision if they have reason to think that the selection criteria were not appropriately applied.

This standard may be a surprise to some and may seem to be asking for unnecessary trouble, but it follows from the need to be explicit and fair in the selection process. Even the best managers may make mistakes in applying the criteria. Respect for employees requires due process in terminating employment, and due process requires the opportunity to appeal decisions. Procedural justice is an important part of any effort to act fairly, and the opportunity to appeal a decision is an essential part of due process.

4. Management should provide significant interim benefits as well as out-placement services.

This is sometimes referred to as being "generous" with benefits and out-placement assistance. "Generous" might not be the right word to use, how-ever, because this is not really a matter of charity; these (former) employees are owed benefits and assistance to compensate them somewhat for the burden they are bearing for the organization.

After Downsizing: The Survivors

Downsizing does not always result in the expected benefits to the organiza-tion because the survivors are often demoralized and insecure (and may even feel somewhat guilty that they remain while some of their colleagues are gone). Downsizing the right way includes respectful treatment of surviving employees in addition to making and implementing layoff decisions appropri-ately. Attention has been given in recent years to ways of healing the wounds left by downsizing.[7] I limit my comments here to three proposed guidelines for the ethical treatment of survivors.

1. Honest and frequent communication of information about organiza-tional issues is essential to begin to rebuild trust.

There has been much emphasis in this chapter on the importance of honest communication. Communication is so fundamental to respectful treatment of employees in restructuring that it cannot be overemphasized. It is inevitable that stress, anger, and distrust will be widespread among surviving employ-ees, and a pattern of open communication is a necessary starting point for diminishing these feelings.

2. Avoid making promises that management might not be able to be keep.

It may be tempting to say, for example, that no more layoffs will be re-quired, but circumstances may not allow that promise to be kept. Unkept promises, however well-intentioned and sincere they were when made, lead to a greater sense among employees that they have been manipulated and be-trayed. It takes a long time to regain the trust lost through downsizing. It is too risky to engage in unrealistic promises or assertions.

3. Employees should not be expected to take on significantly increased re-sponsibilities because of the reduced workforce.

A commitment both to high-quality services and to good working condi-tions requires that there are sufficient persons to do the essential jobs and that these employees have adequate support to function well. Downsizing is justi-fied when it is essential to allow the organization to continue to perform its essential work well. If there are not sufficient persons and adequate resources to do the essential work well, reorganization has not been successful and employees have been made to suffer without sufficient benefit to the community served.

A Concluding Comment

It may be useful to repeat a point from Chapter 8.

Doing a good job of overseeing downsizing and reorganization is an important management achievement and is worthy of recognition. It should not be recognized, however, by bonuses to the CEO or senior management. If it is necessary for the financial stability of the organization to cut the payroll, the compensation of top management should not be increased.

Despite a superior performance by leadership in handling a difficult situation well, it is very difficult to justify paying senior management more at the very time when others are laid off. When payroll costs need to be cut, there is an obvious fairness problem if executives get bonuses or significant salary increases while lower-paid employees get laid off. It is best to find a nonfinancial method of recognizing good management in a time of downsizing.

Ten

Patient Requests for Healthcare Providers of a Specific Race or Sex

One of the characteristics of an ethical manager in American society today is informed sensitivity to the ways in which attitudes toward persons of a different race, sex, nationality, culture, religion, or social/economic position can affect behavior.

Chapter 7 included a brief discussion of the potential impact of these attitudes on the quality of healthcare. There the focus was on the importance of preventing unequal treatment of patients because of attitudes or biases existing among healthcare providers. In this section of the book, focused as it is on healthcare organizations as employers, it is useful to consider management's responsibilities to employees when patients request that they be cared for by persons of a specific race or sex.

When all relevant considerations are taken into account, some such requests are more legitimately honored than others. It is the purpose of this chapter to assist managers in identifying relevant considerations and in distinguishing between requests that should be accommodated and those that should not be accommodated.

The Race of the Caregiver[1]

Case 10.1. M. J., a home care case manager, is not sure how to proceed. She has just had an extended conversation with the patient for whom she is arranging home care. All went well until the patient said that he did not want anyone who is black coming into his home. The patient is an elderly European American who said that he does not feel comfortable around black people and that he especially does not like the idea of a black person walking around in his house. "I'm a strong believer in staying with your own kind. Besides," he continued, "I have a right to decide who comes into the privacy of my own home."

M. J. has had such requests or demands before and has wrestled with them each time. She knows that some case managers do try to provide a home worker of the race requested. They argue that personal care is intimate and private and that compatibility with the caregiver is an important dimension of a good patient experience. Patients, they conclude, should have a worker with whom they are comfortable.

A second reason is sometimes given for acceding to the patient's request for a home care worker of a particular race. To send a black worker to the home of someone who does not want such a person in the house is to place the worker at risk of racial insults or abuse. The patient in this particular case has made a major point of insisting that no black person come into his home; he might be capable of such harassment.

M. J. has heard and considered these arguments before. She is also convinced, however, that there is an important fairness issue involved in not assigning someone to do a particular job simply because of his or her race. In the past, she has always refused to honor requests for home care workers of a particular race. This time she decides that she would like to clarify the policy and practice of the organization. She asks her supervisor whether she should make arrangements that specify a white worker or to tell the patient that the organization will not comply with this request.

It is not surprising that M. J. and others in this situation often find it difficult to know how best to respond to a patient's request or demand for a home health worker of a particular race. As is indicated in the case scenario, some ways of thinking about management's responsibility to patients and employees may seem to suggest that the organization should, in fact, comply with such requests. When priority principles of ethics (Chapter 2) are kept in mind, however, it becomes clear that complying with this request would be a serious mistake. It would be a denial of a basic right in order to accommodate lower-priority interests.

The determination that someone should be prevented from performing a particular job simply because of her or his race is a very harmful form of discrimination. When a factor like race, totally unrelated to the ability to do the job, is used as a basis for deciding who does what work, managers are saying that irrelevant considerations will be permitted to influence work assignments. While there are understandable perspectives that may lead good managers to wonder whether they should honor patient requests for race-based assignments, the bottom line is that such assignments are a violation of worker dignity and a denial of fairness in the workplace.

It may be useful to comment on some of the considerations that are put forward at times to justify accommodating a patient's racial preference in home care work assignments, to explain why these values, concerns, and commitments, even when combined, do not justify race-based work assignments. Such considerations include (1) being an advocate for the patient, (2) respecting cultural differences and personal idiosyncrasies, (3) respecting patient privacy, and (4) protecting workers from unnecessary risk of harm.

1. The use of racial criteria in making work assignments is not justified by an appeal to patient advocacy.

To be a patient advocate is to seek to do what is best for the patient; it is to promote the patient's well-being and to keep that concern from being subordinated to other, less fundamental interests or considerations. To be a patient advocate does not mean, however, that one will accede to any and all patient requests. Especially when patient behavior or staff compliance with patient preferences may be harmful to someone else, it cannot be seen as justified simply because it may make the patient feel more comfortable. The patient is not the only person involved or affected.

A good manager would not allow a patient to subject a home care worker to sexual harassment. Nor should a manager allow a patient to determine the race of the home care worker. In both cases, being a patient advocate does not in any way justify abandoning basic ethical workplace standards.

2. The use of racial criteria in making work assignments is not justified by an appeal to respect for cultural differences and personal idiosyncrasies.

There has been a growing recognition in recent years that patients do come from different cultures and backgrounds and that these differences should be respected, even when healthcare providers do not share the patient's particular cultural beliefs. Further, there is a recognition that individual differences should also be respected, when possible, even when they strike others as strange. We may think that someone else's way of thinking or behaving is odd, but we want to let them live according to their values as much as possible.

This respect is admirable, but it does not mean that a patient's racial preference should be honored. It is important to respect cultural values and personal idiosyncrasies when we can, but not when cooperating with personal traits harms someone else. Not wanting a black (or a white) home care worker is not simply a matter of taste; it is a request that the manager apply a standard that is harmful and insulting. It is one thing to let patients live their own lives according to their own values; it is something else to allow them to dictate a violation of standards of justice and ethics.

3. The use of racial criteria in making work assignments is not justified by an appeal to respect for patient privacy.

A third argument sometimes given for complying with a racial preference request follows from a concern for privacy. The primary expression of this argument is that the home is part of the private sphere in a way that a health-care institution is not. While managers would not honor a request regarding the race of employees caring for a patient in the hospital, some think that the home is different. The home is the place where people can have more control over their environment. In this context, it is sometimes argued, persons should be free to live their lives according to their own personal standards, even if their standards appear to others to be bigoted.

Most of us would agree that an individual's home should be an arena of privacy. That is, people should by and large be able to control who enters their own homes. When they engage an agency to provide care in the private home, however, the home becomes a place in which professional services are provided. Just as one cannot say that professional standards of healthcare cease to exist when healthcare is taken into a private setting, so one cannot say that employment standards cease to exist when work is taken into a private setting. A manager cannot justify substandard healthcare because it is provided in a private home. Nor can a manager justify substandard employee treatment because the work is being done in a private home.

There is another dimension to the privacy argument. Sometimes the point is made that the nature of the care provided by a healthcare worker in a home often involves care that is very personal (bathing, for example) and that a patient should be permitted to decide who is allowed to enter that realm of personal privacy. Personal privacy is an important consideration and, as is discussed below, is sometimes a relevant consideration regarding the sex of the caregiver. While sex may be relevant in this context, race is not. Sexual or physical privacy is related to the gender of the caregiver but not to the race of the caregiver.

4. The use of racial criteria in making work assignments is not justified by an appeal to the protection of workers from risk of harm.

Sometimes, as in the case presented above, the argument is made that a patient's demands regarding the race of home care workers should be honored for the sake of the worker, if not for the sake of the patient. Again, there is an element of a legitimate concern here. Workers should not be exposed to unnecessary risk of harm. Nevertheless, if a patient's racial demands are acceded to, there is no longer just the question of a risk of harm. Harm is, in fact, already being done. In the name of protecting workers, racial discrimination is being implemented. As the history of racism has shown, the desire to protect a racial minority from harm has often been the expressed rationale for limiting their opportunities. A denial of their human dignity is no way to protect persons.

Sometimes, in cases like this, someone suggests informing the healthcare workers of the patient's request and asking them whether they want this assignment. This is another way of trying to protect and respect the worker and of trying to prevent surprises and problems. While understandable, this approach may still give too much legitimacy to the patient's request. If a problem does arise when a worker is providing services in the home, the situation then needs to be addressed like any other problem that occurs in the delivery of home care. To try to prevent problems by not assigning a person of the "wrong" race to a case would make one a major participant in unjustified discrimination.

In a commentary on a case similar to the one discussed here, Adrienne Asch arrives at a different conclusion. She puts particular emphasis on the comfort of the patient, and concludes: "If the client believes that she cannot be comfortable with a suggested person based on anything—personality or appearance, speaking style, ethnicity, or race—those wishes must be honored."[2]

The problem with this approach, it seems to me, is that it does not take seriously enough the harm caused by the way others accommodate an individual's preferences. If honoring the individual's preferences causes harm only to that individual, they should be honored. If honoring the individual's preferences causes harm to others, it is a whole different story. To make work assignments on the basis of race is a direct assault upon the dignity of the staff affected and a reduction of their work opportunities. Preventing a worker from performing jobs because of her or his race is a most blatant form of discrimination. It violates the fundamental principle of fairness, that job assignments should not take into consideration factors that are not related to the ability to perform the job. This is very real harm. And it is harm done by the organization, not (just) by the patient who made the request.

The best approach would seem to be a policy approach: patients who make race-based staff assignment requests should routinely be informed that the agency does not make work assignments based on race. Having clear policy both makes good sense and facilitates responding to such requests. One need not attempt to make any judgments about individual patients and their intentions. It is simply a matter of workplace standards.

It should be noted that this discussion has not included those situations in which the race of the caregiver might be relevant for purposes of providing good clinical care. In psychotherapy, for example, there might be justification to provide a therapist of the same race if the client requests such and has a recent history of issues related to racial questions. In this sort of case, accommodating the patient's request may be appropriate, not because the patient is not comfortable with someone of a specific race but because a same-race therapist may be more effective clinically. These are unusual situations, generally involving psychotherapy, and do not imply any change in the general policy proposed above.

The Sex of the Caregiver

On the basis of the arguments that have just been presented about the importance of avoiding making work assignments on the basis of the race of the caregiver, the reader might expect a similar position on the practice of making work assignments on the basis of the sex of the caregiver. If the two situations are similar in terms of the relevant considerations, the ethical stance should be the same. Ethics requires fairness and consistency; it requires treating similar cases in a similar manner.

Putting ethics into practice also requires making appropriate distinctions, identifying relevant differences between two situations where they exist. Where relevant differences exist, ethics requires that the cases be treated differently. The most important question that needs to be addressed here is the question of whether there are any ethically relevant differences between a patient request for a caregiver of the same race and a patient request for a caregiver of the same sex.

The following three scenarios present different examples of management being faced with the question of whether to attempt to accommodate the request of the patient for caregivers of the same sex.

Case 10.2. A 45-year-old female patient comes in for her yearly exam. The primary care physician, Dr. Jane Smith, discovers an ovarian mass and orders a pelvic ultrasound, which shows that the mass is suspicious for cancer. Dr. Smith now wants to refer the patient to Dr. George Jones, the only gynecologist specializing in cancer surgery who participates in the patient's HMO plan. Dr. Smith has a good working relationship with Dr. Jones; patients seem to like him, and colleagues have high regard for his work. The patient refuses to go to him, stating that she will not see a male physician for this problem. There are female gynecologists and general surgeons in the plan, but Dr. Smith does not think that they are as skilled as Dr. Jones.

What should management of the HMO do if the patient requests that the healthcare plan pay for a referral to an experienced female gynecological surgeon who is not part of the plan?

The next case was presented in Chapter 4.

Case 10.3. The rehabilitation patient is reluctant to engage in scheduled whirlpool therapy because she does not think that she would be appropriately dressed for being in the presence of males who are not members of her family. In her culture, women do not appear in swimwear at public beaches or pools. She requests that she be given privacy and female therapists. Therapists take this request to their supervisor and ask what should be done. They state their conviction that it important to treat all patients equally and that they do not think that patient requests for special treatment should be accommodated.

The last case is the one most similar to the case of racial preference above.

Case 10.4. M. J., the home care case manager who was asked for no home care workers from a particular racial group, now is faced with another request. The patient is a female patient who lives alone and requires assistance in bathing. She requests that only female caregivers come to her home, saying that she does not feel at all comfortable being "exposed" to males alone in her home. M. J. needs to decide whether to try to accommodate this request.

There are two major arguments made by those who support the practice of accommodating requests for same-sex healthcare providers while refusing to accommodate requests for same-race healthcare providers.

The first reason is essentially a quality-of-care reason. Women and men are often quite different in terms of their socialization and sensitivities. The quality of healthcare, at least in many situations, may be significantly improved if the caregiver is sensitive to and respectful of the perspective of the patient. Many women, for example, expect that a female OB/GYN is likely to be more aware of the patient's healthcare needs because a female physician is better able to identify with the patient's sexuality-related feelings and experiences than is a male physician. Men seeking healthcare for sexuality-related concerns might expect that male caregivers will provide better healthcare for similar reasons.

The second reason used to support a practice of accommodation to requests for same sex caregivers is respect for personal privacy. Privacy, including bodily privacy, is a very important value in society and in healthcare. Individuals have a legitimate expectation that their physical privacy will be respected and protected, that their bodies will not be exposed to others, especially members of the opposite sex, without their permission. Separate "women's" and "men's" public restrooms are seen as promoting and protecting an important moral and social value (while separate "white" and "colored" public restrooms are seen as a denial of an important moral and social value). It is necessary in healthcare at times to allow others to observe the naked body, but personal bodily privacy is still seen as something to be respected as much as possible. (Note that this particular meaning of privacy is somewhat different from the privacy of one's home argument in Case 10.1.)

What I have described as the quality concern and the privacy concern often overlap; a patient may expect both better understanding and awareness and better protection of privacy from a same-sex provider. These concerns are stronger in some individuals than in others and stronger in some cultural traditions than in others, but they are quite common in the U.S.

Accommodating requests for same-sex providers involves cost or burdens. It risks being discriminatory by identifying the sex of the caregiver as a qualification for doing certain assignments when sex may not be relevant. This is justified only if, in fact, there are other values being protected by the practice that outweigh the cost (and there is good evidence that these values cannot be achieved as well by sex-neutral caregiver work assignments). A brief comment on each of the three cases may suggest ways of balancing various considerations.

My recommendation in regard to Case 10.2 is that the healthcare plan should not cover out-of-plan surgery for the patient who requests a female surgeon for ovarian cancer surgery. First, there is no reason to think that the quality of surgery in this case is directly related to the sex of the surgeon. Second, the violation of personal privacy involved in having surgery done by a male physician appears not to be severe enough to justify the increased use of shared resources associated with going out of plan. On the other hand, if the issue were a little different, a strong case could be made that the plan has a responsibility to contract with a sufficient number of female OB/GYNs so that patients have the possibility of choosing one for routine gynecological care.

Case 10.3 was discussed in Chapter 4 as an example of the question of a patient's right to respect for cultural values. Most women in our culture would probably not consider whirlpool therapy to be a violation of privacy if males are present. Nevertheless, this patient does make a specific request for same-sex caregivers based on her values of privacy and modesty. As was noted in Chapter 4, this sort of request for special treatment based on the patient's values should be accommodated if it is possible to do so without assuming an unreasonable burden in the process.

What is a reasonable burden to assume to protect patient privacy is related to the extent to which one's privacy is invaded. An unreasonable burden to the organization, one great enough to justify not complying with the request, would generally be a higher-level burden if, for example, a patient objected to her or his nude body being exposed to caregivers of the opposite sex than if, as in this case, a patient objects to being exposed in a swimsuit. Individuals have different understandings of privacy. The healthcare organization, while seeking to accommodate individual differences when feasible, needs to have its own understanding of the meaning and implications of respect for the personal privacy of patients.

Case 10.4 is an example of a situation that presents a strong case for trying to accommodate the patient's request for same-sex caregivers, at least those who assist in bathing. The concern that a female patient may have about being given a bath by a male caregiver with no one else in the building is a concern that reflects a common understanding of vulnerability. If it is possible to assign only female staff to do the bathing without fully disrupting scheduling or resulting in unfair workloads or opportunities, it should be done.

If, on the other hand, requests like these, individually or in conjunction with other requests, mean that work assignments truly would be unfair, the patient should be informed both that the request cannot be accommodated and why the request cannot be accommodated. Even in cases where it is ethically appropriate to accommodate requests for same-sex caregivers, the desire to fulfill the request does not trump all other considerations. There is a clear ethical responsibility to ensure that staff are not overburdened or given too few opportunities simply because of their sex. Just treatment of employees takes priority over accommodating patient preferences.

Conclusion

Developing and implementing ethical standards requires making judgments about the organization's responsibility when requests are made. It is not satisfactory simply to try to please the "customer," to do whatever patients want in regard to the kind of persons that will care for them. Requests for caregivers of a particular race, or excluding a particular race, should rarely if ever be considered sufficiently relevant to the quality of care or to legitimate patient interests to be honored. Requests for caregivers of the same sex may sometimes be relevant in terms of quality of care or legitimate patient privacy interests. In these cases, the requests should be honored if they do not result in unreasonable use of resources or in unfair treatment of staff.

Eleven

Conscientious Objection to Participation in Certain Treatment Options

It is a not always easy to know when members of the professional staff should be exempted from particular patient care situations for reasons of personal conscience. Acceptance of the conscientious beliefs of individuals is an essential part of any society or any organization committed to respecting individuals in their differences. On the other hand, those seeking professional services have a legitimate expectation that professionals will respond on the basis of professional standards, not on the basis of simply personal beliefs. Not every request to be excused from patient care responsibilities because of a conscientious objection should be honored.

The first objective of this chapter is to review some important considerations related to such requests and to propose criteria or guidelines to assist supervisors in determining whether a particular request should be honored.

The second objective is a little different. The discussion of conscientious objection is a good occasion to consider the parameters of an organization's conscientious objection. The healthcare provider organization might decide, on the basis of the governing board's or the sponsor's ethical principles, not to permit certain legal patient treatment options. This practice is reviewed in this chapter in terms of how it relates to patient rights and to demands placed upon employees.

Policy on Staff Conscientious Objection

The expectations of the Joint Commission on the Accreditation of Health Care Organizations have resulted in the preparation of many institutional policies related to requests by staff that they be excused from patient care responsibilities that are in conflict with their ethical values or with their religious or cultural beliefs.

The policies vary, but often include the following features: (1) initial responsibility for determining whether the employee's request should be honored is placed with the employee's supervisor, director, or department head; (2) there is a requirement that the requesting employee continue to provide appropriate patient care unless and until alternative arrangements are made; and (3) if the request is denied at the first level, an appeal is permitted to another person or group.

These are important features, but if nothing more is included, the policy does not assist employees or supervisors in determining whether a particular request should be honored.

Case 11.1. A. H. is a registered nurse working in a long-term-care facility. J. B. is a patient in the home who is suffering from terminal colon cancer. To relieve the pain that has become difficult to control, the doctor has prescribed moderate doses of morphine. The patient has accepted that she is dying and welcomes the morphine prescription.

A. H. requests that she be excused from administering the morphine, based on her belief that this treatment may well cause the patient to die earlier than she would otherwise, by depressing respiration. A. H. argues that it goes against her conscience to give the ordered dosages. Other nurses have no moral problem following the orders.

Should A. H. be excused from the responsibility to provide the ordered care for J. B.?[1]

The claim here on the part of the nurse is that she should not be required to participate in treatment that she thinks is wrong. Some such claims should be honored and accommodated; some should not.[2]

When an employee asks to be excused from certain care responsibilities because of a conflict with values or beliefs, that employee is making one of two different claims. She or he may be saying that (1) "it is wrong to do this" or that (2) "it is wrong for me to do this." An employee making the first kind of claim is expressing a conviction that the patient is not being treated according to professional or ethical standards. An employee making the second kind of claim is saying that the patient is being treated in a way that is not in conflict with the ethics of healthcare, but that the employee's own personal values do not permit participation.

Both are conscience-based claims, but they are different statements that call for different responses. If A. H. wants to be excused because she thinks that the patient is not being treated right, according to professional or ethical standards, the response will need to include efforts to address the issue of the appropriateness of the patient care being provided. This may require a review of contemporary standards on pain management and, perhaps, consultation with the organization's Clinical Ethics Committee.

On the other hand, A. H. may be asking to be excused from the care of this dying patient because she is personally uncomfortable with the amount of morphine that the patient is receiving, even though she agrees that what is being done is fully compatible with general medical, ethical, and organizational standards. She wants to be excused because the care being provided is at odds with her own values or beliefs, which she recognizes as different from those of her professional colleagues in this case.

The conscientious supervisor will seek to discern which of these two kinds of claims the individual is making when someone makes a request to be excused. If it is the second, the response will need to focus only on the question of whether this particular employee should be excused or reassigned. The rest of this case commentary focuses on criteria to be used in responding to the second kind of claim.

Respect for individual conscience is at the heart of respect for human dignity. It needs to be high on the list of moral priorities, even when (perhaps especially when) the individual's beliefs are different from those of most others. On the other hand, healthcare employees need to be counted on to provide the type of care normally associated with their professions.

In an effort to reconcile respect for the convictions of individual employees with professional responsibility and with the institution's service mission, the following guidelines might be helpful.

An employee's request to be removed from certain care responsibilities should be honored when

1. the request is based on conscientious objection to participation in a particular type of treatment or procedure, not a refusal to care for a particular (type of) patient; and
2. the request appears to reflect a consistently held value of the employee; and
3. the care responsibility that the employee wants to be excused from is not fundamental to the profession; and
4. the patient will not be deprived of the type of care at issue; and
5. other caregivers are not asked to assume unreasonable burdens.

When a request to be removed from certain patient care responsibilities meets these criteria, it should be accommodated. The supervisor should assure the employee that the request is perfectly appropriate and should make every reasonable effort to remove the employee from the situation.

If, on the other hand, the request does not satisfy one or more of the five conditions, it should ordinarily be denied (with an explanation of the process for appealing the decision).

It may be difficult at times for a healthcare professional to provide care for a patient who is a substance abuser and repeatedly returns for the same treatment. It may be difficult for a healthcare professional to provide care for a patient who has repeatedly infected others with a sexually transmitted disease or who has a record of child abuse. A member of the staff may have strong moral objections to the behavior of these patients, but if the moral objection is not focused on the type of care they are receiving, a request to be excused from the care should not be given further consideration. Professionals care for patients in need even if those patients have abused themselves or others.

The second condition is sometimes difficult to assess in a particular case, but it can serve as a reminder that what should be respected is the employee's beliefs and ethical commitments, not necessarily every assertion that "I can't do this because it goes against my beliefs." A nurse, for example, might claim that it is contrary to her/his beliefs to use physical restraints on a patient. If this nurse has been involved in the use of physical restraints for years without any expression of concern, there is reason to wonder whether this is the sort of request that should be honored.

The third condition is a recognition that there are some responsibilities that are so fundamental or basic to a particular profession that anyone who has a moral or cultural conflict with that care would have a hard time engaging in the professional role at all. For example, healthcare workers who have an ethical objection to being involved in the care of any patient who refuses obviously beneficial treatment need to be reminded that respect for patient rights is fundamental to the healthcare professions. This may be a sincerely held conscientious objection, but it is not compatible with basic professional responsibility to respect patient refusal of unwanted treatment. As Martin Benjamin put it, "An individual whose moral or religious convictions are incompatible with a common essential type of health care has no business seeking a position in which such care is a routine expectation."[3]

The fourth condition is a very important one. If the patient has a legitimate expectation that a certain kind of care will be provided, the organization has a responsibility to provide that care. When honoring a healthcare worker's request to be excused means that the care or treatment owed to the patient will not be able to be provided, the request should not be honored. Respect for conscientious objection should be subordinated to the responsibility to provide care that meets accepted medical, ethical, and organizational standards.

It is appropriate for the organization to expect and, if necessary, require that other staff assume some burden in order to respect the conscientious objection on the part of an individual. Respect for conscience has little meaning if it is not permitted to inconvenience others at all. There are definite limits, though, to the burdens that should be placed on others in order to accommodate the individual's request. It is not always easy to know what constitutes an "unreasonable burden." Simply making adjustments in patient assignments is not placing an unreasonable burden on others, even if others do not want the changes made. Making unwanted shift changes, especially over a long period of time, might constitute an unreasonable burden.

In applying these conditions to the case above, the supervisor may need to give careful consideration to the third condition ("The care responsibility that the employee wants to be excused from is not fundamental to the profession"). The importance of providing adequate pain relief has become recognized as a central consideration of medical practice and medical ethics.

Assuming that the level of morphine medication ordered in this case is consistent with professional guidelines for pain management, A. H. is asking to be excused from a type of care that the patient has a right to and the organization has a responsibility to deliver. Administering morphine to a dying patient who accepts it may very well be an example of a "common essential type of health care" from which a nurse should not be excused because it is at the heart of what the profession is all about. Nevertheless, respect for conscience means that individuals should not be required unnecessarily to act contrary to their moral beliefs even when these beliefs are at odds with the dominant point of view.

One practical approach to resolving this case might be to honor A. H.'s request the first time it is made, *provided* that conditions 4 and 5 are met. This could then be followed by further discussion with her about pain management ethics and about nursing responsibilities in the organization. It would seem appropriate to notify her that such requests will not be honored in the future because this type of care is essential to good nursing practice. The implications of any refusals to do what is expected should be explained. The one-time reassignment is important, though, to demonstrate respect for her conscientious beliefs and to allow time for her to make the necessary decisions about what to do in the future.

When the Organization Restricts Treatment Options

The healthcare organization may take the position that despite the fact that certain medical interventions or procedures are legal and some patients are seeking them, they will not be provided within this organization because these procedures are considered contrary to the ethical beliefs adhered to by the organization. Abortion is a commonly recognized example, but there are a variety of other procedures as well that are sometimes prohibited within an organization or institution. These include, but are not limited to, assisted suicide (where legal), some forms of assisted reproduction, genetic testing for certain indications, research on human embryos, and sterilization.

Healthcare organizations cannot be entirely neutral. Whether they permit or do not permit staff or institutional participation in a particular procedure, they are sending a message to the public about the acceptability to the organization of that procedure in good healthcare or in good research. Likewise, the ways in which they respond to persons with views different from the official one of the organization speak very clearly regarding their position on respect for diverse points of view.

Though it is both appropriate and desirable for healthcare organizations to take conscientious positions on the types of legally acceptable practices that are and are not to be permitted within the organization, there are some important responsibilities that accompany decisions to restrict patient care options. These responsibilities are both to patients and to staff:

1. Decisions not to permit certain healthcare practices within the organization must be compatible with respect for essential patient rights.
2. Decisions not to permit certain healthcare practices within the organization must be compatible with respect for differing points of view within the organization.

Let me explore briefly some of the meaning and implications of each of these two organizational ethical guidelines for the organization.

Case 11.2. L. S. has been a resident of a long-term-care facility for several years. Two years ago she was diagnosed as suffering from a terminal disease, and she has been in deteriorating health since. During this latest hospital stay, she, her physician, and her family (grandchildren) have engaged in explicit conversations regarding how aggressively to try to prolong life at this point in time. L. S. executed an advance directive several years ago, before she knew she had a terminal condition. In it, she gave medical durable power of attorney to her granddaughter and expressed her wishes not to have life-sustaining treatment attempted when and if it became evident that she would die soon anyway. She wanted "to go with dignity." With her granddaughter's support, she has now requested "Do Not Resuscitate" status and has requested as well that other efforts, like tube feeding and antibiotics, not be used to extend her life. She is ready to die and does not want to fight for extended life any longer. Her doctor has accepted and recorded her position.

When the hospital social worker called the nursing home to prepare for L. S.'s return, she reported the decisions that were made at the hospital. "Then we cannot take her back," was the response. "We do not accept anyone who does not consent to tube feeding when it is necessary for nutrition. Our Board has taken a clear position that we will not be party to starving anyone to death."

In the section above, I noted that one of the conditions that need to be met before a staff member's request should be honored is that the particular responsibility that the employee wants to be excused from is not fundamental to the profession. A similar condition applies here: An organization's refusal to permit a certain care option is justified only if this option is not an essential component of good healthcare. The point is not so much whether we agree with the leadership of the nursing facility in regard to the morality of withholding tube feeding, but whether refusing to accept patients who want that option is a violation of fundamental patient rights.

There is a useful distinction sometimes made in regard to patient rights that may be of significance here. This is the distinction between refusing specific treatment and requesting or demanding specific treatment. These actions are ethically different, at least in regard to the response of others. For a provider to decide not to comply with a patient's wishes when the patient is requesting a particular treatment is to decide what the *provider will do*. For a provider to decide not to comply with a patient's wishes when the patient is saying no to a particular treatment is to decide what the *patient will do*.

The difference between these two types of situations should not be overstated, but treating without consent is imposing one's view on the patient in a way (imposing treatment) that refusing to comply with a request for a particular treatment is not. When an organization refuses to comply with a request for a type of treatment for its own conscientious reasons, it is saying to patient, in effect, "We are not going to do what you are requesting because we do not think that it is right." When an organization refuses to comply with a patient refusal of a particular type of treatment, it is saying, in effect, "We are going to require that you have this treatment because we think it is right."

One essential of good healthcare is respecting a competent person's informed refusal of treatment (except in the unusual circumstances in which such refusal puts others at serious risk of significant avoidable harm). Even when providers think that the decision is wrong (medically or ethically), the decision needs to be honored. The nursing home's tube feeding policy, in this case, appears to be a violation of this right to say no. As such, it fails to meet the requirement that institutional limits on patient care options not violate essential elements of good healthcare.

Sometimes the organization in a case like this will explain that its policy does not force patients to accept unwanted treatment, because patients are not required to come to this facility; they can go elsewhere. If they are informed at the time of admission that the policy requires tube feeding if the patient cannot take food by mouth, and, if they choose to be admitted after being informed, they are consenting to this kind of treatment if needed. If they later change their minds about the consent, they can transfer.

It is important that patients be informed in advance when organizations have ethical standards that restrict the types of medical treatment practices available. The fact that a facility lets prospective patients know in advance what the rules are, however, does not justify rules that infringe on basic rights. The right to refuse unwanted treatment cannot be consented away in advance. It is a fundamental right of consent that should not have to mean transferring in order to be exercised.

The decision of an organization not to permit an optional service (such as elective abortion, elective sterilization, and assisted suicide) is not open to the same criticism as the decision not to care for patients who do not accept certain treatments. There is a difference, noted earlier, between requiring that patients accept certain treatments and refusing to provide a non-medically necessary treatment that the patient requests. Nevertheless, there are important responsibilities involved in decisions not to permit certain treatments.

The healthcare organization has responsibilities to patients who seek services that are not available in this setting. The organization should encourage the clinical staff to inform patients of the options available elsewhere, if they seek that information, so that patients can make informed decisions. If a patient has a legal claim to have a procedure done and requests assistance, clinicians should, at a minimum, inform the patient where he or she can get the information necessary in order to pursue the interest in having the procedure done. To provide the opportunity for a patient to consult with someone else does not mean that one approves of the procedure in this case; it is to recognize, respectfully, their legal option and their moral freedom.

When a patient chooses to go elsewhere in order to receive treatment of the sort not permitted in this organization, an extremely important consideration is the continuing provision of competent and compassionate care during the transfer. "Skilled and humane care should be provided until transfer of care is complete, so that abandonment does not occur."[4] When patients make choices that are contrary to the ethical views of providers, they remain persons to be treated with dignity and respect. Obstacles should not be placed in their way, and the quality of their care should not suffer.

Let me turn now to what organizations can legitimately expect of staff.

Case 11.3. Dr. Jorden, an obstetrician/gynecologist employed at St. Francis Hospital, has been reported by two non-physician employees to be "moonlighting" at a clinic that provides abortions. St. Francis has a clear policy against induced abortions, a policy that is well known in the community. The report, made to the department head, the chief of the medical staff, the hospital CEO, and the Chairperson of the Board, includes a strong statement of expectation that the hospital will quickly "do something" about the fact that one of its physicians is performing abortions. The four individuals who received the memo have scheduled a meeting for the next day to decide what, if anything, to do about Dr. Jorden and how to respond to the memo.

This is a situation that is difficult to resolve, because it involves fairly complex matters of employee responsibilities and rights as well as potential for significant publicity. The right thing to do, all things considered, can be determined only when relevant factors are taken into account. It is possible here, though, to provide some important ethical perspectives that should begin and guide the deliberation.

Employees have a responsibility to conform to legitimate organizational policy in their work as employees. They retain, at the same time, basic freedoms in the outside activities in which they engage. Employees in a hospital that has a clear policy against providing abortions have a responsibility to adhere to that policy in their capacity as employees. These same employees, however, should not be penalized at work in any way, if, on their own time and outside the organization, they support and promote social and ethical positions and/or practices contrary to those of hospital leadership. They retain their rights as citizens to express their points of view, to act according to their views, and to encourage and promote whatever legal behavior they believe appropriate. This distinction between what employees do on the job and what they do on their own is a basic starting point for analyzing issues of this sort:

> Employers have the right to demand work of a specific kind from their employees, and while they are working they can be expected to do certain tasks assigned to them. But no employer has the right to deprive his employees of their civil rights off the job. . . . Employees are properly evaluated for their work on the job, but this evaluation should not extend to non job-related activities as long as these do not adversely affect their job performance.[5]

It is important to start with this basic principle of business ethics and then to assess whether there are any circumstances specific to this case which would make this situation relevantly different. It might be different from the ordinary employer-employee situation if Dr. Jorden had agreed upon employment not to provide abortion services anywhere while an employee of St. Francis. It might be different if Dr. Jorden had such a high-level and visible position within St. Francis that she or he could not practice medicine anywhere in the area without being identified with St. Francis. It would probably be different if Dr. Jorden made use of the St. Francis employment position to recruit patients to the clinic.

There may be extenuating circumstances that would support disciplinary action in regard to Dr. Jorden, but the burden of proof rests with the decision to do so. The same respect for conscience that is found in a policy allowing employees to claim conscientious objection in some situations requires the practice of allowing employees to act contrary to organizational moral positions in their outside activities. In the absence of circumstances powerful enough to meet the burden of proof, the response to the memo should be a reminder of the institutional commitment to respect the consciences of employees.

Twelve

Union Organizing and Employee Strikes

Chapter 9 included Frank Narvan's observation that decisions related to downsizing strategy "become the model. They tell all employees what the new rules are. These decisions set the standard for the ethics of future decisions."[1] How downsizing is handled is one of those defining moments, a loud and clear communication regarding the values that management actually adheres to in its relationships to employees.

This chapter focuses on another defining moment in management's relationship to employees: management's response to union-related activity—organizing efforts and strikes. The importance of this response is hard to exaggerate, especially given the impact on the attitude of employees toward management over the long term. Management's response to employee unionizing efforts and management's strategy when strikes occur inform employees, loudly and clearly, of the nature of management's respect for them.

This chapter does not address the ethical responsibilities of employees or union representatives in organizing or work stoppages. The reason is simple: These comments are written for management about management's responsibility. There are, to be sure, important ethical issues that should be considered by union organizers and employees, but that discussion is for another time and place. In some situations and issues, and this may be one, it is not very helpful to focus on the ethical responsibilities of "the other side." The best starting point for management's reflection on ethics and union-related activity is to consider its own role and responsibilities.

The Right to Form Unions

There is a long-standing and widely recognized ethical principle that employees have a right to form unions. The United Nations Declaration of Human Rights affirms this right: "Everyone has the right to form and to join trade unions for the protection of his interests."[2] Though the precise language often varies from one statement to another, this fundamental ethical principle is frequently noted in discussions of human rights, of business ethics, and of healthcare ethics. One business ethics text, for example, recognizes that "workers have the right to freely associate with each other to establish and run unions for the achievement of their morally legitimate common ends."[3] The United States Roman Catholic Bishops, to cite another example, recognize this right in their directives for Catholic Health Care Services: "the rights of employees to organize and bargain collectively without prejudice to the common good."[4]

The ethical right of employees to establish unions is a human right, more basic than law. It applies to all organizations that hire employees, whether private or public, for-profit or not-for-profit, wherever they are. There is widespread assent given to this right of employees to negotiate through unions, but the meaning of this right is not always well understood.

Basic human rights are of fundamental significance in determining ethical responsibilities. Human rights represent the ways in which everyone, regardless of power, position, or merits, is to be respected simply because of being human. Human rights are so fundamental that governments are not considered ethically legitimate if they do not respect them. Human rights apply within businesses and service organizations; they must be observed in the organization if the organization is to meet minimal standards of ethical legitimacy. When the effort to achieve certain organizational interests puts basic rights at risk, those organizational interests need to be subordinated to the obligation to protect rights.

As a basic human right, the right of workers to form unions makes binding claims upon others. To prevent workers from organizing is to deny them the fundamental human activity of associating with others to achieve their goals. To prevent workers from organizing is to deny them the fundamental human activity of seeking to exercise some control over decisions that affect them directly and of asserting themselves in regard to what they perceive to be just and fair.

In some cases, the right to form unions is understood as merely a right to choose. Respect for the right to form unions is sometimes interpreted as a tolerance responsibility, a responsibility to accept the decision of employees to unionize even though that decision is probably not a good one. It is true that one of the implications of the right to form unions is that the choice of employees regarding unionizing is not to be interfered with, but mere tolerance of employee decisions is not an adequate recognition of the full significance of this human right.

The exercise of human rights should be endorsed, not simply tolerated. Endorsing the right means seeking to create an environment in which employees feel free and supported in making whatever decision they choose to make. It means providing employees with access to the kinds of information about the organization necessary for them to make an informed judgment. Endorsing the human right to form unions means a clear advance acceptance of the union, should the workers so choose, and a commitment to bargain in good faith.

It is not unusual to hear someone say that those organizations that get unions deserve them, that, in effect, unions represent a failure of management. It is often true that disappointment with management action is the occasion for an organizing campaign. It is unfortunate, though, to describe the choice of a union to represent workers as a failure on the part of management. In the first place, such an observation suggests that unions have no positive function, that, in fact, they exist only to counteract injustices or correct mistakes. Unions are a natural result, in some cases, of the need that workers have to participate in decisions in the institutions in which they work and to try to influence decisions that affect them. Unions may not be the only way to participate, but they are, at this time and place, a normal means to achieve that goal.

In addition, describing unions as a failure on the part of management tends to put management in the position of having to oppose a unionizing movement as a way of proving that this management is not really failing. Seeing employee selection of a union as a failure on the part of management puts management too much on the defensive and makes it very difficult to recognize the positive nature of the exercise of this human right.[5]

Unions have made major contributions to fairer wages and to improved working conditions. Seeking to speak with a stronger and more unified voice is a natural way for workers to try to address issues that they consider important. To do this by unionizing is also to be expected, since speaking through unions is often the typical and established way of trying to be heard more effectively in an organization.

Respecting the right of workers to organize and bargain collectively means that management will be fully supportive of employee decision-making regarding unionization. As is considered in more detail below, this means much more than not literally preventing union certification elections or not abiding by the results.

When human rights are taken seriously, they impose weighty responsibilities.

Responding to an Organizing Drive

Case 12.1. Senior management is meeting to begin to plan its strategy regarding a newly announced union organizing effort. The Service Employees International Union is seeking to represent the nurses in the organization. At this time, none of the professionally licensed employee groups is represented by a union. It is agreed around the table that recent layoffs may be the reason that this effort is being undertaken now.

As this first meeting progresses, different strategy issues are raised. One major question is whether management should hire a consultant who has worked with other organizations in cases of unionizing drives involving the SEIU and nurses. While there is some support for this in the leadership team, there is clearly no consensus. After some discussion, the CEO suggests that a decision on this question be postponed until management clarifies its own stance in regard to this organizing drive.

The CEO in this case is probably making a wise suggestion. It is important to be clear on the big picture before making a decision about hiring a consultant. Part of the process of getting clear on stance and strategy may be to review some of the ethical implications that follow from taking seriously the human right to form unions.

The following are several guidelines that may be particularly relevant to the question of how management should respond to an organizing drive.[6]

1. Avoid employing consultants who have a reputation for assisting employers in fighting unionizing efforts.

Some consulting firms have the reputation of being "union-busting" firms. They are known for their services designed to assist an employer's effort to "win" union elections.

There is a message that is sent by the use of such consultants. What it says to workers is that management is willing to use "hired guns" to prevent a union and that management is willing to use the questionable methods that are often associated with these consultants. It was noted above that management's response to employee unionizing efforts is a defining moment in the understanding that employees will have of management's respect for them. The damage done to management's reputation and to the working relationship between management and employees by hiring such consultants is enormous. Even if management is able to maintain control over the tactics used, much damage is done by the very employment of such consultants.

If there is to be any use of consultants, those hired should be known either (1) for their ability to give objective advice regarding labor law or (2) for their reputation for advising management on ways to empower employees as a group or on ways of addressing constructively the kinds of issues that employees are concerned about. A good principle might be for management to consult with the employee group and hire only the type of consultants for assistance during a unionizing drive that the employees do not oppose.

2. It is risky to refer to "winning" or "losing" the organizing campaign.

One of the reasons that it is ethically questionable to hire consultants who have a reputation for helping to "defeat" union organizing efforts is that this is responding to the organizing drive as though one needs to prepare for decisive action in which one side wins and one side loses. Management may, in some cases, prefer that employees not select a particular union to represent them, but focusing on "winning" tends to distort good management practices. It supports a "them" and "us" attitude, suggesting that employees cannot be both pro-union and pro-employing organization. Given the emphasis that is often placed on "winning," this sort of language may also involve some danger of escalation, of using inappropriate means if such means are considered necessary to win.

The point here is not just about language, of course. It makes very little sense to talk about management "winning" in regard to a decision that is not theirs to make. A union vote is a case of employees exercising their right to decide how they want to work together.

3. Give serious consideration to the option of card-check recognition.

Card-check recognition of union representation is an option that may have distinct advantages in many cases. Recognizing the union based on the fact that a majority of employees in the group have signed authorization cards avoids the election process and all the potential for damaging behavior associated with such elections. When the goal is to respect the decision of the majority of employees regarding union representation, there is little reason to pursue the issue further when a majority have signed authorization cards and there is no evidence that the cards were signed under duress. If there is any indication of significant pressure on employees to sign cards, a secret ballot is preferred.

4. Choose the least intimidating methods of presenting management's perspectives on the unionizing effort.

If management determines that there are good reasons to encourage employees not to select a particular union to represent them, they should present these reasons to employees in ways that are respectful of the employees' role in making the decision. The two major ethical requirements of such communication are that it be honest and that it be as non-intimidating as possible.

Honest presentation of management's reasons means that these reasons are not misrepresented. It means that, for example, implications of a decision to unionize are not overstated or distorted. It means that "scare tactics," a description of the worst possible scenarios as though they are the most likely scenarios, are avoided.

Scare tactics are not only dishonest. They are intimidating. Employees are intimidated if they feel threatened with undesirable consequences if they act or speak in support of union representation. Intimidation results from suggestions that job security will be reduced or that leaders in the unionizing effort are not loyal employees or that unions are incompatible with professional responsibility. Any suggestion that employees are less worthy of management's respect when they exercise their basic right to union representation should be avoided.

5. Refrain from negative campaigning.

If management determines that there are good reasons to encourage employees not to select a particular union to represent them, they should present these reasons to employees in ways that are respectful of the employees' role in making the decision. Presenting management's perspectives in terms of the needs of the organization is one thing. Challenging union credibility or engaging in other ways in "anti-union" behavior is the kind of negative campaigning that, even if "successful," makes future working relationships much more difficult.

The first step after the election is over, which needs to be taken very quickly, is to move on. If union representation is voted in, a contract should be negotiated quickly. If union representation is not selected, the issues that employees identified need to be addressed in some other way. In both cases, the last thing that is needed is the distrust and anger that results from negative campaigning.

Employers often view unions as unnecessary and as potentially disruptive of working relationships in the organization. Given this perspective, it is tempting to want to prevent employees from embarking on that route. It is tempting, but the manager who is committed to respectful long-term working relationships will resist many of the practices used in "fighting" unionizing drives and will, instead, seek to live out the practical implications of the ethical responsibility to respect the rights of workers to unionize.

One last comment may be in order on this topic. Union organizers and employee supporters have a similar responsibility to adhere to high ethical standards during an organizing effort. The failure of either management or labor to adhere to ethical standards does not, however, justify any lowering of the ethical level on the "other side." Both have to live with the consequences. To focus once again on management, the choice of the high road, regardless of the tactics chosen by others, will stand management in good stead when the organizing episode is over.

Strikes by Healthcare Professionals

A major characteristic of the understanding of healthcare ethics presented in this book is that healthcare is not just like any other business. Healthcare is fundamentally and essentially a service. Healthcare organizations are best understood as community service organizations. The basic purpose of health-care organizations is to meet the healthcare needs of individuals and to promote the health of the community.

Strikes by healthcare providers are not the same as strikes in some other industries. At the same time, employees in healthcare do not lose their right to bargain collectively. It is important to try to clarify management's responsibility when healthcare personnel strike.

In general, the right to form unions and to bargain collectively implies the right to strike. Workers have a right to form unions and bargain collectively as a means of seeking good wages and working conditions and as a method of having a voice in their work. Unless unions have the ability to withhold labor as a last resort, they are in a very weak bargaining position. Without the right to strike, the right to bargain collectively is effectively denied.

A general right to strike does not mean, however, that a particular strike is right. While a strike can be a legitimate means of pursuing improvements for employees, it often causes harm to individuals, to organizations, and to the public. It is important, therefore, that it be undertaken and/or continued only when necessary to achieve demands compatible with employees' responsibility to the public good and to their employer. The question raised by strikes by healthcare professionals is whether the harm and suffering that may result are justified. Furthermore, the usually legitimate claim of employees of a right to strike may conflict, in this case, with the usually legitimate claim of patients to access to high-quality healthcare services. On the other hand, it may be that the strike demands, if met, will lead to improved quality of healthcare.[7]

Some strikes by healthcare personnel are ethically justified; some are not. It depends on the nature of the issues and on the likely consequences of a strike. Union leaders need to give careful consideration to the circumstances that distinguish justified strikes from non-justified strikes. Here, however, the discussion needs to stay focused on the responsibilities of management in the event of a strike.

Case 12.2. Negotiations have not been going well with the union representing registered nurses in the hospital. The nurses have been working without a contract for several weeks now, but they have recently set a deadline: Unless a tentative contract is reached by the end of the week, they will go on strike. If a strike occurs, the union has informed management, only a small number of nurses will report for work, and they will provide care only in emergency situations.

As the management team prepares for the possibility of a strike, the first question that demands their attention is the question of hiring replacements.

In the midst of patient care concerns and public relations concerns, it is very difficult for management in a situation like this to keep clearly in mind what is most fair to striking employees. Yet attention to that concern is essential.

The precise practical implications of what it means to be fair or just regarding striking employees in a case like this cannot be determined without much more information regarding the specifics of the case. It is possible, though, to provide a few general guidelines that may assist managers think through their specific responsibilities.

1. A judgment on the part of management that the union is wrong in going on strike does not mean that "union-busting" tactics are justified.

Unions are a legitimate means for employees to use to promote their interests. They retain the right to bargain collectively through representation of their choice, even if particular decisions do not appear to others to be good decisions or reasonable decisions. There is a parallel to management here. Management retains the right to exercise its responsibility even if particular decisions do not appear to others to be good decisions or reasonable decisions.

Respecting the right of employees to choose their own bargaining agent requires that management not take advantage of a strike to try to break the influence of the union among the employees. It requires that management continue to speak to employees through their bargaining agent.

One example of questionable behavior is encouraging individual workers to cross the picket line and to report for work during the strike. It is one thing if, in this case, some nurses choose to cross the picket lines on their own. It is something else entirely if management encourages or requests that they do so. Respect for the right of collective bargaining means not asking employees to be strikebreakers.

2. If it is necessary to hire replacement workers in order to provide essential services, these workers are to be recognized clearly and explicitly as temporary replacements, not permanent replacements.

One of the most egregious forms of union busting is to hire permanent replacement workers when employees go on strike.

Workers have a right to form unions and bargain collectively. Without the right to strike, the right to bargain collectively is effectively denied. If workers risk being permanently replaced if they go on strike, the right to strike is effectively denied. Hiring replacements without clearly indicating that striking employees will have their positions back is a clear violation of basic employee rights.

It is understandable that management, in such a difficult situation, will have a very positive attitude toward those who are hired to meet the immediate service needs that have resulted from the strike. Management is likely to feel a sense of loyalty to these workers. This is understandable, but there is a prior loyalty to workers who have already been part of the organization. True loyalty to workers includes respect for their freedom to go on strike, even if one thinks that it is a poor decision.

3. Continued negotiation on a new contract should not be made contingent upon a prior return to work.

When management thinks that a strike is unnecessary and harmful, there may be a temptation to try to put pressure on the union to end the strike by refusing to negotiate until employees return to work. Again, this tactic may be understandable, but it is, in effect, a failure to recognize the basic right of employees to bargain and to strike.

Strikes are disruptive. In healthcare, strikes by professional care providers result in enormous difficulty in providing good-quality care. Good organizational leaders, faced with such disruption and difficulty, are able to find solutions that are fully compatible with respect for employee union-related rights. Even in organizations devoted to providing essential services that cannot all be postponed, fairness to striking employees is high on the list of management's responsibilities.

Union Issues and Ethics Resources

The right of employees to organize as a fundamental human right has not received much detailed attention in the education of most persons in management positions in the United States today. This is true in healthcare as well as in other organizations. This chapter has been an attempt to describe some of the implications for management of understanding union issues as high-priority ethics issues. The implications are challenging and may demand some rethinking in some cases, but the behaviors required by ethics can also be recognized as good practices for promoting respectful long-term relationships between managers and employees.

What is acceptable legally and what is acceptable ethically are often two different things. The "union issue" is complex enough both legally and ethically that management may well benefit from advice and consultation in regard to both dimensions of the issue (but not, ordinarily, seeking both kinds of advice from the same persons). This issue, like others discussed in other chapters, suggests a need to have a resource that managers can turn to as they make decisions about what is the right thing to do in difficult and complex situations.

Resources and mechanisms for aiding in the ethics deliberations of managers in healthcare are discussed in Part 5 of this book.

Thirteen

Responsible Advertising

> At its best, advertising can provide information to help consumers make informed choices. Conversely, it can inflate expectations, create demand, manipulate desire, transform wants into perceived needs, and increase utilization and cost of health-care services.[1]

Advertising has long been recognized as a major tool in efforts to achieve business success. It has long been understood, at the same time, to be an ethically risky business tool. Education in the essentials of business ethics has always included consideration of the ways in which advertising can take unfair advantage of potential consumers or cause other harm. In its initial emphasis on organizational ethics, JCAHO has also recognized marketing and advertising as functions that require clear ethical standards.

Much of the attention given to the ethics of advertising has been focused on the question of whether particular advertising is deceptive or misleading. This is obviously a legitimate and important concern, but as the above quote suggests, there are a number of other considerations that need to be taken into account in the process of developing responsible advertising. This is true of advertising generally; it may be even more true of healthcare advertising.

Before discussing specific ethical issues and standards in healthcare advertising, it may be useful to reflect on the need for high ethical standards in marketing and advertising in healthcare.

Marketing Healthcare Services: The Need for High Ethical Standards

Some marketing methods involve, even if unintentionally, the adoption of a model of business that is not suitable for healthcare. Healthcare marketing needs to be compatible with the nature and mission of the healthcare organization.

In an article recommending the adoption of a "business" model of managing hospitals in order to succeed in an era of competition, Tasker Robinette made a distinction between being a "customer satisfier" and being a "care provider":

> Most of us view the traditionally organized not-for-profit hospital as charitable and humanistic institution established for patient care, community service, scientific research, and training and educational programs. . . . Hospitals must see themselves as customer satisfiers. Once we've made that shift, rational management techniques can work. At first glance, the difference between customer satisfier and care provider may seem insignificant, but it is a *fundamental* difference.[2]

Robinette is correct, I think, in recognizing that there is a major difference between understanding the healthcare organization as customer satisfier and understanding the organization as care provider (even though there are many ways in which care providers need to satisfy their customers).

In the most radical sense of being a customer satisfier, a business recognizes that the customer is boss, the customer is always right, the customer should have whatever he or she wants (and is willing and able to pay for). A business, as a good customer satisfier, essentially gives customers what they want.

A care provider business, on the other hand, recognizes that providing good care does not always mean satisfying the customer; it certainly does not mean always giving customers what they want. Success as a care provider is determined largely by the professional quality of the care provided, not by what the customer wants (whether the "customer" is the one who is cared for, the one who pays for the care, or the one who refers or admits someone for care).

High-quality care does require that customers are satisfied in regard to the nature of the professional and personal interactions they encounter. In this sense, customer satisfaction is essential to good healthcare. This is very different, however, from giving customers the precise type of treatment or testing they might want. Being a good care provider and adhering to professional standards of quality means that a customer will definitely not get what she or he wants at times and will not, in that sense, be satisfied.

This discussion of Robinette's distinction is not intended to play down the importance of giving "customers" of healthcare organizations the respect and deference they deserve. It is not intended to suggest that everyone who talks about the importance of satisfying customers is really seeing no difference between providing professional care and selling clothes. Rather, it is meant to remind healthcare managers that the "customer is queen" model of doing business is more suited to industries that provide goods and services that are not professional in nature.

The marketing of healthcare services needs to be done in a manner that does not make it more difficult to provide high-quality healthcare. This requires that marketing and advertising efforts be undertaken with a clear recognition of the specific nature of healthcare. One of the points made below is that good advertising avoids promoting unnecessary services. This ethics standard makes good sense if one understands healthcare as community service of a professional nature. This standard would make little or no sense in many other businesses.

Common strategies and practices in marketing and advertising have arisen and been developed primarily in customer satisfier businesses. Advertising agencies hired by healthcare organizations may very well have had most of their experience in customer satisfier businesses. Responsible marketing and advertising in care provider organizations therefore requires special attention and effort.

Without management's close attention and supervision, advertising ethics standards for healthcare may very well be violated. This risk exists not because of a disregard for ethics but because of the higher standards required in healthcare. Being higher standards than the generic ones found in most discussions of business ethics, they are not likely to be internalized by marketing professionals without a deep immersion in the nature of healthcare as a service.

Consumer-Directed Prescription Drug Advertising

Case 13.1. As the members of the hospital Ethics Committee were getting coffee and bagels a few minutes before the beginning of their regular monthly meeting, D. M., the Chairperson, decided that she had found the perfect way of introducing the topic for the education portion of the meeting.

The committee was in the process of improving its understanding of "organizational ethics" and had been spending time considering ethical issues related to the functions that the Joint Commission on the Accreditation of Health Care Organizations included in its standards for organizational ethics: marketing, admissions, transfer and discharge, and billing. The topic for this meeting was advertising, and a professor of business ethics from a nearby university had been invited for a discussion of ethical issues in advertising.

D. M. had just overheard part of a conversation between two committee members at the coffee urn. "How are you this morning?" "Fine. And I will be even better as soon as my sniffles clear up." "Do you have allergies? You ever see the Claritin commercials on TV?"

As D. M. greeted the business ethics professor, she asked him if it would be okay if they used the case of advertising prescription drugs to the public as the context for identifying key issues that needed to be considered in regard to advertising ethics and healthcare. She told him that she frequently found herself uneasy when she saw prescription drug commercials on television and that she wanted to take this opportunity to think a little more carefully about the issues and about her reaction.

The advertising of prescription drugs directly to the public has increased significantly in the 1990s and has become quite common. The fact that it is a common practice does not, however, mean that the many questions about its appropriateness have been satisfactorily addressed. The most basic question is whether such advertising is in the public interest.

As has already been noted, advertising ethics has traditionally been dominated by a concern to avoid being deceptive or misleading. This focus, combined with the emphasis in healthcare on the need to provide information on potential risks when recommending treatment, probably accounts for the fact that the major regulation of drug advertising is the requirement that such advertising include a statement on side effects and contraindications. It seems, though, that other considerations related to prescription drug advertising are of more basic ethical importance than the disclosure of risks.[3]

The major community health benefit that might result from prescription drug advertising is educational. Consumers may become more aware of symptoms to call to the attention of their doctors. They may become aware of, and ask their physicians about, new medications that might be improvements over what they are receiving. Public advertising of prescription drugs may provide benefit in increasing awareness both of diseases and of treatment options.

There are, on the other hand, serious risks to the public good associated with this method of promoting prescription drugs. Among the risks identified in a 1995 resolution of the American Public Health Association are these:

> . . . pharmaceutical advertisements directed at the public may be potentially misleading and/or false in that consumers' expectations of the drug's effectiveness may be heightened by the advertising copy;
> . . . heightened consumer expectations may put an undue strain on the physician-patient relationship as patients demand advertised products which may not be appropriate for them;
> . . . pharmaceutical advertisements directed at the public may result in the irrational use of drugs that is detrimental to public health;
> . . . the irrational use of drugs may result in treatment failures from the use of the wrong therapy, patients suffering from unnecessary adverse effects, and the waste of patients' money and scarce national health resources. . . . [4]

Prescription drugs are not to be dispensed and used without the professional judgment of a clinician that medication is needed and that this is the appropriate medication given the patient's needs and circumstances. Public advertising of these drugs clearly has the potential for putting pressure on clinicians to prescribe what patients want or expect rather than what is needed and appropriate. Such advertising has the potential for promoting "irrational use of drugs."

Individual physicians have a professional responsibility to resist patient demands for inappropriate treatment. This responsibility should be supported, not made more difficult, by pharmaceutical companies. It is frequently difficult for physicians to say "no" to patients who present with advertising-driven expectations for specific medication.

The general ethical standard for advertising healthcare services and products is that such advertising should promote public health and high-quality healthcare. To make the point differently, healthcare advertising should not encourage or result in attitudes or values or behaviors that are likely to be harmful to public health or lead to poor healthcare decisions for individuals.

The ways that medical drugs are promoted have effects, whether intended or not, on the practice of medicine and on public health. Some of the effects may be positive, resulting in more fully informed diagnosis and treatment. Some of the effects may be negative, resulting in drug use that is inappropriate or unnecessary or more expensive than necessary. Good healthcare advertising is designed to increase the probability of positive health effects and reduce the probability of negative health effects.

While advertising sometimes has education and information as one of its goals, the primary purpose of commercial advertising is to increase consumption. Increasing sales may, in some cases, do harm to the very people who are interested in using the product. In their public advertising of prescription drugs, pharmaceutical companies may not be able to "serve two masters: the promotional interest of the pharmaceutical industry and the individual's health needs."[5] When there is no absolutely clear evidence that more harm than good results from a particular advertising approach or campaign, the principle of "do no harm" suggests that a very cautious approach.

Putting the emphasis on the need to avoid potential harm is especially important if it is possible to achieve the positive public benefits through other means. Consumer education on available medications can be done separately from promotion. There is a strong case to be made for separating the two efforts, based on the sound ethical principle that situations with potentially conflicting goals and interests should be avoided if possible.

Advertising drugs is not like advertising food or clothes or cars. Drug advertising needs to be guided by the ethical standards relevant to healthcare advertising. The comments made about drug advertising by the American Public Health Association and others offer a good introduction to ethical standards for healthcare advertising.

Ethical Standards for Healthcare Advertising

Among the characteristics of responsible healthcare advertising, according to Kurt Darr, are these: it must "be truthful, fair, accurate, complete, and sensitive to the public's healthcare needs and not raise unrealistic expectations."[6]

He and others also recognize a specific ethical responsibility not to create demands for "unnecessary" services.[7] Allen Dyer, in the statement that was used to open this chapter, provided a similar list of ethical considerations: "At its best, advertising can provide information to help consumers make informed choices. Conversely, it can inflate expectations, create demand, manipulate desire, transform wants into perceived needs, and increase utilization and cost of health-care services."

Most codes of ethics in healthcare organizations, in line with the expectations of the Joint Commission on the Accreditation of Health Care Organizations, express a commitment to marketing and advertising that accurately reflect the services available. Avoiding misrepresentation is basic to advertising ethics, but it is only the beginning. More complete ethical standards for healthcare advertising are proposed here, organized under five different general statements. The headline statements are used only to provide order to the discussion; the full nature of complex responsibilities cannot always be captured in one-sentence statements.

1. Good healthcare advertising promotes accurate expectations.

One very important question to ask about advertising is what message is being sent and/or received regarding expectations. The American Public Health Association, as noted above, is concerned about the public's heightened expectations about a drug's effectiveness as a result of advertising. Even though nothing is promised or put into words, the images presented may encourage or allow someone to conclude that rapid and permanent improvement is likely, when that is not, in fact, the probable case. A consumer may respond to an advertisement by thinking that a drug, or other medical intervention, would be beneficial in the treatment for a condition very different from its intended use.

The message being received may, at times, be different from what is intended to be conveyed. Ethical responsibility means assessing the potential impact in addition to the intended impact and avoiding anything that promotes unrealistic expectations. The American Public Health Association expressed concern about unrealistically heightened expectations because heightened expectations are not harmless. They may, for example, "put an undue strain on the physician–patient relationship as patients demand advertised products which may not be appropriate for them."

What is the message being received if a hospital's advertising suggests that life-saving "miracles" take place frequently with the availability of the latest technology? Clinicians frequently have to contend with unrealistic expectations on the part of family members regarding the chances of survival of critically ill patients with very poor prognosis. It is not such advertising alone, of course, that causes these unrealistic expectations, but it could be a contributing or supportive factor. Again, unrealistic expectations are not harmless. In addition to the strain on doctor-patient/family relationships, they can result in care that is not appropriate and may, in fact, increase or extend a patient's suffering unnecessarily.

2. Good healthcare advertising provides accurate and understandable information.

"Truth in advertising" has long been recognized as an important ethical standard, but the acceptance of the standard does not always make its implementation easy. What should be said, for example, about a commercial that says that the "best doctors" or "caring nurses" are found in the XYZ healthcare system? Is there really any evidence that these are the best doctors, whatever "best" might mean? And is there an implication that nurses at other institutions are not as caring?

In regard to advertising ethics generally, it has sometimes been found helpful to use the "reasonable person" or "reasonable consumer" criterion for assessing whether advertising is deceptive or misleading. Would the reasonable consumer be deceived or misled? The reasonable consumer is one who has been exposed to a great deal of advertising over the years. She or he is sophisticated enough and skeptical enough to know that neither a new car nor a particular cologne is going to produce dramatic increases in one's appeal to attractive members of the opposite sex. The reasonable consumer knows about attention grabbers and about hyperbole and about what is found only in the fine print.

The reasonable consumer criterion works well in many situations in determining whether a particular ad meets the standard of truthfulness. It does not work well in others. Young children, for example, are not yet capable of knowing how advertising works and, therefore, are more easily deceived or misled than "reasonable consumers." Advertising directed at children needs to adhere to a higher standard regarding truth and accuracy.

Adults can also be fairly easily misled by advertising at times, especially regarding professional services that are difficult for the layperson to evaluate. In these sorts of situations, the reasonable consumer is not someone who has much knowledge, experience, or sophistication regarding professional standards. A reasonable consumer *is* likely to know how to process references to the "best doctors" and "caring nurses." It is less clear, however, that the layperson will know how to understand references to a "center of excellence in cardiac care" or to being "fully accredited by NCQA."

The point here is that healthcare is a profession dedicated to serving the public interest. It is in the public interest that healthcare advertising promote an accurate understanding of how the healthcare system works. It is not enough to avoid inaccurate statements. It is necessary, as well, not to take advantage of any lack of knowledge or sophistication.

3. Good healthcare advertising promotes utilization levels reflective of high-quality care.

As was noted in Chapter 3, high-quality healthcare requires the avoidance of underuse (failure to provide proven effective interventions), overuse (unnecessary interventions or treatment for clearly inappropriate indications), and misuse (interventions causing preventable complications). Given the frequent relationship of advertising to the desire to increase use of services, ethical assessment requires a particular focus on the need to avoid overuse. Management's responsibility to make the most effective use of limited financial resources implies a strong responsibility to avoid any advertising that might promote unnecessary use of resources.

In a community sense, an unnecessary healthcare service is one that is already sufficiently available to meet community needs fully.[8] Promoting these sorts of services may have some legitimate purpose in terms of market share, but such promotion carries with it a very real risk of increasing use beyond what is needed. It is clear that, in healthcare as in other areas of life, supply sometimes creates demand. Advertising prescription drugs directly to the public is likely to lead in some cases to the unnecessary use of those drugs in the care of patients who ask their doctors about them. Advertising other healthcare services may lead to overuse as well.

4. Good healthcare advertising avoids promoting harmful values or attitudes or images.

There has been a growing recognition in recent years of the need to focus on the kind of values or attitudes that are being promoted or reinforced in advertising. Advertising often promotes a product or service by taking advantage of values and feelings that exist in potential purchasers—feelings of frustration or unattractiveness, desires for popularity or power or success, a sense of distrust or envy. Advertising targeting women, for example, has often been seen as playing on insecurities and projecting particular models of female beauty:

> As B. Earl Puckett, then head of the department store chain Allied Stores Corporation, put it 40 years ago, "It is our job to make women unhappy with what they have." Thus for those born with short, skinny eyelashes, the message mongers offer hope. For those whose hair is too straight, or too curly, or grows in the wrong places, for those whose skin is too dark or too light, for those whose body weight is distributed in anything but this year's fashion, advertising assures that synthetic salvation is at hand.[9]

Healthcare advertising is not the same as cosmetic and fashion advertising, but it is not entirely different. Any advertising that suggests healthy behavior or promotes ways of making life better can hardly avoid presenting models of health and responsible behavior. Any advertising that uses images or voices of human persons is likely to suggest, for somebody, what is good or what is bad.

Ads for antidepressants in medical journals that consistently include pictures of women, not men, as depressed patients may reinforce the tendency among some doctors to categorize a female patient's health complaints as emotional in nature more quickly than he or she would a male patient's complaints. Billboards that consistently present physicians as middle-aged white males may reinforce the tendency on the part of some patients not to trust physicians who are not white, who are not male, who are foreign-born, who are young.

It is impossible for advertising to be neutral in terms of the attitudes and values and images that are being communicated. Furthermore, it is likely that the message being received is different from the message that was intended. Images and words often communicate on their own, regardless of what is intended. This is especially true in a society in which there is a great diversity of subcultures. The intent can be different from the impact.

Attention to the potential impact of words and images in advertising is no less important than attention to honesty.

5. Good healthcare advertising protects the independence of ethical evaluations.

So far this discussion has focused on the "what" of ethical healthcare advertising. It is useful to comment as well on the question of "who": Who should be involved in assessing the ethical appropriateness of healthcare advertising?[10]

On the one hand, it does not take any special expertise or skill to be able to implement the ethical standards discussed here. On the other hand, asking and answering all the right questions does not just happen. It is essential that proposed advertising be reviewed explicitly in terms of the potential impact. In order to ensure that specific advertising is the kind that serves the public interest, a careful ethical assessment needs to be part of the process leading to decisions. This assessment or review should be undertaken by persons qualified to do the job well.

The right persons for doing the ethical evaluations of proposed advertising are those who are perceptive and sensitive to the potential (including unintentional) public or community impact of promotional materials. Further, these reviewers need to be independent. This means that they are protected from adverse job consequences if they offer critiques or advice that is not desired. They need to be able to "call it like they see it." (The need for ethics advisors whose independence is protected is discussed further in Part 5.)

Conclusion

To describe the healthcare organization as citizen is to recognize that it has a responsibility to promote the public good, particularly a responsibility to seek to improve the health status of the community. One key component of good citizenship is responsible advertising, advertising that promotes the good of the community (or at least does no harm) at the same time that it seeks to achieve other organizational goals.

Fourteen

Environmental Responsibility and the Precautionary Principle

Case 14.1. The hospital CEO has called a meeting of the management team to decide what to do in response to an outside group, made up of environmental activists and others, that is claiming that the hospital is contributing to environmental health problems.

The group, in a campaign called "Health Care Without Harm," argues that the incineration of medical waste is a leading source of dioxin and mercury pollution. In its campaign, HCWH describes dioxin as a known human carcinogen that is also suspected of having a number of other serious effects (on the immune system, on reproductive ability, on fetal and infant development). Dioxin is formed when products containing chlorine are manufactured or when waste containing chlorine is burned. PVC (polyvinyl chloride) plastic is a major source of chlorine in medical waste.

Health Care Without Harm describes mercury as a neurotoxin presenting serious risks to developing fetuses and young children. Mercury, not destroyed in incineration, is released through the smokestack and deposited in the environment. HCWH claims that medical waste may account for 20 percent of all the mercury in the solid waste stream. In healthcare mercury is used in thermometers, in blood pressure devices, in dilators and feeding tubes, in batteries, and in fluorescent lamps.

HCWH has asked this hospital, as well as others, to take immediate active steps to reduce toxic pollution. It is seeking the following actions: (1) using other technologies than incineration, like autoclaving, whenever possible to treat infectious waste; (2) finding alternatives to the use of PVC plastic; and (3) finding alternatives to mercury use wherever possible.[1]

In June of 1998, the American Hospital Association and the U.S. Environmental Protection Agency signed a Memorandum of Understanding. They agreed to undertake activities aimed at the virtual elimination of mercury-containing waste from the healthcare waste stream (with a target date of 2005) and a reduction in the total waste generated by the healthcare industry (with a target of 33 percent reduction by 2005).

It strikes many people as strange that the Environmental Protection Agency and environmental health activists have decided that it is important to target healthcare organizations in their efforts to improve the quality of the environment. It strikes people as strange because they would expect and assume that an organization dedicated to healthcare would not itself be engaged in any activities that might threaten health.

This issue deserves special attention by healthcare managers precisely because it is the healthcare organization itself that is being associated with serious environmental health risks. The issue is both a major challenge and a major opportunity for the healthcare organization in its role as a citizen.

The management team in the case above may not have an easy time determining the hospital's response. This is not only because of the complexity of the issue itself, but also because education in healthcare management ethics has rarely included explicit attention to the implications of environmental responsibility. This chapter proposes some perspectives on this responsibility.[2]

Environmental and Health Risk Assessment

One hospital executive who was faced with an actual scenario almost exactly like the one presented above informed me that management had decided to deal with the incineration issue as "a business decision." That meant, as I understood the context, that they were going to continue to incinerate if it was the least costly manner of handling their waste.

Implied in this response was, I am sure, much more than just a narrow focus on the bottom line. The unstated part of the response was something like this: "Since our incinerator is meeting all applicable emission requirements and since we have no convincing evidence that emissions at this level are harmful to public health, we think that our incineration practices are appropriate." Therefore, the CEO felt justified in focusing on the question of the financial impact.

The basic ethical issue, a difficult one, is how to understand responsibility in the face of uncertainty about the environmental and/or health effects of particular practices. What should be done, for example, in the case presented above? Should management be satisfied that it is acting responsibly when the practices meet federally and state-mandated requirements?

A common approach to determining a business's environmental responsibility is a decision-making model frequently referred to as risk assessment. Risk assessment is a widely accepted standard of ethical responsibility, but it is also coming under much criticism regarding its ability to protect public health. Efforts on the part of environmentalists and public advocates, as in projects such as "Health Care Without Harm," are based on a very different model of environmentally responsible decision making. Some observations on the risk-assessment model of environmental responsibility will help to identify its limitations and some of the reasons why it probably should not be considered satisfactory for healthcare organizations.

A presumption of the risk-assessment model is that environmental alterations, including the releasing of substances into the air or water, are safe until demonstrated otherwise. The burden of proof is on those who question the safety of a practice. Until harm has been demonstrated, a practice may be begun and may continue. The question is whether there is enough and clear enough evidence to stop or prevent or regulate an environment-affecting practice.

One of the implications of establishing the burden of proof in this manner is that serious and widespread harm may occur before there is sufficient evidence of such harm to be judged convincing. And, of course, once a practice has been put in place, there are strong vested interests in continuing without major modifications (and in attempting to debunk evidence of harm).

In the risk-assessment model, only scientific research that demonstrates or predicts a cause–effect relationship to environmental or health harm is sufficient to meet the burden of proof. Unless there is clear evidence that is widely accepted in the scientific community, there is only uncertainty and possibility. Uncertainty is not a sound basis on which to refrain from any environment-affecting activity if there is good economic or other benefit to be gained from this activity. A slogan of those who promote the risk-assessment model of decision making is that "facts, not fears" should govern decisions and behavior.

A problem with this understanding of scientific evidence is that it appears to be at odds with a basic recognition of environmental science: Complex environmental interactions make it very unlikely that we can accurately demonstrate or predict the full impact of any environmental change. What is considered good science for some purposes may not be the best basis for understanding environmental responsibility.

In the risk-assessment model, an organization is acting in a fully responsible manner as long as it does not engage in activities that have been demonstrated to be harmful or that are prohibited. If, on the basis of risk assessment, environmental and health protection regulations are put in place (regarding, for example, the level of emissions of particular chemicals that is considered safe), then the organization has a responsibility to comply with these standards.

Complying with all legal requirements is a minimum standard of responsibility. As has been noted in other places in this work, good business ethics often requires going beyond compliance with legal minimums. What makes issues of environmental health so difficult is that there is sometimes uncertainty about the risks associated with legally acceptable levels of pollution; the long-term implications are not yet known. The risk-assessment model does not encourage the avoidance of uncertain risks and does not put much emphasis on finding alternative and less risky methods of meeting one's goals.

In the case presented above, we can assume that the hospital is meeting all emission standards. Nevertheless, HCWH activists are critical of hospital practices as harmful or as unnecessarily risky. Two things seem to be going on here. One is that HCWH believes that the present legal environmental protection levels may be inadequate to protect health. The second is that they do not accept the risk-assessment model of understanding environmental responsibility.

Environmental ethics does, in fact, suggest a different model. The risk-assessment model of decision making wants "facts, not fears" to govern behavior. Facts, however, are often impossible to establish in regard to the full environmental impact of releasing substances that have health risks associated with them. How much mercury released into the environment is too much mercury? How much risk of producing dioxin in the incineration of PVC plastics is too much risk? Decisions have to be made about how aggressively to reduce the use of mercury and PVC without any clear "factual" answers to these questions. What is needed is a good decision-making model for use when the environmental and health impacts are not clearly established. The risk-assessment model does not seem to put a high enough priority on public health to be a satisfactory guide for healthcare organizations.

Environmental Ethics and the
Precautionary Principle

Concepts and principles used in environmental ethics provide a useful starting point for thinking about how to act in the face of unknown risks. Environmental ethics includes a variety of issues and concerns, but the focus here is limited to perspectives on toxic pollution and hazardous waste disposal.

Thinking about environmental responsibility requires that we think in terms of the realities of ecological systems. The use of resources and the creation of waste constitute pressures on environmental stability. A basic ecological insight is that waste is not neutral. "Whenever we pollute or degrade . . . [the natural environment] with toxins or waste, we are destroying our natural capital and reducing our ability to sustain our civilization. It is that simple."[3]

In interrelated ecosystems, everything is related to everything else. It is ecological wisdom to understand that the release of toxic pollutants in one place can never be assumed not to have a deleterious impact on other parts of the system. Ethics starts with the assumption that even the best scientists cannot always know what the long-term implications of the disposal of hazardous waste are likely to be. What we intend to do does not control the actual consequences.

To be environmentally responsible is to be committed to future well-being. It is not enough to dispose of waste in a manner not expected to cause harm in the short term. Many toxins are persistent. They will remain in the environment and in the food chain for future generations.

Pollution of natural systems is risky. A basic principle of environmental ethics is, therefore, the need for caution. Being ethical, environmentally speaking, is not just an issue of intention or knowledge; it is also an issue of avoiding or reducing the risk of serious potential harm, regardless of intent or knowledge. Because of the great potential for unintended negative consequences of actions that change or affect aspects of the ecosystem, environmental ethics has long been concerned with the burden of proof. Contrary to the risk-assessment model, environmentalists have argued that it is more in tune with what we do know about the environment to place the burden of proof on those who hold that some amounts of hazardous waste are not harmful enough to do any serious damage.

Given the risks of harmful effects of hazardous pollution, *the precautionary principle* should govern decision making when toxins might be introduced into the natural environment. The Rio Declaration at the United Nations Conference on Environment and Development in 1992 called on nations to adopt the precautionary principle. In 1998, an international group of scientists, urban planners, farmers, union leaders, philosophers, environmentalists, physicians, editors, and government officials met at a conference in Wisconsin to define the precautionary principle further. The Wingspread Statement emerged from those deliberations. This statement reads, in part:

> When an activity raises threats of harm to human health or the environment, precautionary measures should be taken even if some cause and effect relationships are not fully established scientifically. In this context, the proponents of an activity, rather than the public, should bear the burden of proof.[4]

The precautionary principle is fundamental to environmental ethics, and its key point is the burden of proof standard. The principle "puts the burden of proof on the potential polluter to prove that a substance or activity will do no environmental harm, rather than on communities to prove harm."[5] It further requires that the process of applying the precautionary principle must be democratic, that is, open and inclusive of those potentially affected.

Sandra Steingraber has articulated two different expressions or applications of the precautionary principle. The "principle of reverse onus" is that "it is safety, rather then harm, that should necessitate demonstration," and the "principle of the least toxic alternative" requires that "toxic substances will not be used as long as there is another way of accomplishing the task."[6]

This last point can be very helpful in focusing attention on alternative substances and methodologies.[7]

Healthcare Ethics and the Precautionary Principle

There are two major traditions in healthcare ethics that can inform thinking about the healthcare organization's responsibility regarding environmental risks. One, found in clinical medical ethics and in research ethics, is the emphasis on the obligation to avoid harm. The other, developed in healthcare management ethics and in public health ethics, is the obligation to meet the healthcare needs of the community. Taken together, the harm principle and the community benefit principle seem to require a precautionary approach toward potentially hazardous pollution.

The Harm Principle

There is a very long and strong tradition in medical ethics regarding the obligation not to do harm in patient care. The Latin maxim *"Primum non nocere"* ("First [or above all] do no harm") is familiar to most healthcare professionals. The powerful interventions available to the physician and the trust that the patient places in the healthcare professional require a strong emphasis on the obligation to be careful: one should not harm patients or put them at risk of harm.

The continuing significance of the harm principle is exemplified by the importance placed on the obligation to refuse to provide an intervention that may cause harm (without proportionate benefit). A physician is not, for example, to prescribe counter-indicated drugs, even when the patient requests the prescription with full knowledge of the likely or potential harmful consequences.

The strength of the harm principle is also indicated by the fact that committees established to protect human subjects in medical research (Institutional Review Boards) have a clear responsibility to protect the individual subject from significant risk of harm even when many other persons may potentially benefit from the research. The good of the many does not justify placing the one at significant risk of major harm.

The harm principle in healthcare ethics is not an absolute principle that insists that harm must be avoided at all times or that any risk of harm is too great. The principle of not inflicting harm and the moral rules following from it are presumptive obligations. That is, such a moral obligation "must be fulfilled unless it conflicts on a particular occasion with an equal or stronger obligation."[8]

Acting in a way that puts others at risk of significant harm is sometimes ethically appropriate because of the responsibility to avoid a greater harm or

to provide a significant benefit, but the burden of proof is on those who advocate the risk of harm. There needs to be both substantive justification (good
reason to conclude that the risk of harm is outweighed by other considerations) and procedural safeguards (methods of ensuring that those who are
most likely to be harmed have their interests considered in the process of
decision making).

The obligation to avoid harm and the burden-of-proof standard for putting
someone at risk of harm are very similar to the ethical perspectives being
advocated in environmental ethics.

The Community Health Principle

Administrators of healthcare institutions and organizations are professionals
dedicated to the mission of providing healthcare, as are clinical professionals.
One difference is that healthcare executives need to focus on the healthcare
needs of all those served by the organization, not just those presently being
provided medical care. Like other professionals, healthcare managers have
codes of ethics, and these codes recognize a responsibility to the community.
As expressed in the words of the code of the American College of Healthcare
Executives, there is responsibility to "work to identify and meet the healthcare needs of the community."

Healthcare has long recognized a public health mission, a responsibility to
ensure the conditions in which people can achieve the highest attainable state
of health. The mission, in a more negative sense, is to eliminate or ameliorate the unhealthy conditions in which people live.[9] This public health responsibility may well lead to a recognition that some widely accepted societal,
business, and governmental practices are questionable and should be trans-
formed. It is largely its public health mission that provides healthcare with its
activist and reformist nature.

The community health principle is an important recognition that healthcare providers have a responsibility not just to those who are directly in their
professional care, but also to the larger group who may be affected more indirectly by their work. The public health effort to help establish the conditions in which people can be healthy implies an obligation to non-identifiable
members of the public.

Though it is often difficult, because of financial and other pressures, for
individual healthcare organizations to focus resources on the community, it
remains very clear that the mission of healthcare institutions is to improve the
health status of the community. Even in hard times, it is a responsibility that
can be ignored only at the risk of losing part of the essential identity of
healthcare.

The language and emphasis of biomedical ethics tend to be individual-
focused. The language and emphasis of community health ethics provide a
necessary societal focus. The harm principle, together with the community

health responsibility, support the need to adopt the precautionary principle in healthcare organizations.

Implementing the Precautionary Principle

Until now, most of the pressure to improve practices regarding medical waste has come from environmentalists (as in the case used to introduce this chapter). As healthcare professionals become more aware of research on the potential health effects of the way that waste is managed, there is likely to be increased demand for changes from within the healthcare field. Regardless of the source of the expressed concern, leaders in healthcare organizations should be quite clear regarding their general responsibility. They need to recognize, accept, and act on the obligation to avoid, to the extent practically possible, the potentially harmful effects of the hazardous waste that is generated in the provision of healthcare services.

A decision to implement a precautionary model of decision making regarding the disposal of hazardous medical waste has several implications.

1. It is important to avoid the temptation to minimize the danger or the nature of the problem.

The risk of damage to human health from exposure to mercury is well known (and is acknowledged in the Memorandum of Understanding between the EPA and the AHA). Mercury affects the central nervous system and can also harm the brain, kidneys, and lungs. The public has become aware of the risks of mercury, especially through the health advisories warning against the consumption of fish from many mercury-contaminated lakes and rivers.

Mercury in medical waste can be released into the environment through incineration. It enters into the food chain, and as it gets passed up the chain, it can become concentrated in the bodies of animals and, ultimately, humans.

Dioxin is one of the most toxic chemicals on earth. "In the world of synthetic chemicals, dioxin has enjoyed the reputation of being the worst of the trouble makers—the most deadly, the most feared, and the most elusive to scientists seeking to unravel the secrets of its toxicity."[10] Though it has been difficult for researchers to determine the exact manner in which dioxin causes damage to human health, its reputation as a dangerous and potent toxin is well established. It can cause cancer, affect both male and female reproductive ability, and damage the immune system.

Dioxin does not break down readily in the environment and, as a result, accumulates in the water and the soil. It accumulates in fatty tissues of animals, as well, and gets concentrated as it is passed up the food chain. The primary exposure to humans is through the food we eat. Dioxin is passed from mother to child during pregnancy and in breast milk and can affect the normal development of the brain.

Healthcare contributes dioxin to the environment directly through the incineration of chlorine-containing medical waste and indirectly through the use of chlorine-based products (dioxin is the result of both the production and the incineration of these products). PVC plastic is a major source of chlorine in medical waste. PVC is use widely in healthcare, including IV bags, tubing, mattress covers, and packaging.

Though both mercury and dioxin are clearly dangerous to human health, there can be some disagreement about the extent to which medical waste incineration increases health risks. Given a natural reluctance to acknowledge that one is involved in harmful practices, it may be tempting to minimize the danger. It may be tempting to accept only those assessments that one would like to hear, those that judge the contribution of medical waste incineration to health risk to be minimal. The precautionary principle of environmental ethics means resisting the temptation to act on a belief that a risk is minimal when the exact extent of the risk is undetermined.

2. It is important to keep cost in proper perspective.

Addressing this issue well (including reduction of waste that needs to be disposed of as hazardous waste) might be one of those win-win situations in which the institution saves money at the same time that it reduces risks to health. While this might be the case, the decision to proceed should not be made on the basis of cost reduction alone. The issue is how to reduce waste and find healthier ways of disposing of hazardous waste in a cost-effective manner.

3. It is important to emphasize alternatives.

Safe alternatives exist for many medical uses of PVC and of mercury. One of the most important responses to the health risks caused by the healthcare industry is to begin to move as quickly as possible to these alternatives and to put pressure, if necessary, on suppliers and producers for a full range of alternatives. This is an example of addressing the problem as much "upstream" as possible.

4. It is important to attend to issues of institutional culture.

There may be a temptation to do the least amount of change and preserve the status quo as much as possible in responding to the need for new ways of dealing with waste. While making the least possible change is understandable because it is the least disruptive of established work patterns, it may also be the least effective and the least cost-effective in achieving health-protection goals.

Conclusion

To describe the healthcare organization as citizen is to recognize that it has a responsibility to promote the public good, particularly a responsibility to seek to improve the health status of the community. The most basic obligation is to avoid harm to public health. The possibility that the healthcare organization may itself be contributing to health problems requires that the issue of hazardous medical waste be high on the agenda of organizations committed to ethics and to the public good.

Fifteen

Community Serving Mergers and Acquisitions

Even the most casual observer of the healthcare industry is well aware that the last decade has been a time of restructuring in healthcare organizations. Acquisitions and mergers are common.

Mergers and acquisitions are more than new organizational arrangements; they are more than disruptive periods to be gotten through quickly in order to get back to the business of providing high-quality healthcare services. They often change the way services are available to the community, and they affect the working environment of employees. Mergers and acquisitions often have major long-term consequences. The focus in this chapter is on selected issues related to the impact of mergers and acquisitions on the communities served by the healthcare organizations.

The Preamble of the ACHE Code of Ethics includes this statement:

> The fundamental objectives of the healthcare management profession are to enhance overall quality of life, dignity, and well-being of every individual needing healthcare services; and to create a more equitable, accessible, effective, and efficient healthcare system.

Mergers or acquisitions are usually given consideration, in the first place, because of an organization's desire to become a more efficient healthcare provider. As proposals are considered and as decisions are made and implemented, it is important to ensure that the pursuit of efficiency does not have negative implications regarding the equitable, accessible, and effective provision of healthcare to the community.

Location of Services

Case 15.1. Because both institutions are experiencing financial losses and because their combined bed capacity is clearly excessive, the two acute care hospitals in the region have begun to negotiate a consolidation of services. One institution is a nonprofit community hospital in a city with a population of approximately 55,000. It serves almost exclusively residents of the city (which has experienced a declining manufacturing base in recent decades). The other hospital is a nonprofit religious-sponsored hospital which was located in the city at one time but moved to a location about ten miles outside the city limits about twenty years ago. It serves patients from all over the county.

The public announcement indicates that not all services will continue to be available in both locations, but that no final decisions have been made regarding what will be offered where. The rumors that have circulated say that most services, including medical, surgical, and obstetrics, will be located in the newer suburban facility and that the city facility will keep only emergency services, a primary care clinic, and a mental health unit.

Shortly after the announcement, a number of city residents and political leaders voice their strong concern about "losing" their community acute care hospital, which is located in a low-income area and has served the city population for a century. For at least some residents, transportation to the suburban hospital will be difficult. Concern is expressed about specific services ("No more babies will be born in the city"), but the major focus of opposition is on the significance of not having a full-function hospital in the city. Another frequently voiced concern is that the merger, if it takes place as rumored, will further reduce the employment base in the hard-hit city. The hospital is now the largest employer.

Both hospitals are committed to and do provide charity care, but the city hospital does considerably more both as a percentage and in actual dollar amounts.[1]

As the leaders of the healthcare organizations make decisions about the location of services, they need to decide what kinds of community issues should be taken into account. Being a good citizen means that the healthcare organization recognizes that it has a responsibility to promote the public good. This means, first of all, a responsibility to improve the health of the community. But it means more than that. It means that in all of its decisions, polices, and practices it is sensitive to the impact of its actions on the public well being.

All businesses and corporations have an ethical responsibility to society. In their text on *Business and Society*, William Frederick, James Post, and Keith Davis explain the meaning of corporate social responsibility this way:

> Corporate social responsibility means that a corporation should be held accountable for any of its actions that affect people, their communities, and their environment. Its implies that negative business impacts on people and society should be acknowledged and corrected if at all possible. It may require a company to forgo some profits if its social impacts are seriously harmful to some of the corporation's stakeholders or if its funds can be used to promote a positive social good.[2]

Those considering this hospital merger should hold themselves accountable for avoiding unnecessary harmful effects on the quality of life of people in the community. This does not have to do only with the types and quality of services available as a result of the merger. It also has to do with negative impacts that may result from decisions made, including results that are not immediately or directly related to health. To be a good citizen means to take into account at all times the potential effects of decisions on the larger community.

In this case, the concerns being raised by city citizens appear to be relevant. Planners should definitely take into account the fact that transportation for patients and families would likely be a greater problem if many services were available only in the suburban location. This is an access issue and is clearly related to the organization's responsibility as a healthcare provider.

Planners should also take into account other probable economic and community implications of decisions about the location of services. There will be some negative public impact in any community where major reductions take place. Assuming that the need to restructure is real, this cannot be avoided entirely. Even if some negative public impact cannot be avoided, there is still the need to minimize the harmful consequences. The first step is to get assistance in assessing the likely impact on the community.

Burdens should be shared fairly, whenever possible. It is a good principle of social ethics, therefore, that those communities presently experiencing greater social ills (such as poverty or environmental degradation) have a greater claim to be spared new negative impacts than those communities that are better off. The information provided in the case is not sufficient for us to know all the implications related to one location or the other. There should be a strong burden-of-proof bias, however, in favor of locating most services in the city. There are good corporate citizenship reasons for a preference for the city location. A closer examination of all factors may tip the scales in the other direction, but the initial information suggests that greater public harm would result from radical cuts in services in the city.

Decisions about which services should be available in which locations are, from a community service point of view, among the most important considerations in mergers or other partnerships. The main point in this limited commentary on the case is that the concerns raised by the citizens in the anonymous city are indeed relevant concerns and should be taken seriously by healthcare leaders. Clearly no one organization is responsible for trying to solve or ameliorate all the social problems that exist. At the very minimum, though, every organization is responsible for not making these problems any worse than necessary.

One additional point should be noted. Healthcare managers and board members are not always in the best positions to understand the social impact of decisions about the location of services. Being a good citizen in this regard means listening in a timely and systematic way to persons from the community who are better prepared to assess that impact.

Conversion from Nonprofit to For-Profit Status

One type of acquisition that is of particular interest in healthcare business ethics is the acquisition of a nonprofit institution or organization by a for-profit company. These acquisitions are not regulated by the federal government, and state intervention varies significantly. Regardless of the legal climate, there are some important issues and some clear ethical responsibilities that need attention.[3]

Nonprofits exist for "community benefit," and the overriding concern regarding conversions is how community benefit is maintained and protected. In this inconsistently regulated area, it may not be enough to be guided by the law. "With no regulation expected from the federal government and limited regulations expected from the states, the responsibility for protecting communities during nonprofit conversions must fall on health care executives and trustees."[4] The primary responsibility for protecting community interests rests with executives and trustees of the nonprofit organization, in their fiduciary responsibility to the community, and most of what follows is focused on their role. Executives of the for-profit company also have a responsibility, however. For-profit businesses are likewise citizens of the larger community and have a social responsibility to prevent or minimize harmful consequences to the community from actions that they take.

None of the emphasis on the community benefit responsibility of nonprofits is meant to suggest that for-profit healthcare companies do not also provide community benefit. They do, both when they provide good-quality care and when they pay fair taxes. The point here is not to compare the community benefit of different types of organizations, but to ensure that the assets that nonprofits have acquired specifically for community benefit are, in fact, fully used for that purpose when conversions occur.

The general responsibility of executives and trustees in nonprofit conversions can be made more specific.

1. Executives and trustees have a responsibility to avoid conflicts of interest as much as possible.

In order to reduce the likelihood that their decisions will be influenced more by their self-interest than by judgments of community benefit, personal gain incentives should be removed from decisions about takeover or price. The best practice is to have clear ground rules from the very beginning of any negotiations. These rules might require, for example, that decisions about the sale will be totally separate from any decisions about future employment or Board service for individuals involved in making the decisions for the nonprofit organization.

At times of possible organizational transition, it is only natural for individuals to be concerned about their own future. And it is only natural that this concern might affect judgment regarding what should be done. The responsibility of nonprofit management and trustees is to act on the basis of their judgments regarding the best way to accomplish the mission of their organization. To the extent possible, therefore, they need to remove themselves from situations in which they may have personal incentive to do less than the best they could do for the community.

2. Executives and trustees have a responsibility to ensure that the sale involves fair market value.

Whether the takeover price paid by the for-profit is fair is not easy to determine. Fairness includes more than a fair price for the nonprofit's assets; "the community benefit that the nonprofit provides also needs to be included in the price of the sale."[5] As leaders of an organization accountable to the community and existing for community benefit, the nonprofit executives and trustees have a responsibility to seek to ensure that the purchase price is fair. This requires a third-party valuation by a qualified firm.

Part of the value to the community is the value that the nonprofit provides in uncompensated care and in other community health initiatives. There appears to be some evidence that for-profit hospitals do not provide as much uncompensated care as nonprofits do.[6] Whether or not that is, in fact, always the reality, nonprofits have a major fiduciary responsibility to the community, which normally includes providing a certain level of uncompensated care. In any acquisition of a nonprofit institution by a for-profit company, it is essential to include provisions that ensure the continuation of uncompensated care and other community health services. Often this is done by including, as part of the purchase agreement, the establishment of a charitable foundation for healthcare in the community.

3. Executives and trustees have a responsibility to disclose the fact that a conversion is being considered and to hold public hearings.

Given the nature of healthcare service organizations and given the special community service responsibility of nonprofit organizations, negotiations about possible sale should not be conducted as purely private business. The community needs to be informed and to have the opportunity to express its concerns. The disclosure, done early enough in the process to allow reactions to be taken into account before any decisions are made, needs to include an explanation of the methodology used to determine fair market value and an explanation of the ways in which community benefit will be ensured. The nature of the proposed deal should be disclosed. Community members need to have an opportunity to express their understanding of the adequacy of the community benefit that will result from the proposed acquisition.

Mergers and Reproductive Healthcare Services

Another merger-related issue that raises questions about the ethical responsibilities of healthcare organizations is the impact of mergers on the availability of reproductive healthcare services. This issue is most pertinent, of course, when the merger is between a provider that has been offering (many of) these services and a provider that takes a strong principled position against providing (many of) these services.

Case 15.2. The two hospitals considering a merger in Case 15.1 find that location is not the only major issue they face in regard to the provision of services. One hospital is St. Ann Hospital, sponsored by a community of Roman Catholic religious women, and the other is City General, a nonprofit community hospital with no history of religious affiliation. St. Ann follows the "Ethical and Religious Directives for Catholic Health Care Services" published by the American Catholic Bishops in prohibiting most practices related to assisted reproduction, contraception, sterilization, and abortion. City General provides and permits a wide range of reproductive healthcare services.

In the merger negotiations, the plan is to offer most services in only one location, not to maintain two separate hospitals. St. Ann representatives told City General representatives very early that their sponsors and the local Catholic bishop would expect any merged organization to include a commitment to follow the "Ethical and Religious Directives."

This case requires an expansion of the analysis done in Chapter 11 regarding an organization's conscientious objection to providing certain types of treatment. There the focus was on the relationship between an organization's conscientious objection and the rights of individual patients and of individual employees. Here the focus is on the relationship between the organization's conscientious objection and the needs of the community it serves.

Within limits, it is entirely appropriate for healthcare organizations to determine on the basis of their own ethical principles which legally acceptable practices are and which are not to be permitted within their facilities. Respect for the consciences of individual providers and those who sponsor healthcare services requires that the community generally accept the decisions on availability made by the leaders of the organizations. Given the potential significance of some healthcare practices on quality of life and the values of the community, individual healthcare organizations are to be commended for making conscientious decisions regarding which practices they judge to be acceptable and appropriate. But there are limits to what the organization is ethically justified in doing in prohibiting certain practices.

One of the limits to the moral rights of organizations to limit what they permit was initially discussed in Chapter 11. The limit is exceeded if an organization refuses to participate in the type of care or treatment that every patient has a basic ethical right to in every institution providing care. The organization is not justified in appealing to its own conscience or ethical standards in these situations.

Most of the differences between the services available in the secular hospital and the Catholic hospital in this case present a somewhat different set of circumstances. The point is not so much whether every patient has a right to expect the full range of reproductive services from every provider, but whether there is reasonable access in the community for those who find these services ethically and medically acceptable. The second limit to the moral right of organizations to limit what they permit is based, then, upon the need to ensure adequate access in the local community to those services normally available in the larger society.

Community members have a legitimate expectation of reasonable access to healthcare services that are generally acceptable to the medical profession, that are safe and effective, and that are not prohibited by law. This includes access to some forms of contraception, sterilization, abortion, and assisted reproduction. That the community has reasonable access does not mean that every institution needs to provide or permit these services. It does mean, however, that the services need to be available in the community without significant burden or difficulty to individuals.

Before the proposed merger, there is good reason to support and endorse the right of St. Ann not to provide the kinds of services that its leaders or sponsors consider ethically unacceptable. Until a merger, there is an option for those who want these services: they can use the facilities of City General. St. Ann's objection to providing these services does not pose a major obstacle to access, because these services are available elsewhere in the community. The situation becomes different, however, precisely because of the proposed merger.

If a merger takes place, and the merged organization does not provide these services, and if there is no other reasonably convenient access to these services for members in the community, then the legitimate healthcare expectations of the community would not be met. This would be a serious failure on the part of the providers to meet the needs of the community they serve.

The healthcare organization is a community service business. It is of the nature of a service organization that its responsibility is determined in large part by the needs of the community. Not every healthcare facility must offer every type of service, of course, and not every acute care hospital has a responsibility to permit every service to which the community has a reasonable expectation of access. If there is only one acute care facility in the community, however, that facility has much less flexibility. This is the situation that would result from the proposed merger in this case.

Since many of the reproductive services are available in outpatient clinics and in doctors' offices, the stand of an acute care hospital does not necessarily mean that these services are not available to the community. Tubal ligation, though, is an example of a service that is often at the heart of the access issue when the only hospital in the community is a Catholic hospital.[7] Ideally, both the community and providers want to protect the community's access and to allow organizations to act according to their own ethical values. Often it is possible to do both. When it is not possible to do both, the basic responsibility of the organization to serve the community takes priority. This responsibility may require some adjustment be made to what it would ideally like to provide or permit.

Before a decision is made to merge the two hospitals into one institution that follows the "Ethical and Religious Directives for Catholic Health Care Services," leaders of the present institutions and the community need to have several points clearly established in order to protect the community's access to reproductive services.

1. The hospital will not restrict the outpatient practices of physicians and other clinicians in such a way that the community's options are severely limited.

Sometimes physicians leasing office space in hospital-owned medical buildings are prevented in their lease agreements from prescribing contraception or providing vasectomies or abortions in their offices.[8] This is another practice that becomes crucially important when there are limited facilities in the community. It is understandable that the hospital would not want practices that it considers unethical to take place in a facility that it owns. In a community in which there is only one hospital, however, this is likely to be restrictive of community options. It may be better not to own such medical buildings.

2. The hospital will not restrict referrals for services not available at the institution.

As discussed in Chapter 11, responsibilities to patients mean that the clinical staff should inform patients of the options available elsewhere, if they seek that information. At the very least, a patient should be informed where he or she can get the information necessary in order to pursue an interest in having the procedure done. To provide the opportunity for a patient to consult with someone else does not mean that one approves of the procedure in the particular case; it is to recognize a patient's legal option and her or his moral freedom.

3. The hospital will permit some procedures not ordinarily acceptable according to the "Ethical and Religious Directives" in those cases in which it would be an unreasonable burden for patients to go elsewhere for these services.

Because the "Ethical and Religious Directives" are sometimes applied without reference to the community served by the hospital, this merger condition may be the most difficult for the Catholic organization to accept. It follows as an essential condition, however, when the starting point is the necessary access of the community, without unreasonable burden, to common safe and effective medical care.

Tubal ligation is an example (though not the only one) in which some accommodation may be necessary. It is not unusual that a decision to be sterilized is made during a pregnancy, with the procedure scheduled for after delivery, in order to avoid another hospitalization. To require that a woman who is planning to deliver at the only local hospital go elsewhere often does present significant burdens. The closest available alternative hospital may not be one at which her obstetrician has privileges; it may be too distant if labor is short; it may not accept the patient's insurance. If the tubal ligation is done at a different time and location from delivery, it requires a separate admission. These types of realities do, at times, pose unreasonable burdens.

If the hospital is to be the only acute care facility in the area, it needs to provide services in a such a manner that those patients who do not agree with the organization's ethical perspectives are not unreasonably burdened. The nature of an "unreasonable burden" is, of course, open to interpretation, but an unwillingness to modify its position at all as a result of being the only facility in the area is not an adequate recognition of the legitimate claims of the community.

4. If these guarantees of community access are not in place, the proposed merger should not be finalized.

If a religiously affiliated healthcare organization finds that these conditions would unacceptably compromise its mission, then it is best to seek an alternative to the proposed merger. The beliefs of leaders of healthcare organizations should be respected as much as possible. There are, however, responsibilities that come with being the sole provider in a community. The community should have access to medically acceptable services that some patients find ethically acceptable. Reasonable access to these services takes priority over the desire of the provider to restrict certain services. In some cases, the best solution may be to avoid being the sole provider.

The Impact on Employees

Developing and maintaining an ethical organization is never easy. It is often even more difficult in times of rapid and significant organizational change. Creating the kind of culture that supports and rewards careful attention to the highest ethical ideals and standards takes time and energy, both of which may be largely devoted to reorganization in times of major changes. Mergers and acquisitions, even when they proceed "smoothly," have a disruptive effect on the involved organizations.

Because of the focus in this chapter on service to the community, the impact of mergers and acquisitions on employees has not been discussed. Whenever mergers or acquisitions are being considered, the impact on the well being of employees should be of great concern. This is especially the case if the reorganization involves downsizing (see Chapter 9). Full attention to the ethical issues in mergers and acquisitions includes careful and guided consideration of issues beyond those discussed in this chapter.

Sixteen

Socially Responsible Investing

In the final chapter of this section on the role of the healthcare organization as citizen, it may be useful to give some attention to the responsibility of the organization as investor. There are various other activities, such as purchasing, that also raise important questions related to the responsibilities of the organization. Responsible investing is, however, of special interest to a number of organizations today.

The ethical responsibility of investors began to receive intense attention during the debate on the role of transnational corporations in South Africa during the apartheid era. Especially in the 1980s, there was widespread debate in the United States about the appropriateness of companies' doing business as usual in a country with such a repressive and undemocratic government. A question for many concerned Americans was whether the very presence of corporations in South Africa tended, regardless of intent, to give support to and strengthen an illegitimate regime. A further question for those who institutionally or individually owned stock in companies doing business in South Africa was whether they themselves, through their investments, were also supporting and strengthening apartheid.

Socially responsible investing involves, in general, a commitment to assessing the impact of the business activity of companies in which one invests. It is an effort to invest in a manner that reflects and/or communicates one's beliefs regarding ethical business practices. It involves making decisions about investments not simply on the basis of projected financial risks and returns, but also on the basis of ethical judgments about business practices.

As an organization invests endowment funds, pension funds, or other monies, it has the same responsibility that it does in all of its other activities—to promote the public good through careful assessment of the impact on the public of institutional or organizational policies and practices.

The term "socially responsible investing" (sometimes called "ethical investing") is not meant to imply that all investing that does not make use of the strategies described below is "socially irresponsible" or "unethical." The difference is, rather, that those who are involved in socially responsible investing are consciously focused, in all or some of their investment-related activities, on considerations related to ethics and to social and environmental impact. Socially responsible investing (SRI) means that there are both financial and social objectives in investing and that both are made an explicit part of investment decision-making.

Those involved in SRI use different strategies or combinations of strategies. Three approaches discussed here are the use of social screens, shareholder activism, and alternative investments.

Social Screens

A common method of socially responsible investing is to use what is sometimes called an "avoidance strategy."[1] Investors avoid investing in companies that do not meet their criteria for social and environmental responsibility. "The negative characteristics can relate to the kinds of products or services that a firm produces, the way it conducts its business, or the location of its activities."[2] The negative screening strategy is designed to bring about a close connection between investors' understanding of what it means to be a socially responsible business and what they support through their investments.

Investors can identify their screening criteria and do their own research on whether companies satisfy these criteria, or they can seek out funds and research organizations that do this on a routine basis. Social criteria can include, for example:

1. The company's employee relations record
   Worker safety, history of union relations, workforce reduction issues, etc.
2. The company's record on workforce diversity
   Discrimination claims, representation of women and minorities in senior management and on the board, etc.
3. The company's environmental record
   The relationship of the company's products to degradation of the environment, the disposal of (hazardous) waste, etc.
4. What the company derives it revenue from
   Addictive products or practices (tobacco, alcohol, gambling), weapons production or sales, etc.
5. The company's record in other countries
   Wages and working conditions of employees, human rights in countries in which facilities are located, etc.[3]

This is not a complete list, but it provides an indication of the range of considerations often found in social screening. Sometimes a particular concern about a company is taken as a reason, in and of itself, to exclude that company from investment (for example, no investment in any company doing business in Burma while the present regime is in power; no investment in any company in the tobacco business). Sometimes the company's record is analyzed in terms of how the weaknesses and strengths in the social record balance out; it is then the whole record that determines whether the company passes the social screen for investment.

The ethical motivation and intent of those who engage in social screen investing is generally one or both of two kinds: (1) preserving the integrity of the investor; (2) seeking to have an impact on business practices.

Being a person or an organization of ethical integrity means that ethical values and beliefs are consistently applied and expressed in all activities. The organization that is committed to just wages, to the promotion of diversity in the workplace, and to environmental responsibility will, it is reasonable to expect, want to express these same beliefs in its investment activity. It is legitimate to wonder about the level of commitment to these beliefs, to wonder about the ethical integrity of the organization, if it chooses to invest in companies with poor records in these areas (unless it is planning to express its concerns as an activist shareholder, as discussed later). It is also legitimate to wonder about the level of commitment to these beliefs, to wonder about the ethical integrity of the organization, if it chooses to invest in companies without giving any consideration to what their record is on these issues.

The second reason for use of a social screen for investment decisions is to communicate to companies what is expected of them, perhaps to provide some incentive for them to reconsider specific practices. To make a decision *not to invest* in a company because it does not live up to the investor's expectations as a socially responsible firm is to say to the company that it is not worthy of support because of some of its practices. It is a form of boycott, economic avoidance designed to bring about change in the company being avoided.

To make a decision *to invest* in a company, when using a social screen, is to say to the company that it is worthy of support precisely because of some of its practices. When using a social screen for investments, investments are always expressions of what one believes is important in the way business is done. How powerful or effective it is to use a social investing screen to communicate to companies regarding their social responsibility is hard to determine. It is true, of course, that companies are concerned about their reputations, especially among investors.

When the integrity of the investor is the reason for the use of the social screen, it is not always important to communicate investment choices to others. When there is a desire to have an impact on business practices, on the other hand, the social responsibility reasons for investment decisions must be made public in some way. Otherwise, it is not going to achieve its goal.

Investing in funds known to make use of social screens normally meets this publicity requirement, because the funds publish their criteria. If such funds are not used, the organization's use of social screens may need to be communicated in some other way in order to influence corporate activity.

Proxy Resolutions on Social Issues

Another way in which investors try to influence corporate behavior is through shareholder activism on social issues. This is a higher level of SRI activity, in that it requires more involvement in the issues and greater expense and energy. Shareholder activism is a form of lobbying, making use of one's role as a shareholder to communicate explicitly with a company regarding practices or policies that the shareholder would like to change.

Contrary to the use of a social screen, shareholder activism requires the investment in companies that are judged not to be acting in the most socially responsible manner. The effort is to try to work from "within," to be involved in the company as a shareholder precisely in order to attempt to bring about some change.

The most common form of shareholder activism is to file a "proxy resolution" on a particular issue (or notify the company that is one is planning to). Shareholder resolutions are questions to be voted on by shareholders, normally at their annual meeting. Filing the resolution gets management's attention focused on the issue.

Case 16.1. A resolution was filed with Aetna in 1998 linking executive compensation to improvement in healthcare quality. The "whereas statements" included the statement that "While there is considerable pressure by investors to increase returns to shareholders, we believe equal weight in company decisions should be given to patient care and quality of services provided."

The resolution called for action on the part of the Aetna Board of Directors:

> Therefore, be it resolved that shareholders request the Board of Directors institute an Executive Compensation Review to develop policies for executive officer compensation that are tied, in significant part, to NCQA [National Committee on Quality Assurance] accreditation status and progress in meeting the corporation's publicly available quality performance objectives (process and outcomes). These policies shall cover salary, bonus, restricted stock awards, long term incentive compensation plans and other compensation.
>
> The result of the review and recommendations for change shall be reported to stockholders in the fall of 1999.[4]

The question here is not what management should do when it receives a resolution of this sort. Rather, readers are asked to put themselves in the position of an institutional investor who owns stock in Aetna. Should one use the position of institutional stockholder to attempt to get Aetna to act in this way? What should the organization do if asked to support this resolution as a co-filer and/or in voting its proxy?

This is just one of many examples of the types of issues on which resolutions are filed each year. For example, various companies are asked, by different shareholders,

- to report on the ways in which they ensure that their suppliers in other countries do not use child workers or violate workers' rights;
- to endorse and implement the CERES Principles on environmental responsibility (CERES = Council on Environmentally Responsible Economies);
- to phase out the use of chorine-based bleaching agents;
- to make greater efforts to ensure that women and persons from minority racial groups are among the candidates considered for board membership.

The list goes on and on. The investors associated with the Interfaith Center on Corporate Responsibility, a coalition of religious-affiliated institutional investors (denominations, religious communities, agencies, pension funds, dioceses, and healthcare corporations), file more than 150 resolutions with over 100 companies in a typical year.[5]

The filing of the shareholder resolution is usually just the beginning of the activity. The purpose of a resolution is to get the company to make a change or to reconsider a particular practice or issue, not just to get a vote of the shareholders. The resolution may be withdrawn if management takes satisfactory action in response to the concerns of the filing shareholders or if serious negotiations or dialogues are under way. "The process is both time-consuming and expensive, which is why most social-issue resolutions have a number of co-filers."[6]

The proxy resolution is part of the strategy of pressing a particular issue with a particular company. It is undertaken by investors who believe that it is part of their responsibility to be actively involved in promoting corporate social responsibility. The filers of the resolution with Aetna are concerned that executive compensation incentives may be out of balance—that they may promote too much leadership emphasis on the bottom line and not enough on the quality of healthcare services. "As stockholders interested in quality care and financial returns, we want to insure that our Board and management focus as much on quality of care as on finances."[7]

The most basic and minimal level of shareholder activism is to be a conscientious proxy voter. A socially responsible investor provides guidance to the investment manager or whoever is responsible for voting the shares. Those who are not involved as filer or co-filer of resolutions of social issues have the opportunity to vote on issues that others have sponsored. The votes are an opportunity for investors to express their beliefs about the way the companies in which they have some ownership responsibility conduct their business. Conscientious Aetna shareholders will want to make an informed decision about how to vote on this resolution.

Filers and management both know that resolutions not supported by management are not likely to pass. Even a fairly low level of support among shareholders does send a message to management, however. With enough support, filers are able to submit the resolution again the following year, thus continuing the opportunity to discuss the issue with management.[8]

Selective and Alternative Investments

A third form of SRI is selective and focused investment, designed to promote particular companies, organizations, or projects. It is usually called "alternative" because it is investment using a different approach from the return-based model. An alternative investment is made precisely in order to support specific practices. There is anticipated return, but alternative investment usually involves a conscious decision to accept a lower return than can be expected from "mainline" investments. It is a decision to trade some earning potential for promotion of practices in which one believes.

An investor that is involved in alternative investment often designates a portion of the total fund to use in this manner. Investments or loans are made in worker-owned enterprises, in credit unions, in development projects in low-income communities, etc. There is a strong alternative investment interest in community development loan funds.

An alternative investor sometimes selects for investment companies that, in the investor's opinion, represent a better way of doing business. An example is Equal Exchange, a for-profit business engaged in food importing, manufacturing, and distribution. Its main products are coffee and tea. Equal Exchange purchases directly from farm cooperatives abroad and pays a minimum price to growers regardless of the world market price. It assists in the development of grower cooperatives and promotes organic farming methods. Equal Exchange has been the recipient of loans and preferred stock purchases from individual investors and institutional investors who support their approach to "fair trade."

Alternative investment is the only form of SRI that consciously accepts a lower return on investments as an expression of its commitment to social responsibility.

The Ethics of Investing

How one invests is not an ethically neutral activity. Some general observations follow about the ethical responsibilities of investors, observations intended primarily for institutional investors affiliated with healthcare organizations.

1. Investing is not simply financial activity; it communicates, whether intended or not, what corporate practices are acceptable to the investor.

Many investors do not intend to express an opinion about corporate practices when they buy or retain stock. Their actions speak loud, however. When they invest in a company that is being criticized for some of the labor practices of suppliers, for example, their action is likely to be read as a statement of support for what the company is doing. Corporate executives keep a very close eye on Wall Street. When purchasers seek their stock, executives can conclude that the investing public supports what they are doing. Whatever the (unknown) intentions of the investor who purchases or retains stock in a particular company, management of that company understands investors as supporters.

Given the fact that a corporation's "success" is so largely determined by how it does on Wall Street, it is essential that socially responsible investors are aware of the message that their investment activity is sending. This is particularly true when public concerns have been raised about some aspect of the firm's behavior. At a time of a growing controversy about the development and use of genetically modified seeds and crops, for example, one cannot invest in a company like Monsanto in a neutral manner. One might *intend* to be neutral on the issue, but the action speaks on its own.

It is a different story, of course, if one buys or retains stock at a time when concerns have been raised about a company in order to speak to the issue as a socially active shareholder. Then the communication that is made in activity related to proxy resolutions is the clearest statement to the company regarding what one believes is socially responsible.

When there are shareholder resolutions on the proxy ballot related to social issues, whether and how the shares are voted are clearly not ethically neutral decisions. They are speaking directly to the company on that issue.

2. Engaging in SRI is fully compatible with the fund manager's fiduciary responsibility.

Fund managers and others responsible for making decisions about investments sometimes raise the question whether using social criteria for investment decisions is in violation of their fiduciary responsibility. They have a responsibility to provide a good return on investment of money that is not their own. This fiduciary responsibility of the agent is often understood to be a responsibility to "maximize" earnings.

Three points can be made about fiduciary responsibility and SRI.

First, there is no reason to assume that making use of a social screen means that one will earn a lower rate of return. Some of the mutual funds that use social and ethical criteria in making investment decisions have done very well financially.[9]

Second, fiduciary responsibility does not mean that one needs to seek to maximize returns regardless of the harm or potential harm to others. Fund management is a business action that carries with it a responsibility to be aware of and to avoid unnecessary negative social and environmental impacts, the same kind of responsibility that attaches to all business actions. Perhaps a better term than "maximize" to describe the fund manager's fiduciary responsibility is "optimize."[10] The appropriate goal is not the greatest return possible, but the optimal return, the best return compatible with all responsibilities and legitimate concerns.

Third, fiduciary responsibility means that fund managers should not independently decide what ethical investment criteria to use in the management of someone else's money. Making use of social investment criteria is an expression of the investor's understanding of acceptable practices. It is important, therefore, that these criteria are developed with adequate contribution from those who are the owners and/or those for whose benefit the money is being invested. This becomes especially important when the investment strategy being considered (such as alternative investments) might mean a lower rate of return than the beneficiaries might reasonably assume.

Alternative investment decisions are often made, as was noted above, with a willingness to earn a lower rate of return. These are conscious decisions by the fund owners that in these cases the level of return should not be the primary consideration. To do what the owners want is obviously not a violation of fiduciary responsibility.

3. Socially responsible investing on the part of healthcare organizations normally requires the use of some negative screens.

Healthcare organizations have a particular responsibility to work for an improvement in the health of the community. There is a special responsibility, therefore, to review their investment guidelines to ensure that they are not supporting, through investments, activities that seriously threaten public health.

A good example (though not the only one) of an industry in which healthcare organizations should not invest is the tobacco industry. The health damage from tobacco use has been so clearly established that the ownership of stock in a tobacco company appears to be in direct contradiction with the mission of healthcare. Even owning stock in order to file shareholder resolutions may be questionable in this case. Shareholder resolutions focus on specific issues, not the primary business of the corporation. The business of the tobacco industry is, at its core, activity that is a threat to public health. Owning tobacco stock appears to be in direct violation the healthcare organization's responsibility.

4. Socially responsible investing requires a commitment of adequate resources.

Socially responsible institutional investing is, first of all, informed investing. To be done right, it requires an understanding of the ethical beliefs that the institution wants to express in investing. It requires, as well, the ability to apply these beliefs to individual companies and/or issues. Even a modest level of activity (such as the development and use of social screen criteria and conscientious voting of proxies) requires a commitment of resources, especially human resources. More active participation in discussions with corporate leaders requires additional resources.

There are risks associated with trying to engage in SRI activities on "the cheap." Too little support for these activities is likely to mean poorly informed decisions, at least at times. This carries with it the risk of misrepresenting the issues or concerns and the possibility of being unfair to corporations. It carries with it the risk of confusing rather than clarifying the ethical and social responsibilities of business.

Being socially responsible in investing means committing the resources necessary to carry out this function well.

Conclusion

The goal in socially responsible investing is not primarily to be "pure," to invest in only those corporations that have unblemished records. There are no pure companies in the sense of having a perfect social record. The goal is not primarily to have "clean hands," to avoid any contamination with companies that are ethically dirty. There are no companies that are without admirable and responsible practices. The primary goal, rather, is to use the investment role in a conscientious attempt to make a difference, to support and promote those practices judged to be socially and environmentally responsible on issues of consequence to the investor.

Sometimes there is an expressed concern that SRI is too negative, that it does not give adequate recognition to all the good that companies are doing. This is a possibility, it is true, but a fundamental concern of ethics has always been to avoid doing unnecessary harm. A primary dictum in clinical ethics is to "do no harm"; a fundamental concept in environmental ethics is the "precautionary principle"; the basic meaning of corporate social responsibility is to avoid "negative social impact." It is not necessarily denying the good that companies are doing to use one's influence to try to reduce any harm that may be occurring. It is focusing on what needs "fixing."

Socially responsible investing is a natural and, it might reasonably be concluded, an ethically necessary expression of the organization's role as a citizen of the larger community.

Seventeen

Components of a Business Ethics Program

Formal ethics programs in healthcare settings can and do make a difference. As someone who has had the opportunity over the years to work with many different Ethics Committees, I have observed a significant impact in clinical ethics. The committees and the programs that they have sponsored have contributed to an increased sensitivity to ethical concerns and to an improving level of education regarding these concerns.

Perhaps the most important impact, as I reflect upon it, is that the existence of an active Ethics Committee is a recognition in the organization that explicit attention to ethics is an important part of providing good patient care. It is a recognition that staff is expected to use some of its time to become better acquainted with contemporary thinking about ethical responsibility. It is a recognition that ethics education is an important topic for in-service programs. It is a recognition that service on the Ethics Committee is a contribution to the work of the organization. The existence and support of Ethics Committees gives credibility and status to efforts to understand the practical implications of ethical standards and principles.[1]

In developing a business ethics program, healthcare leaders are recognizing a need to have a mechanism in the organization for focusing attention on ethical issues in healthcare management similar to the attention focused on ethical issues in clinical care in recent years. As is the case in clinical ethics, the program needs to have visibility and needs to be understood as an educational and quality-promoting program, not as a policing function.

A good business ethics program is designed to implement the best values of the organization in the conduct of its business. It is mission-driven, not compliance-driven. It is designed to promote the achievement of the highest ethical standards in all areas of management, not to set minimal standards of behavior.

Important topics of ethics education and skill development include stewardship of resources, fairness to employees, and responsibility to the community, in addition to high-quality patient care. The preceding chapters have demonstrated some of the perspectives that are brought to the consideration of various policies or practices when they are considered explicitly in terms of ethical values and concerns. If there is value in considering ethical perspectives in the management of the healthcare organization in a systematic manner, then there needs to be a means of ensuring that this happens. It will not happen on its own.

Despite the best of intentions, an explicit focus on the ethical implications of business or management decisions is not easy to maintain in the busy workplace. This chapter describes and discusses some possible components of a systematic focus on ethics in the business of healthcare. The next chapter focuses on an Organizational Ethics Committee as one mechanism for implementing such a program.

Ethics at the Table

Ethics is everyone's business. There is a very real way in which ethics perspectives are represented at any table at which decisions are being made by persons sensitive to their professional responsibilities and to the mission and values of the organization. The ethical organization is one in which a commitment to ethics and an ability to recognize ethical issues are routinely expected of everyone, particularly those in key management positions.

There is a long-running discussion in schools of business administration about the appropriate place of ethics in the business curriculum. Some want separate courses in ethics and/or social responsibility, taught by individuals with particular expertise in the area. Others prefer the model of integrating ethics into functional courses, discussing ethical issues related to marketing in courses on marketing, ethical issues related to finance in courses on finance, and so on.[2]

Opposition to a separate course in business ethics is often expressed as a concern that such a course implies that ethics is separate from or outside of the regular business functions. Support for separate courses in business ethics is often expressed as a concern that, without a separate course, ethics will be treated superficially and/or will be subordinated to functional considerations (which are the faculty member's true expertise). There is a concern, as well, that there will not be opportunity to reflect upon larger questions about the role of business in society without a separate course.

The best answer to the question of the place of ethics in the business curriculum seems to be that, if possible, ethics should be both taught in a separate course and integrated into functional courses. This avoids the implication that ethics is separate from the "real" business functions and avoids, as well, the superficial attention to ethics that might often result when it in simply presented as short discussions in other courses. Faculty teaching functional courses should be prepared to impart sensitivity to many of the ethical issues that relate to these functions, but they are not expected to consider the full range of issues that ethics faculty bring to the discussion. For many students, a course that gives full attention to ethics in all its implications for business opens the mind to considerations that may otherwise not be recognized.

Something similar can be said about the attention paid to ethics in the day-to-day business of most organizations. Yes, ethics is everyone's business. But, for most people, position responsibilities do not allow sufficient opportunity for on-going deepening and expanding of their understanding of health-care ethics. Recognizing and responding to complex ethical issues often takes skill and experience and practice, something that requires more time than most managers have.

Ethics is everyone's responsibility, but without systematic methods for ensuring that it happens, many decisions will be made without explicit attention to all the implications of what it means for the organization to be a good caregiver, to be a good employer, to be a good citizen. Most managers, despite being ethically sensitive and informed, can benefit from assistance in identifying and reflecting on the ethical dimensions of decisions that need to be made.

There are different ways of having ethics represented at the table, different methods of including ethics perspectives as an explicit part of management decision making. I will comment on two methods here.

An Ethics Voice

One method of helping to ensure that ethical issues are not ignored when they should be explicitly attended to is to have someone at the table in all key deliberations whose responsibility it is to make sure these issues get raised and addressed. This is the equivalent of having a separate ethics course in business education. This method provides for the active presence of someone whose first and primary concern is to focus attention on connections between the meeting agenda and such ethical responsibilities as stewardship of resources, fairness to employees, responsibility to the community, or the quality of patient care.

The ethics person (here called an "ethics and mission advisor," though there is no standard terminology) needs to be well versed in the wide range of ethics issues in healthcare management. An ethics and mission advisor has several responsibilities as a participant in senior management-level committees and in other deliberations: (1) to assist in identifying issues that involve judgments about ethical values or the organization's mission; (2) to articulate what is at stake ethically in these cases; (3) to offer suggestions and perspectives on the best ways of addressing these issues; and (4) to assist in finding resources (persons or literature) related to the ethical issues and their resolutions.

There is a big difference between having someone with a particular skill in ethics present routinely and having such a person available or on call. The routine presence of an ethics and mission advisor will, if she or he does the job well, help to surface issues of ethical significance that might need more attention. This can raise the level of ethical awareness in a way that having someone on call does not. It is like having an ethics consultant involved from the very beginning.

Ethics Consultation

A second method of bringing ethics considerations explicitly to the table when management issues are being addressed is to request an ethics consultation. An ethics consultation is a discussion focused specifically on understanding the ethical significance of what is at stake. A consultation occurs, however, only when someone has already recognized a need for such concentrated attention on ethical concerns.

The practice of requesting an ethics consultation is a relatively recent development in healthcare, but it is no longer rare. Most requests are in regard to decisions that need to be made in clinical care, most frequently regarding treatment for patients who appear to be near the end of life. The increased use of ethics consultation has paralleled and in many cases been part of the growth and development of Clinical Ethics Committees.

There are two basic models of providing ethics consultations: an individual ethics consultant and an ethics consultant team or committee. (The term "consultant" in the following paragraphs refers to either an individual or a team.) The normal policy is that ethics consultations are "optional-optional." Requesting a consultation is optional, not mandated, and the requesting party has the option of deciding whether and/or how to follow any advice or recommendation on the part of the consultant. Often a consultation is requested when there is some disagreement between clinicians and patient/family or among the clinical care team regarding what should be done.

The purpose of having an ethics consultation service is to provide assistance, when requested, for those who need to make decisions in situations where the right thing to do is not completely clear. The assistance that is provided is a review of the relevant factors in the case with a guiding focus on the precise implications and applications of patient rights, professional responsibilities of clinicians, and other relevant ethical principles or standards. The role of the ethics consultant is to offer suggestions or recommendations regarding what should be done in the particular case in light of ethical guidelines and the specific facts of the situation.

Ethics consultation in the business or management side of healthcare is so far much less common than it is in the clinical side. The consultation model that has been developed in clinical ethics is an appropriate one for business ethics, though the expertise and qualifications required of the consulting group or individual are somewhat different. Qualifications are considered in the next chapter; here I want to make a few observations on the general nature of business ethics consultation in healthcare.

1. The basic purpose of consultation is to assist decision makers in understanding what is the right thing to do regarding a particular issue, all things considered.

We are all inevitably somewhat limited in our point of view. We see issues and possible responses to the issues from the perspective of our primary professional and organizational commitments and personal interests. One of the major values of an ethics consultation is that it can bring different perspectives to bear on a particular situation (policy, decision, or plan). Consultation provides the opportunity to see what might be thought and said about a situation if the starting point and frame of reference focus on what is at stake, ethically, in these particular circumstances.

Good ethics consultation or advice is not just another perspective among many. If done well, it assists in identifying priorities and in keeping the focus on the big picture. It assists in evaluating options in terms of the basic responsibilities in the management of healthcare services. Assuming an optional-optional model, any recommendations or suggestions that are judged not to be pertinent or helpful need not be accepted.

2. Good consultation includes advice or recommendations, where appropriate, with an emphasis on the rationale for the proposed course of action.

The ethics consultant is in an advisory role. One requests a consultation as a way of seeking additional observations and insights in order to make a better-informed decision. The buck still stops with management; seeking advice is not letting someone else make the decision.

In ethics consultation, suggestions or recommendations on the best way to proceed are usually more helpful than general statements or a clarification of issues or a listing of options. Specific recommendations or advice, if such is indicated by the review, has the advantage of giving the requester specific and practical points to consider. It is especially helpful if the consultant's response includes a statement of explanation as well as proposed ways of proceeding. In determining how to respond to the advice, management can respond to both the recommendations and the rationale.

3. Contrary to the situation in clinical ethics, the normal request for business ethics consultation is based on a desire to get other perspectives in the conversation, not on the fact that there is a disagreement that needs to be resolved.

A request may be made for an ethics consultation regarding downsizing plans because of an interest in making sure that adequate attention has been given to fairness issues. A request may be made for a consultation about a managed care contract because of an interest in making sure that all potential conflicts of interest are carefully explored. A request may be made for a consultation in regard to policy on the allocation of limited blood products in order to get additional perspectives on proposed criteria. The incentive in each of these cases is not to resolve a disagreement but to improve the quality of decision making.

4. An optional model of management ethics consultation will be used only to the extent that managers have reason to expect such a consultation to be beneficial.

A good ethics consultation process can provide useful perspectives to contribute to high-quality decision making, but it will be used only when managers themselves decide to request this kind of assistance. Those managers are most likely to request this service who have had some experience to suggest the value. The experience may have been ethics education, it may have been personal experience on or with an Ethics Committee, or it may been personal reflection or conversation about ethical dimensions of issues.

A business or management consultation service is not able to stand alone or to be a starting point for an ethics program. It works best when it is part of a more complete program that includes ongoing education, review of polices and procedures, and sensitivity to the messages that are being communicated in day-to-day business of the organization. It is fully compatible with, may in fact work best with, some method of routinely including ethics at the decision-making table.

An Ethics Performance Improvement Tool

One of the methods sometimes recommended for attending to ethics in healthcare organizations is the ethics audit, "a formal process of reviewing an organization's policies, procedures, and outcomes from an ethical perspective."[3] Such an audit is best undertaken not as a response to a crisis but to identify potential concerns that need to be addressed before they become serious problems.

An ethics audit might be undertaken, for example, in response to increases in employee complaints or grievances, in staff resignations, in patient complaints, in problems with suppliers, in adverse publicity.[4] As part of an ethics program that addresses issues that go beyond compliance, an ethics audit is designed to identify issues related to the organization's mission and ethical ideals and to develop the educational and policy responses to address these concerns.

An ethics audit might also be called an ethics performance-improvement tool. One such tool begins the process of identifying the practices that need attention by listing a number of ethical standards in the organization and asking reviewers to indicate, in regard to each, whether it works well or is problematic and needs attention. The following are included (along with many other items that tend to be more focused on clinical ethics):

Conscientious objection
  Caregivers are permitted not to participate in treatments that they object to in conscience.
  Caregivers know about and feel free to object.
Allocation of resources
  Treatment is not provided to patients that does not benefit them.
  Financial impact on organization's ability to meet other needs is considered when new equipment, drugs, etc. are purchased.[5]

There is, I think, great value in developing and implementing a tool of this sort. It requires the identification of practices that need to be present in an organization dedicated to high ethical standards. When used regularly, it facilitates early recognition of issues that may need to be attended to. The very fact of identifying and communicating the expectations that are to be used to evaluate ethics performance in various operations within the organization gives direction to management and staff. The tool also provides a framework for working to improve practices in regard to these standards, goals, or ideals.

Education, Education, Education

Though the functions of healthcare Ethics Committees are routinely described as education, policy review, and case consultation, I recall one seasoned professional ethicist describing the threefold function as "education, education, education."

Education is essential to implementing good practice. It is essential, in fact, to developing the skill of recognizing the issues that are of ethical significance. Without heightened ethical awareness, we often do not even recognize the issues that require more careful ethical analysis. One meaning of the "education, education, education" refrain is that it is hard to overemphasize the central importance of education in any good ethics program.

Another way of thinking about "education, education, education" is to recognize that policy review and case consultation are educational in nature. When done well, each involves the identification of and reflection upon, for others, considerations related to best ethical practice in the organization. This is education, just as much as sessions labeled education are education. Almost everything done by an Ethics Committee (or others responsible for ethics in the organization) has educational value.

There are some special challenges in providing business ethics education in a healthcare organization: the content of healthcare business ethics education is not yet clearly defined and resources in healthcare business ethics are limited.

There is an enormous literature in medical ethics. There is an enormous literature in generic business ethics. Both have journals, collections of case studies, textbooks, and professional associations that hold annual national conferences. Both have contributions from academics as well as from practitioners. It is not difficult for one who wants to organize an educational program in business ethics or medical ethics to find many identified issues and many case studies.

There is as yet only a minor literature in healthcare management ethics or healthcare business ethics. There are few textbooks, no journals that I am aware of, few collections of case studies, no professional associations, and no regular national conferences. The literature is growing, and there is much that is relevant to healthcare business management in the medical ethics literature and in the business ethics literature, but it is not yet possible to put together any "standard" list of topics or readings.

One can expect that the key issues will become more clearly defined in the near future and that useful responses to these issues will become more abundant.[6] In the meantime, it is particularly important to seek out as ethics educators in healthcare business ethics those who are familiar with concepts and guidelines in medical ethics, in business ethics, and in social ethics/social responsibility. The ethics educator also needs to be familiar with the special nature of healthcare organizations.

One of the initial tasks in education is to clarify what "healthcare business ethics" is all about. As a possible contribution to that work, I offer these observations:[7]

1. Healthcare business ethics is about more than compliance.
2. Healthcare business ethics is about more than personal ethics.
3. Healthcare business ethics is about more than clinical ethics.
4. Healthcare business ethics is about healthcare organizations, not some other business.

These first points require no further explanation for readers of this book. They have been guiding concepts throughout.

5. Healthcare business ethics is about more than managed care.

Managed care has gotten very bad press in the last few years, largely because of cases of patients not being covered for adequate care by their healthcare plans. Many persons, when they hear the term "healthcare business ethics," immediately think of issues like denial of coverage by health insurers.

Persons more familiar with healthcare may also express a concern about the way doctors are paid in managed care plans, concerned that doctors may have a financial incentive to provide less medical care or less expensive medical care—a situation that is seen as putting the physician in a potential conflict of interest.

There is no doubt that there is a great need for careful ethical reflection on the way business is done in and with managed care organizations. Nevertheless, there would be plenty of work for healthcare business ethicists and committees even if there were no managed care.

6. Healthcare business ethics is about practical guidance for managers.

Let me make references again to a quotation used in the Introduction. Leon Kass said about healthcare ethics over the last generation, "Though originally intended to improve our deeds, the reigning practice in ethics, if truth be told, has, at best, improved our speech."[8]

I have already indicated that I think that more than speech has been improved with active institutional ethics efforts. But I agree entirely with Kass that we need to remember that healthcare ethics should be designed to affect behavior and practice. Thinking about ethics does require us to pay careful attention to the way that we talk about issues, but the goal is not saying the right things. The goal is assisting managers to make better practical judgments.

7. Healthcare business ethics is about healthcare organizations as care providers.
8. Healthcare business ethics is about healthcare organizations as employers.
9. Healthcare business ethics is about healthcare organizations as citizens.

These three statements probably require no further comment at this point. They have served as the organizing concepts for chapters and topics in this book.

Clinical ethicists sometimes provide a listing of content areas and of books and journals that can be recommended for those who, like Ethics Committee members, need a good basic education in bioethics.[9] Defining a standard educational agenda and a recommended reading list for healthcare business ethics can wait. This does not mean, however, that education should wait. It is only through efforts to clarify the ethical responsibilities of healthcare managers that a better understanding of the nature and range of these responsibilities will evolve.

Responsibility for the Business Ethics Program

This chapter has suggested some possible components that could be included as individual institutions and organizations develop their own healthcare business ethics programs. There is not only one model for a successful program.

A successful business ethics program requires the explicit and strong support of top management. It requires, also, clearly identified responsibility for the program and its various components. The overall responsibility for the business ethics program can be placed in an ethics office (not to be confused with a compliance office) and/or in an Ethics Committee.

Given the history and precedent of using committees to direct attention to ethical issues in clinical care, the committee model is likely to be employed in many cases in efforts to address business ethics issues. The next chapter focuses on characteristics, role, and functions of such a committee.

Eighteen

The Organizational
Ethics Committee

With the recent growth of interest in healthcare business ethics, some organizations have asked their existing Ethics Committee to enlarge its charge, to include issues in "organizational ethics" as well as issues in clinical ethics. This may work well in some cases, but is probably not the best approach in most situations. Most Ethics Committee members have developed some expertise in clinical ethics, but are not well prepared to address issues in business or management ethics. The Clinical Ethics Committee, when it performs well, already has a full agenda, probably too full to allow the necessary time and energy to develop a whole new competence.

An alternative to adding additional responsibility to an existing committee is to establish what is often called the Organizational Ethics Committee. This chapter is a discussion of the functions, responsibilities, and membership qualifications of the Organizational Ethics Committee (OEC). Though the OEC is an alternative to adding major additional responsibilities to the existing Ethics Committee, the OEC follows the model of the Clinical Ethics Committee in many ways. It is designed to give the same sort of attention to practical ethics in management as a good Clinical Ethics Committee gives to practical issues in patient care.

Committee Functions and Membership

A good Organizational Ethics Committee is designed to assist managers in their efforts to make decisions that reflect the highest ethical standards of the healthcare business. The committee's agenda is to promote the achievement of these standards in all areas of management. It is an advisory committee, not an enforcement committee.

Like the Clinical Ethics Committee, the OEC can identify its functions as three: education, policy development and review, and case consultation. Among the charge of the OEC are the following:

1. to develop and/or review policies and procedures related to ethically sensitive organizational issues;
2. to serve as a consultative body (or arrange for consultation by others) for discussion of and recommendations on ethically sensitive issues facing management;
3. to provide educational opportunities for consideration of specific ethical issues and for insight into the evolving understanding of healthcare business ethics.

There is at least one significant way in which the consultative function in business ethics is significantly different from that function in clinical issues. Clinical Ethics Committees usually do not report to the clinicians to whom they may make recommendations. Rarely is one of the parties involved in a particular case that comes before the committee also responsible for overseeing the work of the committee. In the work of the OEC, on the other hand, organizational leaders are likely to be those to whom the committee reports as well as those to whom consultation is provided.[1]

Given the realities of life in organizations, it may not be reasonable to expect that candid and potentially unwelcome suggestions will be given to those who are higher in the organizational hierarchy. The independence of those doing business ethics consulting needs to be ensured if the committee is going to be effective and credible.

Clinical Ethics Committees are interdisciplinary committees, with membership that includes physicians, nurses, social workers, and chaplains. Often administration and risk management are represented as well. Many such committees include a community representative or two. Quite often, Ethics Committees have an established relationship with an outside ethicist, who serves as a member of the committee or as a consultant to the committee.

The OEC is also best structured as an interdisciplinary group, but with a somewhat different mix. Key constituencies to be represented in membership of the OEC include management, non-management employees, clinical staff, and an ethicist.

Management

Just as the majority of members of the Clinical Ethics Committee are usually from the clinical care areas, so the majority of members of the committee that addresses issues related to management ethics should be persons in management positions. Though an argument can be made for having representation from some specific departments (such as Human Resources), having the right persons on the committee is more important than representation of specific management functions. What is needed is a core of management-level employees who are or can become skilled in healthcare management ethics and who are able to apply these skills to a variety of situations. What is needed is a group of managers who have the independence and integrity to put commitment to ethical ideals before office politics and their own career-advancement goals.

More attention is given below to qualifications and skills.

Non-management Employees

It is essential that the OEC include some employees who are not in management positions. These should be persons who are capable of and competent in bringing sensitive awareness of issues in the organization to the attention of management. As is discussed later in this chapter, one important characteristic of a good OEC is a sensitivity to the messages, often unintended, that are communicated to employees in the organization by policies and decisions and permitted practices. Management does not always recognize the unintended messages being received by employees as quickly as others in the organization.

Clinical Staff

Healthcare is a particular kind of business, a business that provides healthcare services. A committee devoted to healthcare business ethics needs to include representation from the clinical staff, persons who are capable of contributing a clinical perspective to the connections between management decisions and the quality of care delivered. While I have repeatedly noted that ethical issues relate to all management responsibilities, not just patient care, it is also true that patient care is a major point of reference for assessing the impact and the consequences of organizational policies and practices.

In selecting clinical members of the OEC, it is important to be sensitive to role, power, and status realities in the organization and not to assume, for example, that a physician (or a nurse) can represent the perspectives of all clinical disciplines.

Ethicists

Many Clinical Ethics Committees have included an outside ethicist as a member of the committee in order to have access to the resources and perspectives that can be provided by someone with specialized training and experience. In addition to contributing to the work of the committee as a regular member, the ethicist is frequently asked to lead educational sessions and to be an active participant in any consultations that are requested.

Clinical ethics is extensively developed in both study and practice. The issues, at least many of them, are quite clearly defined. Clinical professionals have often had formal education on principles, and their application and committees have been addressing these issues in organizations for a number of years. Even in the field of medical ethics, as well developed as it is, a professional ethicist is often recognized as an important member of the committee.

The case for including an ethicist on the OEC would seem to be stronger, given the much less well developed field of healthcare business ethics. An ethicist would be able to assist the committee in identifying issues and resources and educational opportunities. At a time when there is increased interest but still relatively few systematic discussions of healthcare business ethics, an ethicist can be especially valuable in aiding the committee in its early stages. If an ethicist is to be associated with the OEC, it is important, of course, to find one with the right qualifications. The very fact that the field is not yet well developed means that professional ethicists are not routinely experienced in working on these issues.

I made the point above that management members of the OEC should have the independence and integrity to put commitment to ethical ideals before their own status in the organization. This point applies to all other members, as well, including the ethicist.

Qualifications: Understanding Organizational Ethics

Case 18.1. The CEO of ABC Medical Center asked the Organizational Ethics Committee to help him prepare a response to a communication from a community activist organization. The group had sent copies of several articles that had appeared in medical journals over the last few years reporting on studies that indicated that the medical response to African American patients was often different from the medical response to European Americans with the same symptoms. ABC Medical Center was asked what it was doing to prevent this kind of race-related inequality of care.

The CEO reported to the committee that he had responded that ABC was fully committed to non-discrimination and that he was not aware of any cases of discriminatory healthcare in the institution. He had told the community group, further, that he would be providing a more extensive response later. He said to the OEC that he was very concerned about the potential public relations issues here, and he asked the committee to give him some recommendations as soon as possible.

This situation can be used to begin reflection on the skills and knowledge expected of members of the OEC.

OEC members need to be able to think in terms of the ethical values that exist in systems and organizations and cultures, not just in terms of individual choices and decisions. That means, for example, that the issue of potential inequality in healthcare is not primarily whether physicians and others are consciously discriminatory, but whether there are discriminatory outcomes regardless of the intentions of clinicians.

The question for the organization is whether there are quality mechanisms in place to catch and prevent unequal treatment. Given the fact that people often act without full awareness of the values and biases that may affect their thinking, management's responsibility to prevent discrimination requires a focus on practice, not intent. One response to the studies showing that race-related inequalities in healthcare do exist in this country is to implement a recommendation like that proposed by H. Jack Geiger: "the routine and on-going examination of racial disparities in the use of services and in the choices of diagnostic and therapeutic alternatives should be part of the quality-assurance protocols."[2] This kind of emphasis keeps the focus on organizational practices and their impact, rather than on the personal goodwill of individuals in the organization.

One of the key qualifications of every member of the OEC is a recognition that management ethics is about doing the job right. It is not primarily about being good and well-intentioned persons.

In the discussion of codes of ethics in Chapter 7, I noted that the culture of the organization plays a key role in shaping behavior. The way that individual decisions get made is often the result of the organization's culture: what is usual practice, what is rewarded, what is "the way things work here." The culture, perhaps even more than expressed beliefs and written standards, shapes decisions. Promoting ethics in the organization means ensuring that the organization's culture supports behavior that reflects high ethical standards.

There are two ways that an organization educates its employees in ethics: the formal message and the informal message. The formal ethics message consists of mission statements, values statements, codes of ethics, and other communications from management regarding institutional values and appropriate practices. The informal ethics message consists of practices and policies that are promoted or tolerated by management or in some other way demonstrated to be acceptable within the organization.

The informal ethics messages often speak much more loudly than the formal ethics messages. What the institution recognizes as acceptable practices, especially those practices that are the result of decisions on the part of organization leaders, express a position on ethics, whether intended or not. Employees (and others who do business with the organization) quickly recognize that behavior speaks louder than words. Ethics is "caught" as well as "taught." Or, to make the point another way, management is teaching ethics even when it is not saying anything about ethics or values explicitly.

One important component of the effort to maintain a high level of awareness of and commitment to ethics in the organization, then, is sensitivity to the messages being sent about what is really important in day-to-day practices. The need is to develop institutional culture that encourages, supports, and rewards conscientious efforts to apply high ethical standards in responding to issues throughout the organization, whether or not the issues are specifically addressed in a code. Promoting ethics is not just about encouraging and educating individuals to act in certain ways. It is also about assessing institutional practices and, if necessary, changing them, in order to achieve outcomes more compatible with the highest ethical standards.

Case 18.2. The Director of Human Resources in a children's hospital received an anonymous memo (with a notation that a copy had been sent to the CEO). The writer identified herself or himself as an employee and requested a review of the hospital's parental leave policy. She or he made reference to a study that compared such policies in children's hospitals and pediatric medical centers with policies in Fortune 500 companies.[3] One of the findings reported in the article was that companies were more likely to categorize maternity leave as disability leave, and hospitals were more likely to categorize maternity leave as sick leave. The benefit categorization affects how much time is actually available, because younger and more recent employees are not likely to have accrued much sick leave.

The memo writer suggested that the hospital consider changing its policy from sick leave to short-term disability. She or he concluded by saying, "it is interesting that an institution devoted to caring for children makes it more difficult for many employees to care for their own children than an organization devoted to profit."

The writer is making a very good point. The nature and details of a parental leave policy do reflect (and communicate to employees) the organization's values in regard to the importance of caring for children. One of the qualifications of members of the Organizational Ethics Committee is the ability to recognize the ethical value choices made in making policy decisions.

Case 18.3. J. P., a nursing student, was walking down the hospital corridor when she was distracted by a loud voice. At the nursing station a physician was angrily berating a nurse in front of two other nurses. J. P. heard phrases like "I expect you to do exactly what I tell you to do" and "This better not happen again." The nurse was in tears.

A little later the nurse sought out J. P. "I'm sorry about what happened before. I just want you to know that I did nothing wrong. I was following hospital policies. Dr. D. wanted me to get an informed consent signed when the patient didn't seem to know what was going on." J. P. said she was shocked by the public nature of the rebuke. "Does this happen often?" "Not too often, and only from a couple docs. We have reported Dr. D. two or three times, but nothing happened. So now we just listen to him and hope he gets over his anger quickly."

Sometimes the true standards of the organization are communicated not by policies or by other overt actions, but by what is not done. When a nurse is publicly and loudly scolded by a physician and this is reported and no action is taken, the organization is saying, in effect, that this is acceptable behavior. It is sending the message that it is okay for doctors to treat nurses this way.

The qualifications for membership on the OEC include the capability of understanding the true ethics standards being promoted in the organization by the messages being sent, however unintentionally.

Qualifications: Personal Characteristics

I suggested above that having the right persons on the OEC is more important than representation of specific departments within the organization and noted, as well, that not every ethicist is the right person for such a committee. There are some personal characteristics that should be considered important for persons serving on the OEC.

The appointment of the OEC gives it the institutional authority to educate and to make recommendations in regard to policies and specific practices. Having moral authority, though, requires that the members of the committee, at least as a group, are recognized as persons who are worth listening to when they talk about ethics. To have credibility, the committee needs to be made up of persons who are credible as spokespersons on business ethics.

There are three personal characteristics that should be considered especially important for OEC members.[4]

1. OEC members need to be willing to develop the necessary knowledge and skills.

Everyone in the organization should be familiar with ethical standards and ideals; ethics is everyone's business. Nevertheless, members of a committee that is charged with assisting others in understanding what is at stake ethically in different decisions and practices need to have a greater than average understanding of healthcare business ethics concepts, principles, and guidelines. They need to become well read regarding the issues and to gain experience in applying concepts, principles, and guidelines to particular situations.

For its credibility, the OEC needs to be recognized as a group that recognizes the issues and understands how these issues are addressed in the evolving literature in healthcare business ethics. Not every member of the committee needs to have the same level of education on the issues, but those who speak and act for the committee need to be well informed, and every member is expected to continue to become better informed. The OEC is expected to apply its developed understanding of ethics to the issue at hand. Contributing to the work of the committee requires work and study.

   2. OEC members should be recognized as persons of integrity and independence.

It is also important to consider the issue of character when identifying qualifications for members of the Organizational Ethics Committee.

In order to do its job well, the committee needs to command the respect of colleagues. It commands respect by providing intelligent, informed, and sensitive commentaries and opinions. It commands respect, as well, by being made up of persons who themselves command respect as persons of integrity. The particular type of integrity that is most important here is integrity in their role on the committee. Committee members cannot command respect in speaking about ethics if they are perceived as concerned about promotion possibilities first and ethics second. The OEC cannot have moral authority if members are perceived as more concerned with pleasing, or not offending, certain persons in the organization than they are with promoting high ethical standards.

As was noted earlier, to be a member of the OEC is to be in a very difficult position, because the committee sometimes offers advice to those who are higher in the organizational hierarchy. It may require a great deal of integrity and independence and courage to speak one's true mind in such circumstances, knowing that those listening have the power to affect one's future in the organization. The committee will have no real moral authority, however, unless committee members are recognized as individuals who do not let self-interest and personal connections determine their perception of what is right.

It is important, of course, that mechanisms be in place to protect OEC members from suffering some adverse consequences as a result of opinions expressed in their work on the committee. Members should be selected who have the personal integrity and independence to resist the temptation to please "the boss," but the burden should not all be placed on the individuals. A good organization builds in protections of the independence of committee members.

   3. OEC members should be persons who passionately care about ethics.

The Organizational Ethics Committee is an advisory committee, not a compliance committee. It does not enforce or "police" behavior. Nevertheless, the committee functions best when members care passionately about what happens in the organization. An Ethics Committee does not function well by being detached and uninvolved. Those who command respect when speaking about ethics are those who care about ethics. They care deeply about avoiding waste of resources, about protecting employees from unfair treatment, about preventing race-related inequality in healthcare, about reducing the potential harmful effects of medical waste, etc.

There may be a risk of misunderstanding involved in using the word "passionate." Sometimes those who feel passionately about an issue will allow emotion to overwhelm practical reasoning. "Passion" sometimes leads to intolerance of other points of view. These are dangers that need to be guarded against, but moral passion in the sense of truly caring about the issues is essential to the work of the OEC. The OEC represents the relevance and importance attached to ethics in the organization, and its members should be recognized as persons with a deep personal commitment and concern.

Getting Started

Organizational Ethics Committees today are at approximately the same stage of development where Clinical Ethics Committees were fifteen to twenty years ago. That is, they are increasingly being recognized as having a potentially significant contribution to make within the organization, but they are not yet functioning in many locations. It may well be that many more such committees will be in existence in the next few years.

The first step toward being an effective Organizational Ethics Committee is to start well. I conclude this chapter with one simple suggestion for the early work of a new OEC: The committee may want to devote considerable time and attention in the early months to self-education.

The most important step in gaining credibility is being competent. As noted earlier, the members of the OEC need to have a greater than average understanding of healthcare business ethics concepts, principles, and guidelines. They need to be competent in applying ethical thinking to particular situations.

In order to improve their ability to do the work of the committee well, and in order to improve the comfort level of new committee members, it is helpful to have some time devoted to serious, organized, and guided education. The ethics resource person asked to guide the committee's education should selected carefully. It may not be easy to find someone familiar with practical business ethics appropriate for healthcare services. When first organized, many Clinical Ethics Committees spent considerable time in their own education in preparation for assuming their various responsibilities and found this to be very helpful. The OEC might follow this example.

One useful approach to self-education is to relate the study topics directly to topics that have been already been identified for possible attention by the OEC. The issues that are initially brought to the attention of OEC can be used to establish the early agenda both in terms of the committee's work and in terms of the committee's self-education. This way work gets done at the same time that the committee is becoming more familiar with business ethics concepts and literature. The educational sessions then have practical relevance.

Notes

Introduction

1. Leon Kass, "Practicing Ethics: Where's the Action?" *Hastings Center Report* 20, no. 1 (January/February 1990): 8.

1. Healthcare Business Ethics

1. Emily Friedman, "What Business Did You Say We Were In?" *Healthcare Forum Journal* 41, no. 4 (July/August 1998): 8–12.

2. American College of Healthcare Administrators, "ACHA Code of Ethics" (1994).

3. Leonard J. Weber, "In Vitro Fertilization and the Just Use of Health Care Resources," in James M. Humber and Robert F. Almeder, eds., *Reproduction, Technology, and Rights* (Totowa, N.J.: Humana Press, 1996), p. 79.

4. As published in *Image: Journal of Nursing Scholarship* 31, no. 1 (First Quarter 1999): 2.

5. Emily Friedman, "Too Much of a Bad Thing," *Healthcare Forum Journal* 39, no. 2 (March/April 1996): 15.

6. William C. Frederick, James E. Post, and Keith Davis, *Business and Society*, 7th ed. (New York: McGraw-Hill, 1992), p. 30.

7. Tom L. Beauchamp and James F. Childress, *Principles of Biomedical Ethics*, 4th ed. (New York: Oxford University Press, 1993).

8. Nancy S. Jecker, "The Role of Intimate Others in Medical Decision Making," *The Gerontologist* 30, no. 1 (1990): 69.

9. Thomas Schindler, "Doing Justice," unpublished.

10. Leonard J. Weber, "Healthcare Management Ethics: Business Ethics with a Difference" (A Review Article), *Business Ethics Quarterly* (forthcoming).

2. Ethics Is Not Neutral: A Framework for Making Decisions

1. Leonard J. Weber, "The Business of Ethics," *Health Progress* 71, no. 1 (January–February 1990): 76–78.

2. "A Model for Making Ethical Decisions," in P. A. Twadell-Soleri and M. A. McDermott, eds., *Education for Parish Nursing: Assuring Congregational Health and Wholeness in the Twenty-First Century* (Park Ridge, Ill.: The International Parish Nurse Resource, 1997), p. 523. For another model, see Laura L. Nash, "Ethics Without the Sermon," *Harvard Business Review* 59 (November/December 1981): 78–90.

3. Ethics, Cost, and the Quality of Care

1. Richard D. Lamm, "Redrawing the Ethics Map," *Hastings Center Report* 29, no. 2 (March–April 1999): 28–29.

2. Leonard J. Weber, "Mixing Ethics and Dollars," *Advance for Administrators of the Laboratory* 8, no. 1 (January 1999): 18–20.

3. James Sabin, "A Credo for Ethical Managed Care in Mental Health Practice," *Hospital and Community Psychiatry* 45, no. 9 (September 1994): 859.

4. James H. Ellis et al., "Selective Use of Radiographic Low-Osmolality Contrast Media in the 1990s," *Radiology* 200, no. 2 (August 1996): 300.

5. Institute of Medicine National Roundtable on Health Care Quality, "The Urgent Need to Improve Health Care Quality," *The Journal of the American Medical Association* 280, no. 11 (September 16, 1998): 1000–1005.

6. Sabin, p. 859.

7. M. Kuczewski and M. DeVita, "Managed Care and End-of-Life Decisions: Learning to Live Ungagged," *Archives of Internal Medicine* 158, no. 22 (1998): 2424–2428.

4. Patient Rights in a Just Organization

1. "Case Study: My Conscience, Your Money," *Hastings Center Report* 25, no. 5 (September–October 1995): 28.

2. Leonard J. Weber and Margaret L. Campbell, "Medical Futility and Life-Sustaining Treatment Decisions," *Journal of Neuroscience Nursing* 28, no. 1 (February 1996): 57.

3. Lawrence J. Schneiderman, Nancy S. Jecker, and Albert R. Jonsen, "Medical Futility: Its Meaning and Ethical Implications," *Annals of Internal Medicine* 112, no. 12 (June 1990): 950.

4. Rosalie A. Kane and Arthur L. Caplan, eds., *Everyday Ethics: Resolving Dilemmas in Nursing Home Life* (New York: Springer Publishing Co., 1990), p.156.

5. Clinicians and Conflicts of Interest: A Focus on Management

1. Manuel G. Velasquez, *Business Ethics: Concepts and Cases,* 4th ed. (Upper Saddle River, N.J.: Prentice Hall, 1998), p. 430.

2. E. Haavi Morreim, "Conflicts of Interest: Profits and Problems in Physician Referrals," *The Journal of the American Medical Association* 252, no. 3 (July 21, 1989): 390–394.

3. Joint Commission on the Accreditation of Health Care Organizations, "Patient Rights and Organizational Ethics" (1997), Standard RI 4.4.

4. Marc Rodwin, *Medicine, Money, and Morals: Physicians' Conflicts of Interest* (New York: Oxford University Press, 1993), p. 55.

5. Ibid., p. 145.

6. Ezekiel Emanuel, "Medical Ethics in the Era of Managed Care: The Need for Institutional Structures Instead of Principles for Individual Cases," *The Journal of Clinical Ethics* 6, no. 4 (Winter 1995): 338.

7. Rodwin, p. 157.

8. James Sabin, "A Credo for Ethical Managed Care in Mental Health Practice," *Hospital and Community Psychiatry* 45, no. 9 (September 1994): 859.

9. Mary Gilliland, "Workforce Reductions: Low Morale, Reduced Quality Care," *Nursing Economic$* 15, no. 6 (November/December 1997): 320.

10. Ibid.

6. A Fair Hearing of Appeals of Denied Coverage in Managed Care Plans

1. An earlier version of this chapter appeared as Leonard Weber, "An HMO Grievance Committee: Ethical Challenges and Opportunities for the Organization," *HEC Forum* 10, no. 2 (June 1998): 201–212. Used with permission.

2. Norman Daniels and James E. Sabin, "Last Chance Therapies and Managed Care: Pluralism, Fair Procedures, and Legitimacy," *The Hastings Center Report* 28, no. 2 (March–April 1998): 27.

3. David Eddy, "Principles for Making Difficult Decisions in Difficult Times," *The Journal of the American Medical Association* 271, no. 22 (June 8 1994): 1792–1798.

7. Organizational Ethics: A Code Is Only the Beginning

1. Lynn Sharp Paine, "Managing for Organizational Integrity," *Harvard Business Review* 72 (March/April 1994): 106.

2. Robert Jackall, "Moral Mazes: Bureaucracy and Managerial Work," *Harvard Business Review* 61 (September/October 1983): 118–130.

3. Paine, p. 112.

4. Steven Z. Pantilat, Ann Alpers, and Robert M. Wachter, "A New Doctor in the House: Ethical Issues in Hospitalist Systems," *The Journal of the American Medical Association* 282, no. 2 (July 14 1999): 171–174.

5. Marian Gornick et al., "Effects of Race and Income on Mortality and Use of Services among Medicare Beneficiaries," *New England Journal of Medicine* 335 (September 12, 1996): 791–799.

6. Jonathan N. Tobin et al., "Sex Bias in Considering Coronary Bypass Surgery," *Annals of Internal Medicine* 107 (1987): 19–25. Richard M. Steingart et al., "Sex Dif-

ferences in the Management of Coronary Heart Disease," *New England Journal of Medicine* 325 (1991): 226–230.

7. H. Jack Geiger, "Race in Health Care: An American Dilemma?" *New England Journal of Medicine* 335 (September 12 1996): 816.

8. Just Wages and Salaries

1. Quoted in Bill Quigley and Manning Marable, "Justice Challenges for Today and Tomorrow: A Living Wage Is Part of the Answer," *Blueprint for Social Justice* 52, no. 6 (February 1999): 4.

2. "The United Nations Declaration of Human Rights," found in Thomas Donaldson and Patricia H. Werhane, eds., *Ethical Issues in Business: A Philosophical Approach*, 5th ed. (Upper Saddle River, N.J.: Prentice Hall, 1996), p. 127.

3. The Commission of the European Community, "The Community Charter of the Fundamental Social Rights of Workers," 1989, summarized in William C. Frederick, James E. Post, and Keith Davis, *Business and Society*, 7th ed. (New York: McGraw-Hill, 1992), p. 144.

4. Robert Pollin and Stephanie Luce, *The Living Wage: Building a Fair Economy* (New York: The New Press, 1998), p. 167.

5. "Redrawing the Poverty Line," *The New York Times* (October 18 1999): A14.

6. Pollin and Luce, pp. 1–25.

7. William Sundstrom, "The Income Gap," *Issues in Ethics* (Santa Clara University Markkula Center for Applied Ethics, Fall 1998): 13–17.

8. For a good discussion of comparable worth, see Sara M. Evans and Barbara J. Nelson, *Wage Justice* (Chicago: University of Chicago Press, 1989).

9. Ethics and Downsizing

1. Joanne B. Ciulla, "Leadership and the Problem of Bogus Empowerment," *Ethics and Leadership: Working Papers* (College Park, Md.: Kellogg Leadership Studies Project,1996), p. 61.

2. Leonard J. Weber, "Ethical Downsizing," *Health Progress* 75, no. 6 (July–August 1994): 24.

3. Frank J. Narvan, *Truth and Trust: The First Two Victims of Downsizing* (Athabasca, Alberta: Athabasca University Educational Enterprises, 1995), p. 48.

4. Ibid., p. 189.

5. An earlier version of this section is found in Weber, "Ethical Downsizing," pp. 25–26. Used with permission.

6. Narvan, p. 48.

7. David M. Noer, *Healing the Wounds: Overcoming the Trauma of Layoffs and Revitalizing Downsized Organizations* (San Francisco: Jossey-Bass, 1993).

10. Patient Requests for Healthcare Providers of a Specific Race or Sex

1. Two earlier versions of this section have been published: Leonard J. Weber, "The Race of the Caregiver: Should Managers Honor Patients' Requests?" *Health*

Progress 76, no. 2 (April 1995): 50–51. Leonard J. Weber and Michael G. Bissell, "Ethics and Race-Based Home Care Assignments," *Clinical Laboratory Management Review* 13, no. 5 (September/October 1999). Used with permission.

2. Adrienne Asch, "Free to Be a Bigot," in Rosalie A. Kane and Arthur L. Caplan, eds., *Ethical Conflicts in the Management of Home Care* (New York: Springer Publishing Co., 1993), p. 229.

11. Conscientious Objection to Participation in Certain Treatment Options

1. This case is adapted from "The Nurse's Appeal to Conscience," *The Hastings Center Report* 17, no. 2 (April 1987): 25.

2. An earlier version of this commentary is found in Leonard J. Weber, "When to Excuse Employees from Work Responsibilities," *Health Progress* 76, no. 8 (November–December 1995): 50–51. Used with permission.

3. Martin Benjamin, "Conscience," in Warren Thomas Reich, ed., *The Encyclopedia of Bioethics*, rev. ed. (New York: Macmillan, 1995), p. 472.

4. Kathleen Haley and Melinda Lee, eds., *The Oregon Death with Dignity Act: A Guidebook for Health Care Providers* (Portland: The Center for Ethics in Health Care, 1998), p. 8.

5. Richard T. DeGeorge, *Business Ethics*, 5th ed. (Upper Saddle River, N.J.: Prentice Hall, 1999), p. 397.

12. Union Organizing and Employee Strikes

1. Frank J. Narvan, *Truth and Trust: The First Two Victims of Downsizing* (Athabasca, Alberta: Athabasca University Educational Enterprises, 1995), p. 48.

2. United Nations Declaration of Human Rights, Article 23, #4.

3. Manuel G. Velasquez, *Business Ethics: Concepts and Cases*, 4th ed. (Upper Saddle River, N.J.: Prentice Hall, 1998), p. 466.

4. National Conference of Catholic Bishops, "Ethical and Religious Directives for Catholic Health Care Services" (Washington, D.C.: United States Catholic Conference, November 1994): #7.

5. Leonard J. Weber, "Labor Unions and Two Concepts of Social Justice," in Adam J. Maida, ed., *Issues in the Labor-Management Dialogue: Church Perspective* (St. Louis: The Catholic Health Association of the United States, 1982), pp. 171–172.

6. Guidelines proposed in this chapter are similar to those found in the "Ethical Guidelines for Labor Relations in Religious and Non-Profit Institutions" (Chicago: Interfaith Committee on Worker Issues, no date).

7. John Pike, "Strikes," *Encyclopedia of Applied Ethics* (San Diego: Academic Press, 1998), pp. 244–245.

13. Responsible Advertising

1. Allen R. Dyer, "Advertising," in Warren Thomas Reich, ed., *The Encyclopedia of Bioethics*, rev. ed. (New York: Macmillan, 1995), p. 76.

2. Tasker Robinette, "Adapting to the Age of Competition," *Hospitals & Health Services Administration* 30, no. 3 (May/June 1985): 10, 12.

3. Lynette R. Bradley and Julie Magno Zito, "Direct-to-Consumer Prescription Drug Advertising," *Medical Care* 35, no. 1 (1997): 86–89.

4. The American Public Health Association, "Direct-to-Consumer Prescription Drug Advertising," A Resolution Adopted in November 1995. Found as an Appendix to Bradley and Zito, pp. 90–91.

5. Bradley and Zito, p. 88.

6. Kurt Darr, *Ethics in Health Services Management*, 3rd ed. (Baltimore: Health Professions Press, 1997), p. 210.

7. Darr, p. 210. Robert Goldman, "Practical Applications of Healthcare Marketing Ethics," *Healthcare Financial Management* 47, no. 3 (March 1993): 46–48.

8. Leonard J. Weber, "Avoiding 'Unnecessary' Healthcare Services," *Health Progress* 75, no. 5 (June 1994): 61.

9. Alan Thein Durning, "Can't Live Without It," *World Watch* 6, no. 3 (May/June 1994): 11.

10. Leonard J. Weber, "The Ethics of Health Care Advertising," *Michigan Hospitals* 24, no. 12 (December 1988): 32.

14. Environmental Responsibility and the Precautionary Principle

1. "Health Care Without Harm: The Campaign for Environmentally Responsible Health Care" (Falls Church, Va.: Health Care Without Harm, 1998).

2. This chapter is a revised and expanded version of Leonard J. Weber, "Medical Waste and Healthcare Ethics," *Health Progress* 81, no. 1 (January–February, 2000): 26–28; 32. Used with permission.

3. Paul Hawken, *The Ecology of Commerce* (New York: HarperBusiness, 1994), p. 38.

4. Quoted in Sandra Steingraber, *Living Downstream* (New York: Vintage Books, 1998), p. 284.

5. Greenpeace International, "Four Principles of Clean Production," no date.

6. Steingraber, pp. 270–271.

7. For additional perspectives on the precautionary principle, see Carolyn Raffensperger and Joel Tickner, eds., *Protecting Public Health and the Environment: Implementing the Precautionary Principle* (Washington, D.C.: Island Press, 1999).

8. Tom L. Beauchamp and James F. Childress, *Principles of Biomedical Ethics*, 4th ed. (New York: Oxford University Press, 1994), p. 33.

9. Jonathan M. Mann, "Society and Public Health: Crisis and Rebirth," *Western Journal of Medicine* 169, no. 2 (August 1998): 119.

10. T. Colborn, D. Dumanoski, and J. P. Myers, *Our Stolen Future* (New York: Dutton, 1996), p. 113.

15. Community Serving Mergers and Acquisitions

1. This case was suggested by Roland E. Kidwell, "Hospital Mergers and the Care of External Stakeholders," presented at the Sixth Annual International Conference Promoting Business Ethics, Niagara Fall, New York, October 1999.

2. William C. Frederick, James E. Post, and Keith Davis, *Business and Society*, 7th ed. (New York: McGraw Hill, 1992), p. 30.

3. This section draws heavily upon Aaron S. Wilkins and Peter D. Jacobson, "Fiduciary Responsibilities in Nonprofit Health Care Conversions," *Health Care Management Review* 23, no. 1 (Winter 1998), pp. 77–90.

4. Ibid., p. 86.

5. Ibid., p. 78.

6. Jay Greene and Sandy Lutz, "Multi-Unit Providers Survey: A Tale of Two Ownership Sectors," *Modern Healthcare* 26, no. 21 (May 20 1996): 61–74.

7. Amy Pyle, "A Collision of Medicine and Faith," *Los Angeles Times* (January 5, 2000) <latimes.com>. See also Rob Boston, "Bad Medicine," *Church & State* 52, no. 6 (June 1999): 9–12.

8. Pyle, p. 5 of 7.

16. Socially Responsible Investing

1. Christopher J. Cowton, "Socially Responsible Investment," *Encyclopedia of Applied Ethics* (San Diego: Academic Press, 1998), p. 182.

2. Ibid.

3. See, for example, "Social Screening Criteria and Proxy Voting Guidelines" (Boston: The Domini Social Equity Fund, 1996).

4. Interfaith Center on Corporate Responsibility, *The Proxy Resolutions Book* (New York: ICCR, January 1999), p. 95.

5. Ibid., "Introduction."

6. "Social Screening Criteria and Proxy Voting Guidelines," p. 2.

7. Interfaith Center on Corporate Responsibility," p. 95.

8. See "Social Screening Criteria and Proxy Voting Guidelines."

9. Richard T. DeGeorge, *Business Ethics*, 5th ed. (Upper Saddle River, N.J.: Prentice Hall, 1999), p. 481.

10. William C. Frederick, James E. Post, and Keith Davis, *Business and Society*, 7th ed. (New York: McGraw-Hill, 1992), p. 46.

17. Components of a Business Ethics Program

1. Leonard J. Weber, "Healthcare Management Ethics: Reflections on Quality," *Research on Ethical Issues in Organizations* (forthcoming).

2. Leonard Weber, Jane Hammang-Buhl, and Leon Levitt, "Who Sets the Agenda? Integrating Ethics into Functional Business Courses," *The Journal of Legal Studies Education* 9, no. 2 (Spring 1991): 205–213.

3. Paul B. Hofmann, "Performing an Ethics Audit," *Healthcare Executive* 10, no. 6 (November/December 1995): 47.

4. Ibid.

5. Mercy Health Services, "Acute Care Clinical Ethics: Organizational Performance Improvement Tool" (Farmington Hills, Michigan, 1999).

6. One example of recent casebook literature is Karen G. Gervais et al., eds., *Ethical Challenges in Managed Care* (Washington, D.C.: Georgetown University Press, 1999).

7. Weber, "Healthcare Management Ethics: Reflections on Quality."

8. Leon Kass, "Practicing Ethics: Where's the Action?" *Hastings Center Report* 20, no. 1 (January/February 1990): 8.

9. Judith Wilson Ross et al., *Health Care Ethics Committees: The Next Generation* (Chicago: The American Hospital Association, 1993), chapter 5.

18. The Organizational Ethics Committee

1. The American Society for Bioethics and Humanities, "Core Competencies for Health Care Ethics Consultation" (ASBH, 1998).

2. H. Jack Geiger, "Race in Health Care: An American Dilemma?" *New England Journal of Medicine* 335 (September 12 1996): 816.

3. A. H. Weiss, E. J. Gordon, and M. E. O'Connor, "Parental Leave: Comparing Children's Hospitals with Fortune 500 Companies," *Archives of Pediatric and Adolescent Medicine* 152, no. 7 (July 1998): 629–633.

4. Leonard J. Weber, "Speaking about Ethics with Authority," *HEC Forum* 4, no. 4 (August 1992): 255–259.

Index

Ability to pay, 32

Abortion: and Catholic Health Care Services, 145; and hospital mergers, 145; restriction of, by healthcare organizations, 104. *See also* Reproductive health services

Access, reasonable, 146, 149

Admissions, hospital, 64–66

Advertising: and avoidance of harmful values, attitudes, and images, 128–129; and cultural diversity, 129; ethical evaluations of, 129; ethical standards for healthcare, 125–129; and ethics codes, 126; and expectations, 126–127; importance of accuracy and clarity in healthcare, 127; prescription drug, 123–125. *See also* Marketing, healthcare

African-Americans: and hospital nondiscrimination policies, 68–70, 174; and racial discrimination by patients, 14–15, 91–92. *See also* Race

American College of Healthcare Administrators, 4, 136, 140

American College of Healthcare Executives, 4

American Public Health Association, 124, 126

Appeals, managed care plan, 54–55; consistency and fairness in, 60–61; and coverage for alternatives to inadequate care, 56–57; and coverage for experimental "last-chance" therapy, 59–60; and coverage for explicitly denied procedures, 58–59; and coverage for out-of-plan providers, 55–56; support by healthcare organizations for patient, 32–33; types of, 55–60

Appropriateness of treatment, 37–38, 58

Archives of Internal Medicine, 33

Audit, ethics, 166–167

Avoidance of harm principle, 40

Avoidance strategy in investing, 151–153

Balanced Budget Act of 1997, 27–28

Benefit vs. effect of medical care, 38

Business and Society, 142

Care, continuity of: and treatment choices, 28; and unreimbursed services, 29–30

Care, quality of: and cost control, 30–33

Caregivers. *See* Employees; Nurses; Physicians

Catholic Health Care Services, 110, 145–149; and abortion, 145; and *Ethical and Religious Directives for Catholic Health Care Services*, 145, 148; and outpatient practices of physicians, 147

Census Bureau, U.S., on income, 76

Code of Ethics, American College of Healthcare Executives, 4; on managers' responsibilities to society, 10

Codes, ethics, 46, 62–63, 64, 65; and advertising, 126; in educating employees, 175; nondiscrimination, 70

Collective bargaining by employees. *See* Unions

Commercial model of healthcare, 3–4

Commission of the European Community, 76

Communication: after downsizing, 89–90; during downsizing, 86–87; during mergers and acquisitions, 144–145; in nonprofit conversions to for-profit status, 144–145; during union organizing drives, 112–114

Community-based ethics, 6–7; and patients' rights, 8

Community benefit of nonprofit organizations, 143

Community health principle, the, 136–137

Comparable worth, 80–81. *See also* Compensation

Compensation: calculating fair, 73–75; and the Commission of the European Community,

Compensation (*continued*)
76; employee, 73–75; executive, 78–80; gap between regular and executive employees, 78; and internal equity, 80–81; just, 73–75; minimum living wage, 75–78; physician, 46–49; and quality of care, 47–48; and United Nations Declaration of Human Rights, 75–76. *See also* Income

Compliance, xi–xii; and avoidance of fraud, 32; and environmental responsibility, 133; and ethics performance reviews, 167

Conflict: and prioritizing of values, 16–19; resolving, between legitimate interests, 14–16

Conflict of interest: definition of, 44–45; in nonprofit conversions to for-profit status, 144; and physician compensation, 46–49; physicians and, 45

Conscientious objection by organizations, 146

Conscientious objection by staff: accommodating, 103–104; and difficult patients, 102–103; distinguishing different types of, 101–102; management criteria for honoring, 102–104; management respect for, 102

Consistency and fairness in appeals process, 60–61

Consultants: and comparable worth in employee compensation, 80–81; employee, 112; ethics, 21, 164–166; and Organizational Ethics Committees (OECs), 172

Corporate social responsibility, 142

Costs: and ability of patients to pay for services, 32; of accommodating patient requests for same-sex caregivers, 98; and appropriate healthcare delivery locations, 31–32; associated with downsizing, 83; and choice of treatments, 26–27, 42–43; and contrast media for radiology, 26; control, 25–26; and coverage for alternatives to inadequate care, 56–57; and coverage for explicitly denied procedures, 58–59; of downsizing, 84–85; employees and control of, 32; and high-risk patients, 15–16, 33; and home care reimbursements, 27–28; impact on patient care of controls on, 32; of medical benefits, 3–4; and medical waste, 138; and out-of-plan providers, 55–56; and physician financial incentives, 46–49; and quality of care, 30–33, 47–48; review mechanisms, 33

Council on Environmentally Responsible Economies (CERES), 154

Cultural diversity, 42–43; and advertising, 129; and downsizing, 86; and patient requests for same-sex caregivers, 96–97; and race as criterion for making work assignments, 93; respecting and recognizing, 39–40

Culture, organizational, 63–64; and hospital nondiscrimination policies, 68–70; and hospitalist model of care, 64–66; promoting ethics

within, 175; and treatment of medical waste, 138

Customers, healthcare patients as, 38

Daniels, Norman, 59–60
Darr, Kurt, 125
Davis, Keith, 142
Decision making: and conflict of legitimate interests, 14–16; and downsizing, 84–85; and ethical principles, 5, 13–14, 19–21, 176; and ethics consultants, 21; and fiduciary responsibility, 156–157; "four reminders" for, 20–21; involving patients in, 41, 42; and location of services, 141–143; maintaining focus for effective, 20–21; by management, and patients' best interests, 49–52; models of, 19–21; in nonprofit conversions to for-profit status, 144–145; and practicality, 21; and priorities among various values, 14–16; and racial discrimination, 14–15; and socially responsible investing, 151–153

Dilemmas, ethical: model for resolving, 19–20

Dioxin, in medical waste, 137–138
Discharges from hospitals, patient, 66–68
Discrimination, gender, 96–99
Discrimination, racial: and ethical decision making, 19–20; by patients, 91–92; and patients' rights, 14–15; and race as criterion for making work assignments, 93–95

Downsizing: and cultural diversity, 86; ethical issues related to, 82–83; and keeping employees informed, 86–87; and performance-related layoffs, 86; and remaining employees, 87–88, 89–90; selection criteria for, 85–87; and seniority, 86; and the separation process, 87–89

Dyer, Allen, 126

Education: ethics, 161–163, 175; and Ethics Committees, 167–169; formal and informal ethics, 175–176; and hospital nondiscrimination policies, 69–70; and Organizational Ethics Committees (OECs), 175–176, 179–180

Effect vs. benefit of medical care, 38

Elderly patients: and Program of All-Inclusive Care for the Elderly (PACE), 15–16; and quality of care, 51–52; and racial discrimination, 14–15; rights of, 40–41

Emanuel, Ezekiel, 47

Employees, 9–10; and card-check recognition, 113; and comparable worth, 80–81; and conflicts of interest, 44–46; conscientious objection by, 100–104; and cultural diversity, 86; and downsizing, 84–90; and gender discrimination, 96–99; and internal equity in compensation, 80–81; and just compensation, 73–75; and limited healthcare resources, 32; and marketplace determination of compensation, 80–81; and organizational culture, 63–64; and Organizational Ethics Committees (OECs), 172–173; and performance reviews, 86; and poverty-level wages, 76–77; protection of, 94–95; and race as criterion for making work assignments, 92–95; racial discrimination of, by patients, 91–92; responsibilities of, 44, 107–108; right to establish unions, 110–111; and scare tactics by management, 113–114; selection criteria for downsizing, 85–87; and seniority, 86; and the separation process, 87–89; strikes by, 114–117; temporary, 116; and union organizing drives, 111–112; and United Nations Declaration of Human Rights, 75–76; wage gap between regular and executive, 78

Environmental Protection Agency, 131

Environmental responsibility: and the community health principle, 136–137; and the harm principle, 135–136; and health risk assessment of particular practices, 131–133; and legal requirements, 133; and the precautionary principle, 134–139; and risk-assessment models, 132. *See also* Waste, medical

Equal Exchange, 155

Equity, internal, 80–81

Ethical and Religious Directives for Catholic Health Care Services, 145, 148

Ethicists, professional, 11–12; medical, 36; and Organizational Ethics Committees (OECs), 173–174. *See also* Ethics consultants

Ethics, business: and adherence to ethical standards, 13; and compliance, xi–xii; and costs vs. benefits, 6; developing programs, 161–162; and environmental responsibility, 131–132; and healthcare ethics, 5; and hospital nondiscrimination policies, 70; and integrity, xii–xiii; literature in, 168; the need for, 11–12; and practicality in decision making, 21; and prioritizing of values, 16–19; professionals, 11–12; and socially responsible investing, 155–158

Ethics, clinical, xiii–xiv

Ethics, community-based, 6–7

Ethics, healthcare: and ability of patients to pay for services, 32; and accreditation standards related to organizational ethics, 62–63; and business ethics, 5; codes, 46, 62–63, 64, 65, 70; and the community health principle, 136–137; and compliance, 133; and conflict of legitimate interests, 14–16; and conscientious objection by staff, 100–104; and consistency and fairness in hearing appeals, 60–61; and corporate social responsibility, 142; and cost control, 25–30; and coverage for alternatives to inadequate care, 56–57; and coverage for experimental "last-chance" therapy, 59–60; and coverage for explicitly

denied procedures, 58–59; and coverage for out-of-plan providers, 55–56; decision making and, 19–21; and discrimination, 68–70; and downsizing, 82–90; and effect vs. benefit of medical care, 38; and employee compensation, 75–78; and environmental responsibility, 130–139; evaluations of advertising, 129; and executive compensation, 78–80; and futile treatments, 37–39; general concepts of, 168–169; and guidelines for honoring individual rights, 42–43; and the harm principle, 135–136; and hospital admissions, 64–66; and hospital nondiscrimination policies, 68–70; and individual rights, 36–43; informal messages, 175–176; and just compensation of employees, 73–75; literature in, 168; and managed care plan appeals, 55–60; and medically necessary procedures, 58; and patient discharge procedures, 66–68; and patients' rights, 7–8, 36–39; performance reviews, 166–167; and physician financial incentives, 48–49; and the precautionary principle, 134; and quality of care, 30–33; and quality standards, 10–11; and restriction of specific treatment options by healthcare organizations, 104–108; and socially responsible investing, 150–153; standards for advertising, 125–129; and unreimbursed services, 29–30

Ethics, investing, 155–158

Ethics, justice-based, 7–9; and consistency and fairness in hearing appeals, 60–61; definition of, 8–9; and employee compensation, 73–75; and internal equity in compensation, 80–81; and living wage compensation, 75–78

Ethics, medical, xi, xiii–xiv; and costs, 25–26; education, 8; literature in, 168

Ethics, organizational: and Organizational Ethics Committees (OECs), 171–174; qualifications of committee members, 174–179

Ethics, social, 142

Ethics audit, 166–167

Ethics Committees: Clinical, 171, 173–174; and clinical issues, 7–8; considering conscientious objection by staff, 102; and education, 167–169; and ethics and mission advisors, 163–164; and ethics consultants, 164–166; importance of, 161–162; Organizational, 171–174; and prescription drug advertising, 123–124. *See also* Organizational Ethics Committees (OECs)

Ethics consultants, 164–166; as advisors, 166; purpose of, 164–165. *See also* Ethicists, professional

Ethics education, 179–180; formal and informal, 175–176; importance of, 161–162

Ethics and mission advisors, 163–164

Executive compensation, 78–80

Expectations: and advertising, 126–127; of patients, 37; and restriction of specific treatment options by healthcare organizations, 145–149

Fair market value, 144
Fairness: and downsizing, 83, 85–87, 87–89; in employee compensation, 73–75; in executive compensation, 79–80; and patient discharge procedures, 67–68; and race as criterion for making work assignments, 95; and racial discrimination, 91–92; and socially responsible investing, 155; in treating patients of culturally diverse populations, 40
Fee-for-service compensation, 46
Financial incentives: for executives, 79–80; for physicians, 46–49
Financing, healthcare: and Balanced Budget Act of 1997, 27–28; and Medicare reimbursements, 27–29; raising rates or reimbursements and, 29
Focus, 20–21
For-profit organizations, 143; vs. nonprofit organizations, 6–7
Fraud, 32
Frederick, William, 142
Friedman, Emily, 3, 6
Futile treatments, 37–39; and effect vs. benefit of medical care, 38

Geiger, H. Jack, 70, 175
Gender: patient requests for caregivers based on, 96–99
Government involvement in healthcare, 5

Harm principle, the, 40, 135–136
Harvard Business Review, 63–64
Hastings Center Report, xiv
Health maintenance organizations (HMOs). *See* Insurance, health; Managed care plans
Healthcare: ethical principles and decision making, 5; government involvement in, 5; as a social or public good, 5
Healthcare Forum Journal, 3
Home care and high-risk patients, 27–28
Hospitalist model, 64–66
Hospitals: admissions, 64–66; conversion from nonprofit to for-profit status, 143–145; discharge of patients from, 66–68; executive compensation in, 78–80; impact of hospitalist model on, 65–66; liability, 40–41; and location of services, 141–143; and long-term care, 37–38, 51–52; nondiscrimination policies, 68–70, 174–175; and outpatient practices of physicians, 147; and referrals for services outside the organization, 147–148; Veterans Administration (VA), 29–30
Human resources. *See* Employees

Human rights: to establish unions, 110–111. *See also* Individual rights

Incentives, financial: amounts of, 47; controlling the use of, 48–49; in healthcare organizations, 46–47; and promoting good physician practice patterns, 48–49; and quality of care, 47–48
Income: employee, 73–75; gap between regular and executive employees, 78; patients' low, 69; poverty threshold, 76–77
Individual rights, 7–8, 14–15; and conscientious objection by staff, 100–104; to establish unions, 110–111; and futile treatments, 37–39; guidelines for honoring, 42–43; in healthcare organizations, 36–43; and hospital liability, 40–41; and individual self-interest, 18–19; Jehovah's Witnesses and, 56; and organizational interests, 17–18; priority of, 16–17; and racial discrimination by patients, 91–95; and staff conscientious objection, 100–104. *See also* Human rights; Patients: rights; Self-determination in healthcare
Individual self-interest: and community good, 18; and individual rights, 16–17; priority of, 17
Informal and formal ethics messages, 175–176
Insurance, health: advocacy for individual patients and, 32–33; appeals procedure in, 54–55; and consistency and fairness in hearing appeals, 60–61; and coverage for alternatives to inadequate care, 56–57; and coverage for experimental "last-chance" therapy, 59–60; and coverage for explicitly denied procedures, 58–59; and coverage for out-of-plan providers, 55–56; and high-risk individuals, 3; and patients' rights to covered services, 31; payment systems, 33, 47; and physician financial incentives, 47; regulations, 53–54. *See also* Managed care plans
Integrity, xii–xiii; 63–64; and Organizational Ethics Committees (OECs), 178; and socially responsible investing, 152
Interfaith Center on Corporate Responsibility, 154
Investing, ethical. *See* Socially responsible investing

Jecker, Nancy, 8
Jehovah's Witnesses, 56
Joint Commission on the Accreditation of Health Care Organizations (JCAHO), 46, 62–63, 70; on advertising, 121, 126; and conscientious objection by staff, 100–101

Kass, Leon, xiv

Lamm, Richard, 25
Last chance therapy, 59–60

Layoffs. *See* Downsizing
Living wage compensation, 75–78
Locations, healthcare delivery, 31–32, 141–143

Managed care plans: appeals procedure in, 54–
55; and consistency and fairness in hearing
appeals, 60–61; and coverage for alternatives
to inadequate care, 56–57; and coverage for
experimental "last-chance" therapy, 59–60;
and coverage for explicitly denied procedures, 58–59; and coverage for out-of-plan
providers, 55–56; and physician financial
incentives, 47, 48–49; rights of members of,
53–54. *See also* Insurance, health
Management, healthcare: and adherence to
ethical standards, 13; after downsizing, 89–
90; and appeals decisions, 60; and avoidance
of scare tactics in response to union organizing, 113–114; and card-check recognition of
union representation, 113; communication
with patients, 33; and conflicts of interest,
45–46; and conscientious objection by staff,
100–101; and consistency and fairness in
hearing appeals, 60–61; decision making by,
13–14; decision making and patient best interests, 49–52; and the decision to downsize,
84–85; and employee consultants, 112; and
employee separation, 87–89; and ethics consultants, 166; and executive compensation,
78–80; in for- and not-for-profit organizations, 6–7; and general concepts of healthcare ethics, 168–169; and hospital nondiscrimination policies, 69–70; and informal
ethics message conveyed to employees, 175–
176; and integrity, 63–64; and justice, 38;
and negative campaigning against unions,
114; and organizational culture, 63–64; and
Organizational Ethics Committees (OECs),
172–173; and organizational integrity, 63–
64; and patient discharge procedures, 66–68;
and patient discrimination based on gender,
96–99; and patients' rights, xiii–xiv; as a profession, 4; and quality standards, 10–11; and
race as criterion for making work assignments, 93–95; response to strikes, 116–117;
response to union-related activity, 111–114;
responsibilities of, 9–10; responsibility for
ethics programs, 169–170; role of, in teaching ethics, 175–176; and selection criteria
for downsizing employees, 85–87; and temporary employees hired during strikes, 116;
and treatment of patients as "customers," 38
Management and integrity, xii–xiii, 63–64
Marketing, healthcare: and business model of
healthcare, 121–122; ethical standards for,
125–129; and ethics codes, 126. *See also* Advertising
Marketplace determination of compensation,
80–81

Medical loss ratios, 3
Medically necessary procedures, 58. *See also*
Treatments
Medicare: and payment for long-term care, 51–
52; reimbursements, 27–29
Mercury, in medical waste, 137
Mergers and acquisitions, 140; and abortion,
145; and Catholic Health Care Services,
145–149; communication during, 144–145;
and conflicts of interest, 144; and conversion
from nonprofit to for-profit status, 143–145;
and corporate social responsibility, 142; and
fair market value, 144; and location of services, 141–143; and reproductive health services, 145–149; and restriction of specific
treatment options by healthcare organizations, 145–149
Minimum wage, 75–76. *See also* Income

New England Journal of Medicine, 70
Nondiscrimination policies, 68–70. *See also*
Race
Nonprofit organizations, 6; and community
benefit, 143; conversion to for-profit, 143–
145; and employee compensation, 76–77; vs.
for-profit organizations, 6–7
Nurses: assistants, 77; conscientious objection
by, 101; and quality of care, 50–51; relationships with physicians, 176–177; and strikes,
115; and unions, 111–112

Organizational culture, 63–64; and hospital
nondiscrimination policies, 68–70; and hospitalist model of care, 64–66; promoting ethics within, 175; and treatment of medical
waste, 138
Organizational Ethics Committees (OECs):
and clinical staff, 173; establishing, 179–
180; functions and membership, 171–172;
integrity of members of, 178; management
members of, 172–173; necessary skills for
membership, 177–179; and non-management
employees, 173; qualifications of members,
174–179. *See also* Ethics Committees
Organizational integrity, 63–64
Organizations, healthcare: and accommodating
conscientious objection by staff, 103–104;
and accommodating cultural diversity, 39–
40; and accreditation standards related to
organizational ethics, 62–63; and adherence
to ethical standards, 13; and alternatives to
inadequate care, 56–57; and avoidance of
harm principle, 40; as citizens, 9–10, 143;
commercial model of, 3–4; and community-
based ethics, 6–7; and the community health
principle, 136–137; and compliance, xi–xii;
and conflicts of interest, 44–46; conscientious objection by, 146; and consistency and
fairness in hearing appeals, 60–61; as

Organizations, healthcare (*continued*)
  contributors to conflicts of interest, 45; conversion from nonprofit to for-profit status,
  143–145; and corporate social responsibility,
  142; and cost control, 15–16; and cost-effective care policies, 49–50; and coverage for
  explicitly denied procedures, 58–59; and discrimination, 68–70; and employee compensation, 75–78; and employee separation, 87–89;
  employees, 9–10; and ethical issues associated with downsizing, 84–85; and ethical
  principles, 6–7; ethics codes, 46, 62–63, 64,
  65; and ethics and mission advisors, 163–164;
  and ethics performance reviews, 166–167;
  and executive compensation, 78–80; and feasibility of accommodating cultural diversity,
  40; for-profit, 6–7; and futile treatments,
  37–39; and guidelines for honoring individual rights, 42–43; and the harm principle,
  135–136; and high-risk individuals, 15–16;
  hospitalist model of, 64–66; individual rights
  in, 36–43; and informal ethics message conveyed to employees, 175–176; and insurance
  appeals procedure, 54–55; as investors, 150–
  151; and involving patients in decision making, 42; and just compensation of employees,
  73–75; liability, 40–41; and location of services, 141–143; managers, 9–10; and medical
  loss ratios, 3; and nondiscrimination policies, 68–70; not-for-profit, 6, 76–77; and
  Organizational Ethics Committees (OECs),
  171–174; and out-of-plan providers, 55–56;
  and patient discharge procedures, 66–68;
  and patient refusal of specific treatments,
  37–38, 42, 106–107; and patient requests for
  caregivers of a particular race, 91–95; and
  patient requests for same-sex caregivers,
  96–99; and patients as customers, 121–122;
  and poverty-level wages, 76–77; and prioritizing of values, 16–19; and Program of All-
  Inclusive Care for the Elderly (PACE), 15–
  16; and race as criterion for making work
  assignments, 92–95; and respecting cultural
  values, 39–40, 42–43; and responsibilities of
  physicians, 42; and restriction of specific
  treatment options, 145–149; restriction of
  treatment options by, 104–108; roles of, 9;
  and selection criteria for downsizing employees, 85–87; service model of, 3–5, 6–7; as
  targets of environmental health activists, 131
Out-of-plan providers, 55–56
Outpatient practices, 147

Paine, Lynn Sharp, 63–64
Patients: and ability to pay for services, 32; African-American, 69; and appeals procedure
  in managed care plans, 54–55; and avoidance
  of harm principle, 40; best interests and
  healthcare management decision making, 49–
52; and conscientious objection by staff, 101–
  104; and consistency and fairness in hearing
  appeals, 60–61; and cost control, 25–30; and
  coverage for alternatives to inadequate care,
  56–57; and coverage for experimental "last-
  chance" therapy, 59–60; and coverage for
  explicitly denied procedures, 58–59; culturally diverse, 39–40; as customers, 121–122;
  discharge of, from hospitals, 66–68; and effect vs. benefit of medical care, 38; elderly,
  14–16, 29–30, 40–41, 51–52; and Ethics
  Committees, 7–8; expectation of reasonable
  access to healthcare services, 146; expectations, 37, 126–127; and feasibility of accommodating cultural diversity, 40; and futile
  treatments, 37–39; high-risk, 15–16, 27–28,
  33; and hospital admissions, 64–66; and
  hospital liability, 40–41; and hospital nondiscrimination policies, 68–70, 174–175; impact
  of cost controls on, 32; and institutional
  interests, 40–41; insurance appeals, advocacy
  for, 32–33; and limited healthcare resources,
  31; low-income, 69; and organizational conflicts of interest, 45–46; and out-of-plan
  providers, 55–56; privacy, 93–94, 97–99; and
  quality of care, 30–33, 51–52; racial discrimination by, 14–15, 91–95; refusal of
  specific treatments, 31, 37–38; requests for
  caregivers of a particular race, 91–92; requests for same-sex caregivers, 96–99; and
  respecting cultural values, 42–43; and restriction of specific treatment options by
  healthcare organizations, 145–149; rights,
  xiii, 7–8, 14–15, 36–39, 42–43, rights in
  managed care plans, 53–54; rights to services covered by insurance, 31; and special
  care, 67–68; and truth in advertising, 127;
  VIP, 68. *See also* Elderly patients
Patients Rights and Organizational Ethics
  standards, 46
Payment systems, 46–47
Performance reviews, 86
Personal beliefs and conscientious objection,
  100–104. *See also* Individual rights
Physicians: compensation, 46–49; and conflict
  of interest, 45; and Ethics Committees, 7–8;
  financial incentives and good practice patterns, 48–49; financial incentives for, 46–49;
  and hospital admissions, 65; out-of-plan, 55–
  56; outpatient practices of, 147; and patient
  discharge procedures, 66–68; and patient
  expectations, 126; and patient self-determination in healthcare, 37–38; and patients'
  right to refuse specific treatment, 37–38;
  and prescription drug advertising, 125; and
  recommended treatment, 37–38; relationships with nurses, 176–177; responsibilities
  of, 42
Pollution, 134. *See* Environmental responsibility

Post, James, 142

Poverty, 76–77

Practicality in decision making, 21

Precautionary principle, the, 134; and the community health principle, 136–137; and the harm principle, 135–136; implementing, 137–138

Prescription drug advertising, 123–125; American Public Health Association on, 124; and expectations, 126–127; and quality of care, 128

Priorities: in ethical decision making, 14–16; and principles of business ethics, 16–17

Privacy, patient, 93–94; and requests for same-sex caregivers, 97–99

Problem solving, 19–21

Program of All-Inclusive Care for the Elderly (PACE), 15–16

Proxy resolutions, 153–155

Public good: and the community health principle, 136–137; healthcare as, 5; promotion of, by healthcare organizations, 10; and socially responsible investing, 150–151

Puckett, B. Earl, 128

PVC plastic and medical waste, 138

Quality of care: and African-American patients, 69; and cost control, 30–33, 49–50; cost-effective, 30, 49–50; and healthcare advertising, 127–128; and healthcare delivery locations, 31–32; and hospital nondiscrimination policies, 68–70; and low-income patients, 69; minimum standards of, 30; and patient requests for same-sex caregivers, 97; and patients as customers, 121–122; and physician financial incentives, 47–49; and race, 69; and restriction of specific treatment options by healthcare organizations, 105–106; review mechanisms, 33; and strikes by employees, 117

Quality standards, 10–11, 30

Race: as criterion for making work assignments, 92–95; and hospital nondiscrimination policies, 68–70, 174–175; patient requests for caregivers of a particular race, 91–92

Radiology: and contrast media choices, 26–27; and cost control, 26–27; and quality of care, 49

"Redrawing the Ethics Map," 25

Reimbursement: and fraud, 32; unreimbursed services, 29–30, 179–180

Reproductive health services: and Catholic Health Care Services, 147–149; and hospital mergers, 145–149. See also Abortion

Resources, limited: effects on employees of, 32; and insurance payment systems, 33; and

quality of care, 31; and unreimbursed services, 29–30

Responsibilities: and decision making, 19–21; and corporate social responsibility, 142; fiduciary, 156–157; in nonprofit conversions to for-profit status, 143–145

Rights. See Individual rights; Patients: rights

Risk, 16; assessment and environmental responsibility, 131–133

Robinette, Tasker, 122

Roosevelt, Franklin D., 75

Sabin, James, 59–60

Salaries. See Compensation

Schneiderman, Lawrence, 38

Screening. See Social screening

Self-determination in healthcare, 37–38; and futile treatments, 37–39. See also Individual rights; Patients: rights

Self-interest, individual: and community good, 18; and individual rights, 16–17; priority of, 17

Seniority, 86

Separation process in downsizing, 87–89

Service model of healthcare, 3–5; and for-profit organizations, 6–7

Sex: patient requests for same-sex caregivers, 96–99

Shareholder activism, 153–155

Social screening, 151–153, 157

Socially responsible investing, 150–151; and avoidance strategy, 151–153; ethics of, 155–158; and fiduciary responsibility, 156–157; and Interfaith Center on Corporate Responsibility, 154; and proxy resolutions, 153–155; and screening criteria for investments, 151–153; and selective and alternative investments, 155; and shareholder activism, 153–155

South Africa, 150

Standards, ethical, 13; and decision making, 13–14

Steingraber, Sandra, 134

Strikes, 114–117; temporary employees hired during, 116

Tavistock Group, 5

Toxic pollution. See Environmental responsibility

Treatments: and accommodating cultural diversity, 39–40; alternative, 37; and avoidance of harm principle, 40; avoiding useless, 42; choice and cost control, 26–27, 31; conscientious objection by staff to specific, 100–104; and continuity of care, 28; and coverage for alternatives to inadequate care, 56–57; and coverage for experimental "last-chance" therapy, 59–60; and coverage for explicitly

Index

Treatments (*continued*)
denied procedures, 58–59; and effect vs. benefit of medical care, 38; and feasibility of accommodating cultural diversity, 40; futile, 37–39; and medically necessary procedures, 58; and out-of-plan providers, 55–56; patient refusal of specific, 37–38, 42, 106–107; recommended, 37–38; restriction of, by healthcare organizations, 104–108, 145–149; and self-determination in healthcare, 37–38; unreimbursed, 29–30
Truth in advertising, 127
Tubal ligation, 148. *See also* Reproductive health services

Unions: and card-check recognition, 113; management response to, 109–114; and negative campaigning by management, 114; organizing drives, 111–112; right of employees to establish, 110–111; and scare tactics by management, 113–114; and strikes by employees, 114–117
United Nations Declaration of Human Rights, 75–76, 110
United States Roman Catholic Bishops, 110
Unreimbursed services, 29–30, 179–180

Values: and healthcare business ethics, 16–19; in advertising, 128–129; and decision making, 19–21; and organizational culture, 63–64; regarding cultural diversity, 39–40
Velasquez, Manuel, 44–45
Veterans Administration (VA): hospitals, 29–30; and medical ethics, 29–30

Wages. *See* Compensation
Waste, medical: and alternative products, 138; and costs, 138; dioxin in, 137–138; mercury in, 137; PVC plastic and, 138. *See also* Environmental responsibility
Work assignments, 92–95. *See also* Employees

Leonard J. Weber has been on the faculty of the University of Detroit Mercy since 1972. His work is focused on practical ethical concerns, particularly in healthcare and in business. He was selected to be the John L. Aram Visiting Professor of Business Ethics at Gonzaga University for 2000–2001. Weber has published more than seventy articles and is the principal author of the "Case Studies in Ethics" column in *Clinical Leadership & Management Review*. He serves as an ethics consultant to several healthcare organizations and is past president of the Medical Ethics Resource Network of Michigan. He is an enrollee-elected member of the Board of Directors of Health Alliance Plan, a non-profit managed care organization.

CPSIA information can be obtained
at www.ICGtesting.com
Printed in the USA
LVOW11*1421211116

513926LV00010B/165/P